Power and Betrayal
in the Canadian Media

Power and Betrayal in the Canadian Media

DAVID TARAS

broadview press

Canadian Cataloguing in Publication Data

Taras, David, 1950–
    Power and betrayal in the Canadian media
Includes bibliographical references.
Updated ed.
ISBN 1-55111-464-X

1. Mass media – Social aspects – Canada. 2. Mass media – Political aspects – Canada.   I. Title.

P92.C3T37 2001   302.23'0971   C2001-930162-6

Broadview Press Ltd. is an independent, international publishing house, incorporated in 1985.

North America:
P.O. Box 1243, Peterborough, Ontario, Canada K9J 7H5
3576 California Road, Orchard Park, NY 14127
Tel: (705) 743-8990; Fax: (705) 743-8353
E-mail: customerservice@broadviewpress.com

United Kingdom:
Turpin Distribution Services Ltd., Blackhorse Rd., Letchworth, Hertfordshire SG6 3HN
TEL: (1462) 672555; FAX (1462) 480947; E-MAIL: turpin@rsc.org

Australia:
St. Clair Press, P.O. Box 287, Rozelle, NSW 2039
TEL: (02) 818 1942; FAX: (02) 418 1923

www.broadviewpress.com

Broadview Press gratefully acknowledges the financial support of the Book Publishing Industry Development Program, Ministry of Canadian Heritage, Government of Canada.

PRINTED IN CANADA

Contents

Dedication   vi

Acknowledgements   vii

ONE   **Putting the Media Under the Spotlight**   1

TWO   **Media, Citizens, and Democracy**   29

THREE   **Convergence and the High Waves of Media Change**   61

FOUR   **Fragmentation Bombs: The New Media and the Erosion of Public Life**   93

FIVE   **Chilled to the Bone: The Crisis of Public Broadcasting**   117

SIX   **The Worst Assignment: Reporting National Unity**   141

SEVEN   **Bringing You Hollywood: Private Broadcasters and the Public Interest**   171

EIGHT   **The Winds of Right-Wing Change in Canadian Journalism**   199

NINE   **Confronting the Future**   219

Update 2001: Media Conglomerates, the CBC, and Canadian Democracy   227

Notes   241

This book is dedicated to the memory of my mother:

Sheila Taras

She lit up the lives of all those who knew her.
She will be deeply missed by the family that loved her.
But she will always be with us in our hearts.

Acknowledgements

The best part of writing this book is the opportunity to thank those who helped make it possible. Don LePan and Michael Harrison of Broadview Press offered encouragement, made valuable suggestions, and were patient and understanding throughout. Eileen Eckert edited the book with great skill and with a keen eye for grammatical and stylistic errors. She was a pleasure to work with.

Christopher Dornan of Carleton University, Catherine Murray of Simon Fraser University, former *Calgary Herald* publisher Kevin Peterson, and another reviewer who wishes not to be identified were immensely helpful. They contributed generously with their time, pointed out errors and conceptual blind spots, and gave me valuable perspectives. I owe them an enormous debt of gratitude.

Researchers Mark Simpson and Sherry Hergott also deserve a great deal of credit. They did first class jobs digging for information, conducting interviews (in Mark's case), and sharpening my thinking. Barbara Jenkins did a wonderful job transcribing my interview tapes.

Sylvia Mills, my administrative assistant in the graduate program in Communication Studies at the University of Calgary, saved the day on numerous occasions. Her spirit and professionalism have made the graduate program the success that it is today. Marion Hillier, also a member of the administrative staff, was always gracious and generous when I needed her help.

Two Deans of the Faculty of General Studies, Michael McMordie and Beverly Rasporich, were supportive in ways that went beyond the call of duty. They helped ensure that the faculty remained a congenial and progressive place in which to work.

I am grateful to the Social Sciences and Humanities Research Council of Canada for its financial support and hope that I have lived up to the trust that the Council has placed in me.

I would like to thank all of the journalists who graciously agreed to be interviewed. Their experiences and reflections added immeasurably to the book.

Most important were the efforts of those to whom I am bound by the warmth and glow of love and family. My father, Irwin Taras, has been a pillar of strength, my idol and my inspiration throughout my life. Without his faith in me I would never have been able to have an academic career. My wife, Debbie Taras, made all the difference. Her golden heart and great spirit have lifted me in ways that I can never repay.

My two sons, Matthew and Joel, and my two stepsons, Michael and Daniel, have filled the house with their unquenchable energy, curiosity, and creativity. They always brought me down to earth and taught me about how children really use media. Matthew helped his father solve various computer glitches and promises to read this book.

Finally, this book is dedicated to my mother, Sheila Taras, who died while the book was being written. Her relentless optimism and confidence were the greatest gifts that a mother could give to her son.

Any errors in fact and judgment are mine alone.

ONE

Putting the Media Under the Spotlight

Opening Salvos

The main argument in this book is that the Canadian media system is in the midst of a profound crisis. The media in Canada have been recently shaken by a number of cataclysmic developments – developments that have shifted the geological plates on which the media have rested comfortably for decades. A vast technological revolution, perhaps the most sweeping since Gutenberg's invention of the printing press, is changing the very nature of mass communications, and almost all national cultures – Canada's included – are being ceaselessly bombarded by powerful international forces. The publicly financed Canadian Broadcasting Corporation (CBC), long the backbone of the broadcasting system, is threatened with extinction. We are witnessing not an abrupt execution but a slow, lingering death. Newspaper ownership has fallen into the hands of a small handful of individuals, and Hollinger Inc., controlled by media baron Conrad Black, has gained a stranglehold on the industry. And lastly, the quality of journalism has deteriorated. Our local newscasts and front pages are dominated by blood-and-gore crime stories, celebrity news, sports hype, and the latest tidbits from the world of entertainment, while reports about political and social policies rarely grab the spotlight unless they feature high-octane confrontation or pathetic victims. To paraphrase media columnist Howard Kurtz, "there is a cancer eating away at the news business – the cancer of boredom, superficiality and irrelevance – and radical surgery is needed."[1]

The combined force of these changes is weakening the capacity of Canadians to communicate with each other and see their own reflection. It is damaging the democratic process, narrowing rather than broadening our perspectives on the world, and limiting our capacity to achieve great things together. Despite the surface impression that Canadians now have the world at our fingertips because we enjoy more media choices than ever before – that we are media wealthy – the reality is that Canadians are becoming media poor. Simply having a larger assortment of the same thing is not the same as having many different choices. The situation is made worse by the failure of media moguls to put the needs of the country and its citizens on at least a par with their own interests, and by governments and a regulatory system that have failed to curtail their power – that have allowed a few powerful individuals and corporations to call the tune.

While there are hopeful signs – countervailing trends that are working to make the mass media more open and democratic, more interactive and populist – these developments are being overshadowed by larger and more foreboding forces.

The charge of betrayal made in the title of this book stems from my belief that while the owners of the mass media operate businesses and must serve the interests of investors, they also have an obligation to serve the public interest. Unlike other businesses, they have been given unique and privileged access to a resource that belongs to the public – a resource so scarce and limited that it almost guarantees profits. The trusteeship model of the mass media holds that owners, in exchange for this extraordinary right of access, must address the needs of Canadians not just as consumers but as citizens.[2] They must act as a public forum and be a public meeting place, even as they market their wares (namely the size and characteristics of their audiences and readerships) to advertisers.

But owners are only partly to blame. Politicians and regulators bear a great deal of responsibility for the current crisis. There are instances in which politicians have gone over the top – muscling, bullying, and interfering with the news business. In other cases, they have sat on their hands and done nothing, too intimidated, too afraid to take actions that would incur the wrath of powerful media owners. Questions also have to be asked about the performance of the Canadian Radio-television and Telecommunications Commission (CRTC), the government-appointed body that acts as the harbour master over the vast sea of Canadian communications policy, regulating everything from cable licences to phone rates, from satellite services to TV stations. The CRTC's questionable rulings have not gone unnoticed. In April 1998, a large number of Liberal Members of Parliament in Ottawa, concerned that the CRTC had been captured by the very industries that it is supposed to regulate, called for an inquiry to determine if the interests of the public were being properly represented.

According to William Baker and George Dessart, there are six functions that media owners should undertake on behalf of citizens: they should be

> provid[ing] information, discussion, and debate on public affairs, attempting to enlighten the public, thus making it more capable of self-government; serving as watchdogs over government activities, thus safeguarding the rights of the individual, providing entertainment; serving the economy by bringing together the buyers and sellers of goods and services through environments welcoming to advertising, and maintaining their own financial independence and thus presumably staying free from the undue pressures of special interests.[3]

I would suggest that in the Canadian context another obligation needs to be added to these lofty goals: owners should reflect Canadian identity, presenting Canadians with a reflection of their own country in all its magnificence and with all of its warts and blemishes. Sharing a border with the largest economic, military, and entertainment power on the planet, plagued by deep linguistic and regional differences, and having undergone a series of painful national unity and constitutional crises in its most recent history, Canada must depend on its media system to be a cultural and information lifeline in a way that other countries need not.

While these standards may be exacting, and indeed expensive, ones to meet, they are part of the democratic bargain. The mass media are as much a part of the democratic system as are Parliament, the Supreme Court, or provincial governments. And while these other institutions all operate within a system of checks and balances – MPs are accountable at election time, the power of the Supreme Court is circumscribed by law and thus by Parliament, and provincial governments must face the electorate and govern both with and against Ottawa – the mass media seem to have few such constraints. Increasingly in Canada, they have power without accountability. The responsibility for that failure, for that betrayal of public interest and public responsibility, falls on many shoulders.

Our Central Public Squares

To a large degree, the mass media constitute a society's meeting ground, its central public square. This doesn't take away from the importance of society's other vital meeting places: legislatures, schools and universities, churches and synagogues, clubs and charitable organizations, the socializing that takes place at sports events and, of course, gatherings at kitchen tables and at neighbourhood coffee shops and watering holes. But the mass media stretch to include the entire society. They reach everywhere. They envelop and surround us. As Joshua Meyrowitz, a leading American media scholar, has pointed out, "someone or something that does not appear on television does not fully exist in a social sense."[4] For the vast majority of the population, television and to a lesser extent radio, newspapers, and magazines make political leaders and events real. They give them substance and legitimacy and place them in context. The vast majority of Canadians have never visited the House of Commons (or Ottawa for that matter) but have come to "know" Jean Chretien or Preston Manning based almost exclusively on having seen them on television.

Author and environmentalist Bill McKibben believes that television in particular is so pervasive that it has literally invaded our lives, becoming one of the places in which we live: "electronic media have become an environment of their own – ... to the list of neighborhood and region and continent and planet we must now add television as a place where we live. And the problem is not that it exists – the problem is that it supplants."[5]

The essential lifeblood of a healthy democratic society is the degree to which it is open to new ideas, different points of view, and controversial issues. A public space is by its very nature combative and chaotic and filled with popular myths and obsessions. It is a place where passions can be vented and demons fought and slain. But it is also the place where the essential work of a society takes place – the place where ideas are formulated and debated. If the public space is closed off to people with unpopular views or ideas or to important information, then a society risks becoming rigid and atrophied, losing its turbulent and vital energy.

Jay Rosen, a professor of journalism at New York University, has argued that the primary mission of our communications media and indeed of journalism in general should be "to make politics 'go well,' so that it produces a discussion in which the polity learns more about itself, its current problems, its real divisions, its place in time, its prospects for the future."[6] This does not mean that we must forgo our basic diet of sports and entertainment, ambulance-chasing journalism, and tabloid media on which we have been gorging for so long but simply that we should leave parts of our public space open for other kinds of messages and for alternative views and perspectives.

Scholars such as Jürgen Habermas and James Carey have documented the emergence of the "public" as both an idea and a powerful political reality. The notion that there is a public whose needs and wishes must be reflected and satisfied by those who govern coincides with the emergence of the mass media. The essential linchpin of the democratic experience is that citizens will have the opportunity to learn about and then discuss, evaluate, and act on the issues and policies that affect them.

To the German philosopher Jürgen Habermas, the "public sphere" is confined to a precious but narrow segment of society:

that arena not controlled by governments or corporate interests.[7] It is a place where conversations can occur freely, insulated from threats, intimidation or propaganda, and where reasoned arguments can prevail. In Habermas's view, a golden age of political freedom occurred among the bourgeois classes in seventeenth- and eighteenth-century Europe. Their struggle for a free press — a press critical of those who held power — was the necessary precondition for the emergence of democracy. In Colonial America, the formation and notion of a public began curiously enough in pubs — that is, in public drinking houses. Travellers would describe what they had seen on their journeys and their observations were often recorded in log books placed at the end of bars. These logs were then printed and circulated. But the open congeniality of the public houses created a life of their own. Sam Warner, an American historian, has described the formation of public attitudes in Philadelphia just prior to the American Revolution: "gossip in the taverns provided Philadelphia's basic cells of community life … Every ward of the city had its inns and taverns and the London Coffee House served as central communication node of the entire city … Out of the meetings at the neighborhood tavern came much of the commonplace community development … essential to the governance of the city."[8] With the advent of newspapers a new dynamic took over. As James Carey, a distinguished communication scholar, has pointed out: "The public was a specific social formation: a group of people, often strangers, gathered in public houses to talk, to read the news together, to dispute the meaning of events, to join political impulses to political actions."[9] Thus the "public" emerged from interactions that people had with each other, and through knowledge of political developments that they received from the press.

The French philosopher who brilliantly chronicled the emergence of American democracy, Alexis de Tocqueville, described the critical role that newspapers played in creating a democratic culture:

> … a great many men who both want and need to get together cannot do so, for all being very small and lost in the crowd, they do not see one another at all and do not know where to find one another.

> Then a newspaper gives publicity to the feeling or
> idea that had occurred to them all simultaneously
> but separately ... The newspaper brought them to-
> gether and continues to be necessary to hold them
> together.[10]

While we tend to idealize those earlier times – envisioning neighbours meeting in warm and rustic town halls on winter evenings
where people could reason with their friends and voice their opinions without fear – this was hardly ever the reality. The public
sphere, whether the agora in ancient Athens or the famed New England town hall meeting, was almost always a place of privilege. Only
the wealthy and powerful could participate. Women, men without
money or social standing, and members of minority races and reli-
gions were never part of the "public." Even in Norman Rockwell's
famous painting, *Freedom of Speech*, which celebrates the simplicity
and honest virtues of a typical town hall meeting in small-town
America, no visible minorities and only a single woman are present.

Today, the notion of a "public" is at best an amorphous and somewhat artificial construction. We have come a long way from the tangible, ale-soaked world of the public house. What we know about
the composition of the public, and its various moods and sentiments,
is served up to us by pollsters and interest groups who have the
capacity to create as much as reflect public opinion. Scholars such
as Elihu Katz argue that television is the principal means through
which a public is now created and assembled.[11] The power of television is that it gives viewers a sense of intimate witnessing, of seeing people and events for themselves. It draws them into "imagined
communities," to use anthropologist Benedict Anderson's term, and
into central civic places – into town squares – that didn't exist before.[12] According to British scholar Robert Hartley:

> Nowadays there is no physical public domain, and
> politics is not "of the populace." Contemporary poli-
> tics are representative in both senses of the term;
> citizens are represented by a chosen few, and poli-
> tics is represented to the public via the various me-

> dia of communication. Representative political
> space is literally made of pictures – they constitute
> the public domain.[13]

For decades, Canadians shared common experiences based on the simple fact that they came together at the same time to watch the same television programs. We all in some sense shared the same living room. The country was united by predictable civic rituals: sitting down together to watch the news before bedtime or being together with friends to watch the Grey Cup on a Sunday afternoon in the late fall. Common boundaries were created as Canadians en masse watched the same programs, attended the same political or sports events, cheered the same celebrities, and laughed at the same jokes.

Television has for at least a generation been the central nervous system that has linked the country together and linked the country to the world. The statistics on television use are astonishing, some would say frightening. Over the past 30 years the number of hours that Canadians have spent watching television per week has fluctuated "within the narrow band" of between 21 and 23.[14] This means that a typical Canadian will spend almost a full day watching TV every week. Or to put it another way, more than 10 years out of an average lifetime is spent in front of the TV set. More than one in five Canadians routinely watch TV while eating dinner, and close to half of all Canadians have a TV in their bedrooms.[15]

The Mandate Review Committee on the CBC, NFB and Telefilm, which reported to the federal government in 1996, made the following devastating observation: "By the time our kids reach the age of 12, they will have seen approximately 12,000 hours of television – twice as much time as they will have spent in school. And eight times the hours they will have devoted to doing homework. Schools may be educating our children. But for better or worse, it's television that's teaching them."[16]

Joshua Meyrowitz described the central role that TV plays in our lives this way: "We begin peering at TV through the bars of cribs and continue looking at it through the cataracts of old age."[17]

The televising of epic events such as the assassination of U.S. President John F. Kennedy, the launching of astronauts into space, the Watergate hearings, the Vietnam War, and more recently the funeral of Diana, Princess of Wales, and the grand jury testimony and impeachment proceedings against President Bill Clinton have become landmarks of historical and generational memory around the world. In Canada, the Canadian victory in the Canada-Soviet hockey series in 1972, Terry Fox's courageous run for cancer research, the dramatic final days of the Meech Lake negotiations in 1990, the standoff between Natives and the armed forces at Oka, and the long, agonizing night of the 1995 Quebec referendum when the fate of the federation hung precariously in the balance, have been indelibly inscribed in the country's collective consciousness. Television's coverage of the drama and devastation of the Red River flood of 1997, and the blackouts and deprivations of the ice storm that ravaged Quebec and Eastern Canada in Winter 1998, produced an extraordinary outpouring of concern and sparked grassroots volunteer and fund-raising efforts across Canada. These TV "moments" brought the country together – in some cases in triumph, and in other cases in pain.

Despite all of the changes now occurring that are likely to diminish the reach of mainstream Canadian television, such as the cable explosion and the Internet revolution, close to two and a half million people still assemble at ten and eleven o'clock each night to watch *The National* on CBC and *The CTV Evening News.* At moments of crisis or when stories are particularly compelling, audiences can balloon to well beyond these numbers. Studies confirm that a large majority of Canadians rely on television as their main source of news. For instance, a survey conducted at the University of Western Ontario found that 57 per cent of adults turned to TV as their primary source for news as against 28 per cent who relied on newspapers and 9 per cent who depended on radio. A sizeable portion of the population, perhaps as much as one-third of the public, get virtually all of their news from television.

TV viewing varies considerably among Canadians in different regions, and in different age and income groups. Francophones tend to watch more TV than anglophones, women watch slightly more than men, and those over 65 years of age watch far more than teenagers and young adults. The most significant barometer of TV viewing, however, is income and education. The higher one's education and socio-economic status the less television one is likely to watch and the more likely one is to read books and newspapers.

But TV creates a public in other ways. In the 1980s and 1990s a wave of populism swept through television. The rise of talk television with its live audiences and phone-in lines is the most obvious example of this phenomenon. Talk TV is relatively inexpensive to produce, and TV executives thought that they could capture viewers by appearing to give ordinary people a place and a voice. These shows are characterized by a democratic levelling with hosts such as Oprah Winfrey, Maury Povich, or Ricki Lake often taking the role of public prosecutors questioning, judging, and ultimately finding authority figures, whether they be doctors, corporate leaders or government officials, guilty of some kind of abuse. Hosts rev up the audience so that audience members join the fray, sticking their own pointed daggers (verbally at least) into the authority figures or institutions that are under attack. Of course, not every show turns into an inquisition. Robert Hughes, a noted cultural critic, believes that these shows often have a confessional aspect to them, as guests and audience members confess their sins and seek absolution from society, much as they would do in a church or synagogue.[18]

Other interpretations tend to see these shows as little more than appeals to people's worst instincts, a race to the bottom of the television trash heap. These programs have been described as "festivals of dysfunction" because of their glamorization of freakish and outlandish behaviour and their often shameless exhibitionism. Geraldo Rivera did programs on female boxers and visited a topless doughnut shop. Jerry Springer is notorious for setting up confrontations among his guests that lead to screaming matches and fisticuffs. In May 1998, Springer featured programs about husbands who find out their wives are sleeping with their best friends, wives who reveal the men who were really the fathers of their children to their unsuspecting husbands, family members confronting a pimp whose stable includes a mother and daughter prostitute team, secret homosexual and lesbian sex lives, and the reunion of a women with the high school sweetheart who rejected her. *Washington Post* media critic Howard Kurtz has condemned talk TV in the harshest terms: "By parading the sickest, the weirdest, the most painfully afflicted before an audience of millions, these shows bombard us with sleaze to the point of numbness. The abnormal becomes ordinary, the pathetic merely another pause in our daily channel surfing ... We become desensitized by the endless freak show."[19]

Media scholar Wendy Kaminer is a little more charitable. Although she sees these shows as preoccupied with blame and victimization and "self-centred individualism," Kaminer believes that they also serve viewers by focusing on recovery and self-improvement. There is a steady stream of advice on relationships, health care, and consumer buying that may be crucial for many viewers who cannot afford access to professional help.[20]

Even CBC's staid flagship news program, *The National,* has tried to tap into the populist impulse. Its main device is the town hall in which citizens are brought in from across Canada to confront political leaders or discuss burning issues such as unemployment or national unity. The town halls have sometimes been criticized for being too choreographed and for "beating up" politicians, but they have often resulted in healthy exchanges that have put political leaders on public view in a unique and dramatic way. The CBC has perhaps taken its boldest step with a program called *Jonovision.* Directed at teens, the show allows young people to discuss various predicaments in which they have found themselves with Jono, the host, and a studio audience. *Jonovision* also polls members of the studio audience and home viewers about topics relevant to teens such as the minimum wage or whether or not it's "sweet" to have a tattoo.

Moreover, television programs now invite the audience to participate in other ways. Indeed, one can argue that TV is driven by a relentless pursuit of the audience, a ceaseless catering to its wishes. Programs made in Hollywood are meticulously tested before they ever go on the air. The response of viewers to characters and story lines are surveyed by various means so that unpopular wrinkles can be ironed out of shows. Sets and camera angles are thought through so that those watching can feel at home – can in effect "come in and sit around the table." And most important, the verdict of the public, its judgment, is registered in nightly ratings that determine whether programs will remain on the air. Much as was the case with the gunslingers of the Old West, there are only two kinds of shows, the quick (those that can build a large audience quickly) and the dead (those that can't).

Ratings seep into and permeate every aspect of the television business including TV news. In one television newsroom in Calgary a picture of a professional-looking women in her thirties hangs on the wall. The journalists have nicknamed her "Liz." Liz is there because she represents the target audience and reporters are reminded to keep her interests in mind when doing their stories.[21] While much of the academic literature on news reporting stresses the degree to which journalists are shielded from audience demands, and the extent to which they respond to pressures from their managers and from news sources, the entire tilt of television news in the 1990s was toward giving the viewers the news they wanted rather than the news that journalists believed that they should have or needed to know.

MSNBC, the web site and all-news TV channel operated by Microsoft and NBC, has perhaps gone the farthest in moulding and reconfiguring itself to meet audience demands.[22] In effect, they have put the audience in the driver's seat, made the audience into the producer. The system works this way: viewers are asked at the end of every news story whether they would recommend the story to other viewers. They can rate each story on a scale of 1 to 7 by moving a slide bar. MSNBC has responded to this instant rating system by altering its news lineup to feature more stories on health and science and more "news you can use." Critics are concerned that reporters will be judged not according to the quality of their journalism but on the number of times their stories make the top-10 list.

CNN offers its viewers similar but more limited choices. Audience members (that is, the majority of those who call a 1-800 number) can choose a story that they wish to see aired on the next broadcast from a short menu of possible stories.

Some journalists might look back with nostalgia to the time not very long ago when audiences had less influence over the content of news shows. For instance, when Fred Friendly was president of CBS News during the 1960s, he proudly referred to himself as "the Hand on the Big Switch."[23] Today, journalists are concerned that they are slowly losing control of the big switch.

As part of this populist wave, virtually every TV program and network maintains an elaborate web site to keep viewers appraised of schedules or the latest developments on a show. Viewers can contact each other through chat lines, and contact stars or producers directly via e-mail. CNN Interactive, CNNSI and CNN All Politics, The Discovery Channel, ESPN's Sportzone, and MSNBC maintain perhaps the most impressive sites. In Canada, a turning point of sorts occurred during CTV's coverage of the 1996 World Figure Skating Championships. On a single night over 800,000 viewers visited the web site that CTV had created especially to cover the event.[24] One can argue that TV viewing has now become integrated with the Internet so that watching TV and surfing the Net go hand-in-hand. People turned to television, for instance, when news first broke about Princess Diana's death in 1997, but many of them then went to news web sites in order to get more information. These sites also rerouted their visitors back to television by informing them about upcoming specials on Diana. Similarly, when the last episode of *Seinfeld* aired in May 1998, numerous network and fan sites buzzed with information, commentary, advertising, chat and rumours about the much ballyhooed last program and its contents.

The CBC's most visited web site is *CBC Newsworld Online*, which attracts between 35,000 and 50,000 page views per day. The site provides regular updates on news stories, frequently using real-time video. Some CBC programs have geared their sites to attract particular target audiences. CBC Radio's *Ideas*, arguably the most intellectually sophisticated and challenging program offered by any broadcaster in North America, has tailored its site to younger listeners and tries to maintain an ongoing dialogue with a quite sophisticated and highly literate audience. In June 1998, the CBC launched *Infoculture*, an online service that it claims is the country's most comprehensive source for arts and cultural reporting. A similar site was inaugurated by Radio Canada in December 1997.

Of course, television is not the only medium with the power to construct a public. Newspapers and radio are pivotal in organizing and shaping community life, and the World Wide Web is both loosening old ties and constructing new ones. Having more time and space for commentary and opinion than television does, they help frame public consciousness and debate.

Let's take radio. One only has to be reminded of the sense of loss that occurred when CBC-Radio's *Morningside* was cancelled after host Peter Gzowski decided to leave in 1997. Gzowski, whose raspy voice and folksy down-to-earth congeniality was as much a part of the morning for Canadians as a cup of coffee, had become a national icon, and the show drew audiences of 1.5 million listeners daily. Robert Collison described the show as "the country's village bulletin board."[25] While the new morning show, *This Morning*, hosted by Michael Enright and Avril Benoit, has a great deal of *Morningside*'s emotion, verve and panache and will no doubt have its own unique identity, the CBC's decision to discard such an important marquee may be an indication of the fierceness of the storm that has engulfed the corporation, and the extent to which traditions can be easily swept aside in the rush to appear "new" or to at least demonstrate to others that changes are being made.

But it has to be recognized that most radio is intensely local. Although Canadians still listen to a great deal of radio – tuning in for an average of 21 hours per week in 1997 – for most Canadians radio listening tends to be bracketed into drive time or morning listening at home and is dominated by FM easy listening, country and hot rock.[26] All AM radio formats reported losing money in 1997, while FM radio showed a healthy surge in profits from $63.7 million in 1996 to $90 million in 1997. Women tend to listen to radio slightly more than men, and those between 55 and 64 tend to listen just a little more frequently than others.[27]

Even hot line shows tend to be wedded to local markets. Although satellites and syndication have produced huge followings of tens of millions of listeners for American "shock jocks" and "morning zoozanies" such as Don Imus, Howard Stern and Rush Limbaugh, and for the on-air therapy of Dr. Laura Schlessinger, the same phenomenon has not occurred for home-grown Canadian shows. True, CBC-Radio has national talk shows such as the venerable *Cross-Country Checkup* hosted by Rex Murphy (who also does a weekly pop culture segment on *DNTO – Definitely Not The Opera*), and there are sports call-in shows such as *Sports Coast to Coast* and shows that offer financial advice to callers such as *Canada's Smart Money Show* that reach a national audience. Rhona Raskin's *Rhona at Night* is Canada's answer to Dr. Laura. But typically talk radio in Canada tends to stew in local juices.

According to some studies, radio talk shows draw an audience of "regulars" – mostly older male callers who tend to hold sharply conservative views and who use talk shows for the ego gratification of hearing themselves talk, to vent steam on a particular topic, or as a surrogate companion. Howard Kurtz, author of a book on talk radio and television entitled *Hot Air*, believes that the medium has become "fertile ground for the stereotypical angry white male" who feels increasingly disenfranchised and voiceless in the new economy.[28] Kurtz also sees talk radio as little more than a sideshow. "By appearing on talk shows," he claims, "you have a certain name ID with .01 percent of the people."[29] There are others, however, such as Benjamin Page of Northwestern University, who argue that talk radio can be a potent political force because it can galvanize citizens to take action about issues that they care about. Callers are a "vocal minority" who have the potential to ignite "firestorms" if their concerns catch on and powerful interests become involved.[30]

David Barker of the University of Houston paints an entirely different picture from the one drawn by Kurtz. Barker argues that talk show listeners, while certainly predominantly male, older and more conservative than their non-listening counterparts, are not necessarily the motley collection of lonely and disenfranchised voices that Kurtz and others claim they are. In fact, the very opposite is true. Barker found listeners to be wealthier, more involved, and much more likely to vote than were others. Given the potency of such a group, the real power of talk radio "may be in creating 'opinion leaders,' who

then exert influence on their spouses, friends, children, congrega-
tions, students and employees."[31]

To my knowledge there have been no studies of hot line audiences conducted in Canada. But it would be fascinating to see
whether there is a "Rafe Mair effect" in British Columbia or Canadian politics in the same the way that there has been a Rush
Limbaugh effect in the U.S.

Most interesting, perhaps, is the way in which radio has been able
to reinvent itself. In fact, many observers view radio as one of the
new media, not because the technology is new but because radio is
continually experimenting with new formats and breaking new
ground. Far from being left in the distant wake of television's power,
radio has adjusted by becoming more populist and more open to
audience participation. Radio stations know that unless audiences
come to identify with their formats, they won't survive for long.

While broadcasting dominates much of the media landscape,
newspapers have retained their position as the notice boards and
chroniclers of civic life. With over 5.1 million newspapers sold every
day in Canada in 1997, newspapers remain among the key linch-
pins of a national community.[32] While much has been written about
the decline of newspapers, reports of their demise, to use an old
phrase, seem to be greatly exaggerated. At first glance, however,
the future of newspapers does not look to be particularly rosy. The
loss of leisure time (the time crunch that many families find themselves in), the advent of the Internet, which cuts into readership and
threatens to usurp advertising, and the decline in literacy, particularly among the young, have taken their toll. Surveys of people who
have dropped their newspaper subscriptions indicate that as many
as 40 per cent do so because they believe they no longer have time
to read the papers – that the "papers just kept piling up," while an
additional 20 per cent believe that they have "better things to do."[33]
These realities are borne out by statistics. Christopher Dornan, Director of the School of Journalism and Communications at Carleton
University, reports that the industry in Canada endured a precipi-
tous decline in readership during the 1990s, dropping from more
than 5.8 million papers sold daily in 1989 to a little over 5.1 million

in 1997.[34] A similar collapse in readership occurred in the United States – a survey taken in 1995 revealed that only 43 per cent of those contacted had read a newspaper the day before, a figure that was down substantially from 73 per cent in 1967.[35] In another survey taken in 1994, only 24 per cent of respondents expressed "a great deal of confidence" in newspapers, a drop from 51 per cent in 1988.[36]

At the same time, there is much talk about a newspaper renaissance and the prospect of a "new golden age" for the industry. The boom economy of the late 1990s has jacked revenues to record levels; advertising lineage increased by 7 per cent in 1997, the greatest annual increase since 1972.[37] The high tide seems to have lifted all of the newspaper boats as every one of Canada's newspaper chains garnered sizeable profits in 1997. Newspapers still attract approximately 43 per cent of all advertising dollars in Canada as against only 33 per cent that go to television.[38] And newspapers are moving to protect their domination over classified ads (the meat and potatoes of economic survival for most newspapers and perhaps even for the industry as a whole) from the threat posed by Internet competitors by going online themselves. As newspaper baron Conrad Black expressed the need to rise to the challenge: "Failure to protect classified in this way will result in the loss of the entire classified business. We do not intend to sit like suet puddings and allow this to happen."[39]

Media commentators such as Pete Hamill and Jon Katz argue that newspapers are likely to become more important than ever in what Australian scholar John Keane has described as "the era of communicative abundance."[40] They believe that newspapers can be a vital information "clearinghouse," telling readers what's important, what to pay attention to and what to ignore.[41] Hamill wants newspapers to be the institution that "corrects, verifies and debunks," in effect guiding readers through the vast forest of information they have to traverse each day.[42] These observers fear that newspapers will not live up to this challenge, that they will find it easier to follow rather than lead the other media. It's easier, after all, to reprint the public relations packets given to them by the major entertainment giants, pass along the rumours that sometimes pass for truth on the Internet, and repackage wire service stories.

One interesting development is that economic forces are conspiring to make newspapers more national in scope, and therefore more important as instruments of national integration. The *Globe and Mail* and Conrad Black's newly launched *National Post* now battle against each other in cities across the country. At this point the *Globe* remains "the kingdom and the power" of the Canadian newspaper industry because of its unique capacity to penetrate the governmental and business elites of the country and to set the national agenda with its commentary and investigative reporting. Its grey respectability attracts wealthier and better-educated readers, and its Report on Business section, its op-ed pages, and its arts reporting have made it must reading for a variety of different readerships.

Conrad Black's *National Post* is likely to take a sizeable bite out of the *Globe*'s readership and its advertising. Armed with a stable of top columnists such as Mordecai Richler, Diane Francis, Alan Abel, and Andrew Coyne, having the chain-link fence of the Southam news service and its reporters across the country at its disposal, able to offer advertisers space in the national paper as well as in Southam papers across the country, and with deep pockets, it will put the *Globe* under heavy assault. Conrad Black has boasted of having learned how the newspaper game is played during a brutal battle for the London newspaper market with Rupert Murdoch. Black's *Daily Telegram* was nearly bled white in a nasty prolonged price war with Murdoch's *Times*.

There are, however, what some see as ominous clouds threatening the Canadian newspaper industry. In a development that is almost unprecedented in a democratic country, a single individual, Conrad Black, now owns the lion's share of Canadian newspapers. Indeed one can argue that for all intents and purposes, Black has become the newspaper industry in Canada.[43] Black now controls 60 of Canada's 105 daily newspapers. He owns all of the major dailies in British Columbia, Saskatchewan, Prince Edward Island, and Newfoundland. His papers reach over 2.5 million readers daily, approximately 45 per cent of all circulation in Canada. And whereas 70 per cent of daily circulation in Canada is in the hands of just three chains – Hollinger/Southam, Thomson, and the Sun – 75 per cent of American circulation is controlled by 19 American chains.[44] And while almost 25 per cent of American newspapers are independently owned, only the *Toronto Star* – a large publishing empire in its own right – can be considered independent of other newspaper chains.

Some would argue that Black's stranglehold is especially disturbing because Black is an ardent and passionate political warrior. He has strong right-wing opinions, tends to hire journalists who share his views, and knows that newspapers are formidable political weapons. With such overwhelming power clutched in Black's fist, diversity is being threatened. The issue is not censorship or interference by Black or other media managers with what newspaper journalists write, but with the self-censorship that journalists impose on themselves. Some journalists feel that if they push the envelope too far, that is, consistently advocate positions that Black and his managers will find irksome, then their careers will languish. They will be cut off at the knees, banished into newspaper obscurity, into professional oblivion. Not only will they not find themselves rising in the organization, but there are now far fewer rival organizations to go to. One of the guarantees of journalistic freedom is that journalists could always walk across the street and work for someone else. The fear is that there will now be only one side of the street.

The same holds true for advertisers, who in many cases must either accept Black's rates or not advertise in newspapers at all.

Another concern is with Black's strategy of strip mining his newspaper properties. According to some critics his repertoire usually includes slashing staffs, reducing local coverage, relying on more chain and wire service stories, and squeezing papers for every ounce of profit. Papers begin to fit a cookie-cutter mould; they lose their unique character and certainly their gusto for hard-hitting investigative journalism.[45] Others contend that Black is willing to invest in a select number of prestige papers such as the *Daily Telegraph* in Britain, the *Jerusalem Post* in Israel, and the *Ottawa Citizen* in Canada, making them into showpieces; they are laced with editorials, commentary and political coverage.

According to some observers, Black's dominance of the Canadian newspaper industry contains the potential for a widespread abuse of power. While Black may be cautious and circumspect in shaping editorial policy, and indeed be the best imaginable corporate citizen, keeping only a distant eye on papers in his far-flung empire, the possibility for intervention into Canadian politics is always there. As Lou Clancy, a former managing editor of the *Toronto Star* has described the situation: "It may not necessarily be bad, but the potential is always there for it to be dangerous."[46] John Honderich, publisher of the *Toronto Star*, has called for another federal royal commission similar to the Kent Commission (1981), which investigated the concentration of newspaper ownership. According to Honderich: "Sixty per cent of the papers in this country are now controlled by one man. Is this healthy for this country? Is it not important that some of the politicians look at these issues and find out whether there's enough diversity? I think it's a very serious question and one that should be examined very carefully."[47]

The other great question surrounding newspapers is whether the newspaper as we know it will be washed away by the revolution now taking place in new information technologies. Suffice it to say that for now at least newspapers remains an indispensable, perhaps even the indispensable, pillar of community life. Indeed, it would be difficult to imagine what life would be like, how cities and communities would function, if newspapers ceased to exist. That's exactly what happened in Pittsburgh, Pennsylvania, in 1992 when newspaper workers went out on strike, effectively closing down both of Pittsburgh's newspapers. The city was frozen: attendance at sports events, movies and the theatre plummeted, job hunters were left stranded, people missed sales and funerals and lost track of local events, and political life seemed to take place in a vacuum – a game without spectators. The public space that the newspaper had created had become a hollow shell.[48]

As is the case with newspapers, there are threats to the Canadian magazine industry looming on the horizon. While stalwarts like *Chatelaine* (with a circulation of close to one million circulation in English and French), *Maclean's* (500,000 circulation), *L'Actualite*

(188,000), *Canadian Living* (553,000), and *Alberta/Western Report* (40,000), have managed to thrive, most Canadian publications are buried beneath an avalanche of U.S. imports. Approximately 50 per cent of all magazines sold in Canada are American, and U.S. magazines have captured roughly 80 per cent of newsstand sales.[49] The problem is that major advertisers such as Ford, Microsoft, or Universal Studios know that they can reach large numbers of Canadians by advertising in U.S. magazines. Because of this spillover, many of them choose not to advertise in Canada. This has the effect of weakening the Canadian industry.

For decades the federal government subsidized the industry through discounts on postal rates, the levying of customs tariffs, and the imposition of tax penalties on Canadian advertisers who bought space in foreign publications. These protectionist measures – this active intervention – was the margin of survival for more than a few Canadian magazines. In 1997, however, the World Trade Organization (WTO) ruled that much of the protectionist wall that Canada had erected was illegal under international trade law and that it had to be dismantled.

Ottawa continues to resist such international pressures and has moved in particular to outlaw "split-runs." Split-runs are spin-off editions of major magazines such as *Time* and *Reader's Digest*. Both of these publications incidentally do a booming business in Canada – *Time* has a circulation of approximately 315,000 and *Reader's Digest* reaches well over 1,500,000 Canadians in French and English.[50] Canadian editions of these magazines take the bulk of their editorial content from their regular U.S. editions, add a smattering of Canadian content, and offer Canadian advertisers rates that are more attractive than those available to American advertisers.[51] Canadian editorial content is often little more than an add-on, a bit of puffery that adds little to public debate or knowledge about Canada. A nightmare scenario for the magazine industry would be if Canadian laws continued to be struck down by the WTO and the country became inundated by split-run editions of U.S. magazines. According to one estimate, as many as 80 U.S. magazines are prepared to launch split-run editions.[52]

The newest public meeting place is the World Wide Web. The magic of the Web is that it offers audiences a "Milky Way" of choices. People can connect worldwide on any conceivable topic and link up with literally any institution or organization. The Web is an endless display shelf, library, and shopping centre. But some argue that its effect is to splinter and fragment audiences into bite-size morsels, into small, exotic and specialized communities, rather than to bring citizens together in a common meeting ground. Moreover, while television, newspapers and radio reach mass audiences, the Internet is still the preserve of a privileged elite. Approximately 25 per cent of Canadians over the age of 16 use computers at home, work, or school, but only about 13 per cent can be described as regular users.[53] Moreover, a survey of Internet usage conducted by *Survey.Net* found that web surfers were predominantly unmarried males in their 20s who were well-educated and earned over $40,000 a year.[54] A BBM Media study revealed that while 57 per cent of Canadian households with an annual income of $60,000 or more have Internet access, only 19 per cent of those with less than $20,000 are hooked up.[55] Many citizens are locked out of the information causeway because the costs of PCs, telephone lines and servers, let alone the cost of subscriptions to what is available on the Web, are beyond their means. The Internet (but also cable and satellite television) has created new class divisions based on access to information: some people are information rich, with a lavish smorgasbord of choices available to them, while others are information poor — stuck on the bread and peanut butter of the old media.

Although the World Wide Web is poised to bring revolutionary changes, it has yet to challenge conventional television's formidable authority and massive reach. For instance, a study of Internet use during the 1997 Alberta provincial election revealed that only a small minority of the voting population, less than 35,000 in total, visited party or media web sites during the election.[56] Estimates of the percentage of U.S. voters who visited politically oriented sites during the 1996 U.S. presidential election range from 6 to 14 per cent.[57] In terms of reaching and assembling mass audiences the "old" media remain king of the castle.

This does not mean, however, that the group that *Wired* magazine calls "digital citizens" can be ignored.[58] In contrast to the popular image of high Internet users as anti-social techno-freaks who live in their own sheltered worlds, a survey published in November 1997 found that members of the digital community were more likely to vote, were better informed about politics, and had greater confidence in their ability to "control" change than non-users. Internet activists were also far more suspicious of TV and newspapers than were others — only 13 per cent expressed a lot of confidence in the old media's accuracy or fairness.

The Line of Attack

This book will examine the dramatic changes taking place in the Canadian media. The future may indeed be spectacular in terms of new technology, but it may also be bleak in terms of the choices that are being made available to Canadians as citizens rather than as consumers. My worry is that public spaces, while appearing to be more open and democratic, are being choked by powerful commercial forces and monolithic trends. In some senses we are moving not to wider thoroughfares but to narrower and narrower side streets — streets that are beginning to all look the same. A healthy democracy depends on open lines of communication and a fundamental respect for the views of citizens. Anything less can lead to dangerous distortions and a disfiguring of the democratic process. My contention is that the media window, the portal through which we view our country and the world, is becoming increasingly distorted by the stained glass of conglomerate power, a failing journalistic culture, and governments and regulators who have been too weak to fight for real diversity.

What has deepened the crisis is that several large waves of media change are crashing in on us at the same time. The cumulative effect of these giant waves is extraordinary — in fact, governments and citizens have had difficulty coming to terms with the scope of the changes that are taking place. And the pace of media change is so rapid that it is difficult even to chart the latest developments without quickly becoming out of date.

In the next chapter, entitled "Thinking About Media, Citizens and Democracy," I attempt to map out some of the debate that surrounds the role of the media by describing four ways in which the media shape public attitudes. I will offer four contending interpretations or frameworks that will place the role of the media in society in some context. These four views are not mutually exclusive; they don't cancel each other out. There is a sizeable measure of truth in each of them. My hope is that by providing these frameworks, I can shed some light on the crises that pockmark the face of the Canadian media. The goal is to address nagging questions about the role that citizens play in a democracy, and how the nature of citizenship, and indeed of community, is undergoing drastic changes in the new media age.

Chapters three and four will look at the big picture in a different way, examining the changes in technology and global markets that are altering the media landscape. I will focus on two simultaneous trends, convergence and fragmentation. Convergence describes a media revolution taking place at a number of levels. First, technologies are in the process of being merged – broadcast TV, cable TV, the telephone, libraries, satellites, and computers are all being integrated with each other. Second, global alliances among major corporations are being forged to a degree that is virtually unprecedented in world history. Today, a handful of gigantic corporations control almost all of the world's media. Third, there is a convergence of news and entertainment. News is now selected to include stories that have entertainment value, and those stories are increasingly told in ways that will shock, titillate or arouse emotions. The fourth great convergence is the blending of cultures. The same cultural messages now resonate worldwide with little regard for borders or boundaries. The special and unique flavours of local and community life are being swamped by an international shopping centre culture. Some critics fear that international convergence will erode national loyalties and even national consciousness. While the phenomenon of convergence is championed by those who see these developments as ushering in a new era of prosperity and togetherness, others see dark, foreboding clouds on the horizon.

A second and to some extent competing trend is fragmentation. The argument made in chapter four is that the cable explosion, the 500-channel universe that it is likely to bring, and the Internet revolution are splintering audiences into narrower and narrower segments, into tiny slivers. Almost every conceivable identity, interest, hobby, organization or business now has its niche somewhere in the digital universe. Some observers see this new media kaleidoscope as expanding our choices as never before – as a boon to free speech and democracy. The new media horizon is so limitless that no dictator could possibly keep track of it, let alone control or suppress it. The floodgates of opinion and debate have been permanently opened. But other observers are disturbed not only by the anarchy that characterizes much of the new media but by the threat that it poses to the media's capacity to bring large numbers of citizens together at one time and in one place. The public squares created by the old media are being threatened by the juggernaut of the new media. Where convergence is weakening the nation-state by elevating power and authority to an international level, fragmentation erodes the nation-state by jeopardizing its ability to maintain a common system of communication, a common culture.

Chapters five, six, and seven describe the crisis that now envelopes Canadian broadcasting. My main concern is that the publicly financed CBC, which is the spinal cord for national communication and identity, is being weakened by government budget-cutting and jeopardized by the licensing of numerous but often less effective competitors, each of which cuts into the CBC's audience. Although the CBC remains the largest journalistic organization in Canada and has a mandate to cover public affairs with a depth and thoroughness not expected from the private sector, the public broadcaster has been under political siege for much of its history. Chapters five and six deal with the extraordinary political pressures – the intense political heat lamp – that the CBC has been under almost continually since the 1960s. Prime ministers of every stripe, stung by critical reporting, afraid of the repercussions of controversial programming, and mired in the struggle over Canadian unity have at times attacked, cajoled, interfered with, and used the public broadcaster as a political football. These chapters describe how the politics of broadcasting have influenced the broadcasting of politics. My fear is that the great public squares once created by CBC programming have been trampled by too many political footsteps.

In chapter seven the spotlight shifts to private broadcasters. While some of the focus is still on the controversy that surrounds the mandate and financing of the CBC, my main argument is that private TV networks or ownership groups are not so much broadcasters as they are "rebroadcasters." They make the lion's share of their profits by buying American shows "off the shelf" in Hollywood and then delivering them to Canadian audiences and advertisers. My concern is that while this may be a lucrative business practice for CTV, CanWest Global, or Shaw, it has done little for the country. The current economics of Canadian television, indeed the tilting of the TV game board by the CRTC to favour private broadcasters, has produced relatively few instances of memorable Canadian programming, and little that teaches the country more about itself and its prospects for the future. The chapter questions the rationale that underlies current broadcasting policy in Canada.

Chapter eight describes the ascent of right-wing views and influences in Canadian journalism. This chapter will sew together a number of different themes: the "attack culture" in journalism and the cynicism toward government that it breeds, Conrad Black's ideological views and his lock on newspaper ownership, and the rise of right-wing pundits on TV and radio talk shows. What is interesting, of course, is that conservative groups have always claimed that journalists are too liberal, and that the media undermine traditional values. This belief has almost become a mantra, repeated so often that it has taken on a life of its own. I put this claim to the test by looking closely at the current trends in Canadian journalism.

The thread that weaves its way through the book is the issue of the media's responsibility toward the people and the country that they serve. James Carey has written, "[W]e should value the press to the precise degree that it sustains public life, that it keeps the conversation going among us, and ... we devalue the press to the degree ... it turns us into silent spectators."[59] The onus for keeping the democratic conversation going, for keeping it alive, falls not only on working journalists but on politicians, regulators, owners, and citizens themselves. We all have a responsibility to ensure that the society as a whole is as open as it can possibly be to a diversity of ideas. Author James Fallows claims that the media are now demonstrating the same degree of arrogance and disrepair that infected the U.S. military during the quagmire of the Vietnam War, or that plagued Detroit's Big Three automakers during the 1970s when they were sleepily going about their business oblivious to the emerging threat from the Japanese.[60] The problem is that there is no Viet Cong army waiting to assault the media citadels, and no Toyotas or Hondas waiting to drive Canadian media organizations off the road. The Canadian media system and its power holders are deeply entrenched.

My purpose, to use Walter Lippmann's famous phrase, is to "turn the beam of a searchlight" on the media itself. The main focus is on whether the public spaces that the media create remain open to new messages and ideas or whether only the voices of powerful commercial interests are being heard. My worry is that the growth of huge media conglomerates, the lack of support for public broadcasting, and the failures of contemporary journalism are creating a narrower and more limited media world. The Canadian media system and the Canadian political system with which it is so deeply enmeshed are risking the democratic equivalent of heart disease – the arteries that carry the flow of democratic discussion are hardening and clogging up. The beginning of wisdom and action is to recognize that a crisis exists. This book is meant to sound an alarm in the hope that Canadians will care.

TWO

Media, Citizens, and Democracy

The premise of democratic government, the basis of the democratic ideal, is that power rests with the people. This is the essential foundation on which the Canadian governmental system rests. Populist politicians such as Reform Party leader Preston Manning express their continuing faith in "the common sense of the common people." Former U.S. President Ronald Reagan would pay homage to the collective wisdom embodied in the concept of "We the people" – the famous first phrase of the preamble to the American constitution. The notion at the heart of the democratic ideal is that "the people" have an intrinsic sense of what is right and wrong, and that they can be trusted to make wise judgments based on their instinctive feelings and real-life experiences. Legendary journalist Walter Lippmann described what he called the "dogma" of democracy as the belief that "the knowledge needed for the management of human affairs comes up spontaneously from the human heart."[1] This classical view also holds that political leaders who stray too far from grassroots opinion, from the sensibilities of ordinary citizens, have not only lost touch with the nurturing power of ordinary citizens but have been corrupted in some way. The public is seen in reverential, almost majestic terms.

The role that the public plays in a democratic society such as Canada is often difficult to grasp in concrete terms. There are a number of contending interpretations about how public opinion is formed and how the power of public opinion manifests itself as a political force. Each of these explanations sees the role played by

29

citizens from a different perspective. Not surprisingly, each model views the media as playing a critical role in constituting or constructing the public. But each of these frameworks interprets the power of the media differently.

My intention in this chapter is to explore four of these explanations in some detail. Although I have strong views about each of these perspectives, I will not argue that one of these interpretations is the single correct perspective. The truth is multi-layered and multi-faceted, and each perspective shines some light on the reality of public opinion formation. But it is also the case that some of these explanations shine more brightly than others. The objective is to provide readers with a number of possible explanations – a number of lenses – for understanding the pivotal role that the media play in shaping and reflecting opinion.

What these perspectives have in common is that they portray distortions in the democratic process. They each represent fears by scholars and commentators that the marketplace of ideas, the vitality of the central meeting places of our society, are at risk in some way. They each suggest that unless there is drastic reform or rethinking, these cancerous cells will spread – infecting, weakening, and perhaps even overwhelming our democratic institutions.

I would like to dismiss at the outset the notion that the mass media do not have an influence on public affairs or public opinion. After at least three generations of studies about media effects by communications scholars and indeed by advertisers and marketers, such notions can rightfully be dismissed as poppycock. To argue that the media do not have at least some effect on the shape of public life is the equivalent of arguing that the world is flat or that Tinkerbell and the Tooth Fairy are real. The question is what kind of effects the media have on society, not whether the media have effects.

Democracy Without Citizens

According to what can be called the democracy without citizens perspective, the public "tends to be unstable, unconstrained, uninformed and not ideological."[2] The public is amorphous and easily swayed and lacks even basic rudimentary knowledge about public affairs. The gap between our idealized view that the public is made up of engaged and concerned citizens and the reality of widespread ignorance and cynicism is startling.

Walter Lippmann was perhaps the leading advocate for the position that the public could not be trusted to understand the complex realities of the political world. The problem, according to Lippmann, is first that people see reality through the tinted glass of their own definitions and prejudices, and second, that the press presents them with a distorted version of the truth. Lippmann wrote in his book *Public Opinion*, first published in 1922, that the press was "like the beam of a searchlight that moves restlessly about, bringing one episode and then another out of the darkness into vision."[3] The press never allows the public to see the complete picture because it can never illuminate events long enough for them to be completely seen and understood. Issues that make headlines one day can be gone the next. Political leaders simply "cannot govern society by episodes, incidents and eruptions."[4] Therefore faith in the public is misplaced; it is at best a mirage, a "phantom."[5] In Lippmann's view, only the small number of people who are actually involved in events directly or follow them closely are in a position to make meaningful judgments.

Lippmann's elitist perspective has some support from studies that have documented the abysmal lack of awareness that many citizens have about public life. Despite the avalanche of news and information that descend on citizens each day, very few messages about the political world seem to penetrate or seep through the permafrost of public awareness. Surveys by American researchers find that a majority of Americans cannot identify the party that controls Congress or name the Speaker of the House of Representatives. In one survey only one in five Americans could identify words from the Bill of Rights, the most sacred document in the pantheon of American politics.[6] In another survey, only a minority, again fewer than one in five, could name a single member of President Bill Clinton's cabinet.[7]

Moreover, surveys also show that despite all of the commentary about voters and political ideology, only a small percentage of citizens – at best one in ten – can usefully define terms such as "liberalism" and "conservatism."[8]

Even more shocking is that surveys suggest that young people seem to be growing up in a historical vacuum with little basic knowledge about important historical figures or events. In one survey, at least half of those interviewed could not identify towering twentieth-century leaders such as Winston Churchill or Joseph Stalin and two-thirds did not know that the American Civil War was fought between 1850 and 1900.[9] A survey conducted in 1995 by the Pew Research Center for the People and the Press found that barely 20 per cent of 18-to-29-year-olds follow the news at all.[10]

Canadians do not fare much better. In a "national citizenship exam" conducted in 1997 by the Dominion Institute, 45 per cent failed to answer 12 out of 20 questions. Only 48 per cent could identify "Confederation" as the event that brought the original provinces together to form the Canadian federation, fewer than one-third of those surveyed could name the Canadian Charter of Rights and Freedoms as the part of the constitution that guaranteed essential freedoms, and only 8 per cent knew that the Queen was the Head of State in Canada.[11]

A history survey of 18-to-24-year-olds taken in 1997 produced equally dismal results.[12] Only 54 per cent could identify John A. Macdonald as Canada's first Prime Minister, fewer than 40 per cent knew that Confederation took place in 1867, and just 35 per cent recognized that D-Day signified the Allied invasion of Nazi-occupied France in 1944. Most disturbing, perhaps, was that only 10 per cent of the Canadian youth that were questioned could identify the "Quiet Revolution" as the period of momentous change that shook and transformed Quebec and Canadian society in the 1960s.

American media scholar Robert Entman has argued that we have become, in effect, a "democracy without citizens."[13] People are so turned-off, tuned-out, uninformed, and uninterested that they are no longer an important element in the political system. The political system, well-oiled by elite groups and geared to their interests, is able to grind along paying only lip service to the interests and needs of those who are governed. Roderick Hart of the University of Texas has coined the phrase "cameo citizenship" to describe the effect that television has in narcotizing voters. Hart uses the term "cameo" to refer to the little dramas that television creates to represent public life. As Hart explains: "One of the subtlest effects of television is that it gives viewers the feeling that someone else is minding the store and that they, consequently can turn to other pursuits."[14]

One explanation offered for the public's lack of awareness, its high political illiteracy rate, is that television, the principal lens through which the public sees and is informed about the world, has become an ineffective tool for educating citizens. Television news stories are so visual, so sensational, so fixated on personalities, so fast-moving, so fleeting, and so intent on entertaining that they give viewers almost nothing tangible to hold on to. News stories have what Todd Gitlin, one of America's most important media scholars, has described as the "style of substance" but not its content.[15] Bill McKibben has compared TV to "invisible ink," the memory of its images easily washed away because they leave viewers with little that is worth remembering.[16] Jonathan Schell is another scholar who believes that TV news lacks the sticking power necessary for learning. According to Schell, "[T]elevision is powerful because it can dominate the moment. It is weak because it cannot outlast the moment — cannot make an impression that endures."

Moreover, politics no longer sells. Politics has taken a back seat to celebrity news, entertainment news, business news, sports news, and lifestyle news. The large media conglomerates that own the TV networks but also own major chunks of the world entertainment industry have a stake in promoting their own products — movies, books, celebrities, sports teams, etc. — as news stories, and in appealing to audiences with news stories that are "lite and less filling" in order to boost ratings.[17] Often dealing with arduous and complex disputes over issues such as health care or the constitution or with international conflicts, political stories are often too difficult and awkward to fit into an infotainment package. Soon a self-fulfilling prophecy is at work. When political stories are ignored or downgraded by the media, the message to audiences is that political issues aren't really important. Consequently the audiences' appetite for political stories diminishes.[18]

CBS News anchor Dan Rather described the current state of television news in the following way:

> They've got us putting more and more fuzz and wuzz on the air, cop-shop stuff so as to compete; not with other news programs, but with entertainment programs (including those posing as news programs) for dead bodies, mayhem and lurid tales.
>
> They tell us international news doesn't get ratings, doesn't sell, and, besides, it's too expensive. ... Thoughtfully written analysis is out, "live pops" are in. Hire lookers, not writers. Do powder-puff, not probing interviews. Stay away from controversial subjects. Kiss ass, move with the mass and for heaven and the rating's sake don't make anyone mad – certainly not anybody you're covering, and especially not the Mayor, the governor, the senator, the President ... or *anybody* in a position of power.[19]

Some observers shift the blame from the owners and producers of network news, who are the pushers of the new infotainment drug, to the nature of television itself. The argument is that TV watching is for the most part a profoundly passive experience. Russell Neuman cites one study in which respondents could recall only one story out of 20 that were aired in a TV news program they had just watched.[20] Neuman's rough "rule of thumb" is that viewers will remember only 5 per cent of stories without prompting, while another 45 per cent can be recalled with some help from researchers. The contention is that for most people, TV viewing is dead time. It is a time to "veg out," to shut down, to forget the cares of the day. It's a time to retreat from the world rather than be engaged in its concerns. Consequently, TV images wash over the viewers leaving them with few traces of thought or information.

Most commentators and observers view the increasing disenfranchisement and disengagement by the public with despair and warn of the dangers that this poses to the health and vitality of the democratic process. But there are others who take an elitist position, contending that this is the natural state, the natural condition, of a democratic society. The premise of the elite argument is that public debate is dominated by elites and by a relatively small attentive public – wealthier and better-educated citizens who follow and care about public policy issues. For Walter Lippmann, for instance, it's not just that public debate is, and should be, dominated by elites but that these elites are the backbone of a democratic society. The political system rests on their shoulders. In fact, Lippmann devised a scheme that would allow a "specialized class" to control information and thus save democracy from the mass hysteria, prejudice, and ignorance of the uneducated masses.

The public debate is largely framed by politicians, Wall or Bay Street, powerful lobbies such as the Business Council on National Issues in Canada, think tanks financed by big corporations and wealthy contributors such as the American Enterprise Institute in the U.S. or the C.D. Howe Institute in Canada, labour unions, and single-interest groups, whether they be ethnic, religious, or supporters of a particular cause such as the National Citizens' Coalition. Public opinion, which can be volatile, moves to the beat of elite opinion. These groups and interests marshal and construct public opinion. Elites set the tone, define the parameters, and dominate the news.

For all of his popular appeal, U.S. President John F. Kennedy strongly admired and adhered to Lippmann's conception of democracy. In 1962, he stated:

> The fact of the matter is that most of the problems that we now face are technical problems, administrative problems. They require sophisticated judgments which do not lend themselves to the kinds of social movements that involve the citizenry and which stir the country. They deal with problems that are beyond the circumspection of most men.[21]

Of course many media scholars would agree that the interests of the most powerful groups and corporations in our society are both reflected in and buttressed by media reporting. Indeed, there seems to be a widespread consensus in the scholarly community that media reporting fixates almost exclusively on the views of political and economic elites. Studies by scholars such as Lance Bennett, Daniel Hallin, and Herbert Gans have shown that coverage of important issues is "indexed" to the opinions of powerful policy makers.[22] To begin with, large numbers of journalists are stationed on Parliament Hill or at the White House, and others report on issues involving important interest groups or on events sponsored by powerful organizations. Indeed much of the news is made up of what the powerful are doing or saying.

Political debate as portrayed on the evening news or on Sunday morning political panels usually features "I said, you said" or "you're a jerk – no, you're a jerk" exchanges among leading politicians, journalists, or interest group leaders.[23] Indeed, virtually all that television presents, and that Canadians see, of the parliamentary system is the clatter and shouting of Question Period in the House of Commons in which the Prime Minister and members of the Cabinet are engaged in nasty spitball exchanges with the leaders of the opposition parties. In addition. reporters, who almost invariably frame issues in "pro or con" terms, turn to experts or interest group spokespeople to defend one side or the other in their stories. Thus the news is top-heavy with the views of what Canadian sociologist Richard Ericson and his colleagues describe as "authoritative knowers," and public debate echoes the prevailing sentiments of the political elite.[24] Ordinary citizens almost never appear in discussions of important issues except as story props, victims, or wrongdoers.

Two leading scholars, John Fiske and Herbert Gans, have reminded us that ordinary citizens usually make the paper or appear on television news only when their houses burn down, when they are in car crashes, suffer from hepatitis C, are accused of a crime, or when their loved ones die in a grisly murder. As Fiske has observed about the "tabloidization" of ordinary people by the media, "Almost always this entry into the public is in the role of victim – a spectacular exaggeration of their normal social position."[25]

Some observers argue that senior journalists are now part of the very elite that they report on. Senior journalists are not only well paid and well educated and enjoy comfortable lifestyles but they are employed by large corporations whose tentacles reach into key sectors of the economy. Many are celebrities in their own right. They are recognized on the street, given the best tables at restaurants, courted by powerful politicians and interest groups, and given awards for their service to the community. The American media critic James Fallows describes the power of those media pundits who view society from their seats in the "luxury-skyboxes":

> Assurance fluffs up their every pronouncement, because they have permanent thrones. There are no term limits on pundits. The breezy disdain they display for Bill Clinton is akin to the condescension that country club members have for the golf pro. ... While they assail elected officials for pandering to special interests, their own speakers' fees are skyrocketing and those who call their ethics into question are dismissed ... as little "weenies" who are "jealous."[26]

Media critic Jon Katz has observed the same phenomenon:

> Consider the big fees that some of the most prominent members of the bloated Washington press corps take from institutions and lobbies that they cover. Consider the reporters scrambling to cash in on book and movie deals sparked by the stories that they cover. Or the parties that magazine editors in New York give and are given, with celebrity guests arriving in limousines. Journalists have lost their sense of outsiderness, the detachment from power that was at the heart of the moral power that fueled the press for years.[27]

Canadian journalists may not be in the same league as their Washington counterparts in terms of fame or salaries, but few would deny that "celebrity" journalists such as Jeffrey Simpson of the *Globe and Mail*, the CBC's Peter Mansbridge or Avril Benoit, Mike Duffy of CTV, or Vancouver talk show host Rafe Mair have far more influence and are much better connected to "the powers that be" than any ordinary Member of Parliament.

An American political scientist, Timothy Cook, has extended the argument even farther. He contends in his book, *Governing with the News*, that the news media are "not merely a part of politics; they are part of government."[28] The news is, in effect, a "coproduction" between news organizations and government institutions with journalists "so intertwined with the work of official Washington that the news itself performs governmental tasks."[29]

Interestingly enough, in his best-selling book on the Clinton administration's relationship with the news media, entitled *Spin Cycle*, Howard Kurtz paints a not dissimilar portrait.[30] While the relationship is mired in suspicion and antagonism, reporters are described as linked far more to the White House than to their readers and audiences. Needing access to the President and other decision makers in order to carry out their work, dependent and tied to their sources for the latest information and gossip, and both feeding off and wary of each other, White House reporters develop their own agendas, agendas far removed from the concerns of ordinary citizens who live outside of the "Beltway."

While the Lippman position emphasizes that elite domination is not only part of the natural order of things but necessary to the smooth functioning of democracy, others believe that the disenfranchising of citizens by the modern media is deeply corrupting and dangerous.

The strongest claim that television has been the chief culprit in alienating citizens from public life and in discouraging civic involvement has been made by Robert Putnam, Director of Harvard University's prestigious Center for International Affairs. Putnam believes that television has led to the collapse of what he calls "social capital."[31] His central premise is that the stock of social capital – the degree to which citizens trust in and are connected to the life of their communities – has fallen drastically over the last 40 years.

Whether measured by the number of people involved in charitable organizations or school boards, who attend church or synagogue, who visit friends and neighbours, and who trust in the workings of the political system, social capital has plunged to record lows.

Although Putnam's argument is drawn from American experience, the supply of social capital in Canada has diminished sharply over the same period. The percentage of Canadians who were members of service organizations fell from 23 per cent in 1975 to 12 per cent in 1995. Membership in religious institutions also dropped precipitously – from almost 6 out of 10 people in 1975 to just 3 out of 10 two decades later.[32]

While voter turnouts for Canadian federal elections have averaged 75 per cent since the Second World War, only 70 per cent voted in 1993 and 67 per cent in 1997. The 1997 election produced the lowest turnout in fifty years. Less than 50 per cent of those who were eligible voted in the 1996 U.S. presidential election, the lowest turnout since 1924.

In addition, cynicism about politicians and political institutions has rocketed into the stratosphere. In 1980 less than 40 per cent of Canadians who were surveyed described politicians as incompetent and unprincipled. By 1990 a sizeable majority believed that politicians couldn't be trusted to do the right thing.[33] A survey taken in 1997 found that only 15 per cent of Canadians thought that politicians were trustworthy; lawyers, hardly figures of public virtue, were trusted by 24 per cent of the public and journalists by 32 per cent.[34] Politicians have sunk to the point where they rank not much above car thieves, leaders of crackpot religious cults, and members of biker gangs.

Surveys taken in the U.S. show a similar loss of faith and trust. In 1964, 60 per cent of those surveyed believed "that the government would generally try and do the right thing." By 1994 only 10 per cent believed that it would.[35] Only 22 per cent of those surveyed in a 1997 poll expressed confidence in the U.S. federal government. But opinion polls also reveal that strong currents of disapproval exist toward almost all of the major societal institutions. Between 1973 and 1993, confidence in the education system fell from 37 to 22 per cent, while confidence levels for organized religion dropped from 35 to 23 per

cent. Lowest on the hit parade of public esteem was the media itself
— faith in journalism dove from 23 to 11 per cent.[36]

According to Putman, the downward slide in trust, identification
and involvement coincided with the emergence of television as the
primary means of mass communication. While he examines a
number of other possible factors, all the evidence points to TV as
the smoking gun. As Putman argues, "[J]ust as the erosion of the
ozone layer was detected only many years after the proliferation of
the chlorofluorocarbons that caused it, so too the erosion of ... social capital became visible only several decades after the underly-
ing process had begun."[37]

Putnam has two explanations for why television is to blame for
the crisis that infects civic life. The first is TV's so-called "displace-
ment" effects. People who are watching TV (and TV-watching con-
sumes over one-half of our leisure time) have less time to spend
talking to their neighbours, attending city council meetings, doing
charity work, reading books or newspapers, or going for walks with
family members. TV has to a large degree "privatized" leisure time.
In fact, Bill McKibben reports that we have become so insular, so
cut off from others, so house-bound, that a large majority of the
population, almost three-quarters, no longer know who their neighbours are — a shattering commentary on contemporary society.[38]

The late author Jerzy Kosinski, who wrote a book later made into
a movie entitled *Being There*, about a man whose only meaningful
experiences came from watching television, was disturbed by the
degree to which young people preferred experiences from the media world to real-life situations. He was disturbed by the extent to
which it had become far easier and more interesting for children to
sit in front of a TV set or play video or computer games than explore the neighbourhood, play road hockey, or go to a play, a con-
cert, or a museum. Kosinski's brutal observation was that, "We've
reached the point now where people — adults and children alike —
would prefer to watch a televised ball game than to sit in some far
corner of a stadium, too hot or too cold, uncomfortable, surrounded
by a smelly crowd, with no close-ups, no other channel to turn to.
Uncomfortable — like life often is."[39]

The second phenomenon identified by Putnam is what George Gerbner and other scholars have referred to as television's "mean world" effect.[40] There is a considerable body of scholarly evidence to suggest that heavy TV viewers come to see the world as a more violent and frightening place than it actually is. The endless nightly parade of crime and depravity, carnage and mayhem, that is depicted on the evening news, on talk and tabloid television, and in TV drama has created a perception that the world is troubled and unsafe, gloomy and sinister. The TV world is littered with victims and "victim news." Indeed, a study of nightly news shows on the major U.S. networks found that crime is by far the most frequent topic for news stories, and that the number of crime stories zoomed by 721 per cent between 1991 and 1996.[41] Although the murder rate plummeted by 20 per cent during the period of the study, TV was awash with crimes by celebrities and criminals who had been turned into celebrities. Another American survey, the National Television Violence Study, revealed that violence had increased by 14 per cent on prime-time TV shows between 1994 and 1997.[42] The cumulative effect of so much violence, according to Putnam, has been to produce a society of poisonous distrust, a society in which there is less willingness to depend on others, pay taxes, or let children play by themselves without adult supervision.

TV has created an interesting paradox. Polls taken in 1997 show that most Canadians believed that the crime rate had gone up over the previous five years. Perhaps as a consequence, Canadians also supported "get tough" laws and an end to "coddling" criminals.[43] But the perceptions differ from the reality. The reality was that the murder rate was at a low-water mark, its lowest in decades, and that the incidents of violent crime had been falling since 1994. John Wright of the Angus Reid Group believes that Canadians have been hypnotized by the media's "mean world" effect: "People are sensitive to it because it makes news, because it's in their face every single day."[44]

Putnam's claim is that television, in creating its own public space, in assembling its own huge audiences, has reduced other public spaces – the spaces in which genuine human interaction takes place.

Whatever the validity of Putnam's argument, the "democracy without citizens" perspective maintains that citizens are for the most part inattentive bystanders and spectators to the drama of modern political life. Power is wielded and mass opinion is shaped by those at the top of the societal pyramid. Some, like Walter Lippmann, approve of the situation, arguing that reasoned debate can take place only at this level. Those at the pinnacles of power make the system work. Others, such as Putnam, believe that the media are the main culprits in keeping citizens disinterested, in creating the pervasive and poisonous distrust that now seems to dominate our public spaces. This new culture of distrust is destroying the social capital that is the lifeblood of a democratic society.

Citizens Without Democracy

The "citizens without democracy" perspective is the flip side of the "democracy without citizens" position. Those who adhere to this perspective believe that the portrait of an unsophisticated and un-caring public, an unthinking mass, drawn by elite theorists like Walter Lippmann is a grave distortion of reality. Citizens are not passive and gullible; they are active thinkers capable of making ra-tional choices and of knowing where their interests lie. Or as one scholar has put it, "If we're so dumb, how come we made it to the moon!" People, according to this view, have an instinctive feel for what is right and wrong, and they actively resist messages that don't ring true or that don't conform to their needs and beliefs.

This perspective has its origins in the Enlightenment, the intel-lectual and political revolution that challenged the tyranny of feu-dalism and the power of despotic regimes in Europe and America in the eighteenth and nineteenth centuries. Philosophers such as Rousseau, Locke, Paine, and Jefferson represented the power of a new mercantile class but also a new spirit of inquiry and openness in science and religion. The Australian scholar, John Keane, has characterized the energy that guided the Enlightenment in the fol-lowing way: "Enlightenment: to lighten through reason, to illuminate and alleviate the world, to make it less dense and heavy, to open it up by enabling brightness to contest darkness, as when trees are felled and a free and open space is created in a forest."[45] But its basic thrust, its revolutionary impetus, was its populist inspiration, its belief in the "natural worth of the common man."

Populists are well aware of the unrelenting and unforgiving nature of the forces that are aligned against them. The problem is that elites often distort the message. Citizens are often prevented from receiving the information that they require by an alliance of interests that John Fiske calls "the power bloc."[46] And far from being seen as the saviours of democracy, these powerful groups and institutions are viewed as the opposition. Citizens must be continually on guard, ever vigilant, against efforts to manipulate the truth.

Edward Herman and Noam Chomsky have gone the farthest in popularizing what they call the "propaganda model."[47] In their view, society is characterized by grotesque inequalities in wealth and power and by deep class conflict. Those at the apex of power have designed a media system whose primary goal is to "manufacture consent" from those who are at the bottom of the heap. News is "filtered" though a series of constraints – corporate control of the mass media, the power of advertisers, the dominance of "official" sources, the influence of right-wing media critics, and the existence of enemies – so that the public receives a highly contrived and sanitized view of reality. According to Herman and Chomsky, "The elite domination of the media and the marginalization of dissidents that results from the operation of these filters occurs so naturally that media news people, frequently operating with complete integrity and goodwill, are able to convince themselves that they choose and interpret the news 'objectively' and on the basis of professional news values."[48]

Most scholars who are adherents of the political economy or critical approach to communication have moved away from a crude propaganda model. While they recognize the domination of established interests, they see the battle for media control as a tug-of-war in which the public can sometimes have enough muscle to pull the rope in its direction. Robert Hackett of Simon Fraser University, among the country's leading experts on media and politics, has written extensively about the concept of hegemony as it applies to the Canadian media. Employing a framework of analysis first developed by Antonio Gramsci and later embellished by political economy or critical theorists (admittedly these terms cover a wide panoply of views) such as Theodor Adorno, Raymond Williams, Stuart Hall, Todd Gitlin and John Fiske among others, Hackett sees hegemony as the power of established institutions to impose a set of values, a way of thinking, an ideological world view on those "below." As Hackett and his colleagues have described hegemony:

> The major social institutions that generate ways of understanding the world generally (although not necessarily deliberately or without opposition) reproduce a whole system of values, attitudes and beliefs – ideology – that in one way or another supports the established order and the social interests that dominate it. … Hegemony is never completely or finally achieved; it is always contested or resisted, as alternative and oppositional meaning systems (such as environmentalism or feminism) struggle for political and cultural change. But when hegemony is more or less successful, ordinary people themselves accept hegemonic ideology: it becomes enmeshed with the "common sense" through which people make their lives and their worlds intelligible.[49]

Douglas Kellner, a professor of philosophy at the University of Texas-Austin, has described how the concept of hegemony applies to the media: "[A] hegemony model of media power would analyze how the media produce identities, role models, and ideals; how they create new forms of discourse and experience; how they define situations, set agendas, and filter out oppositional ideas; how they set limits and boundaries beyond which political discourse is not allowed."[50]

Political economy or critical scholars argue that the media exercises "social control" and "systems maintenance." These theorists contend that television shows convey messages about society that support and endorse the power of political and economic elites. Shows celebrate and glorify commercial values, male dominance, rugged individualism, patriotic virtues, and the effectiveness of established institutions such as the police, corporations, and the courts. Studies of media coverage of the Persian Gulf War of 1991, for instance, found that news shows were not only on-side with American government policy but had become veritable cheerleaders for the troops in the field. Viewers were covered in a swath of patriotic sentiments.[51] The reality, as media scholar and critic Todd Gitlin has written, is that: "Television radiates ideology which means nothing more or less than a set of assumptions that becomes second nature: even rebels have to deal with it ... Television can no more speak without ideology than we can speak without prose."[52]

The problem is that the political influence of television often goes unnoticed or is not taken seriously. This is because everything on TV is wrapped in the guise of entertainment. TV appears to be innocuous, even frivolous, like eating cotton candy rather than a solid meal. TV, the old joke goes, is just chewing gum for the eyes. Others have criticized the "idiot box" for creating mindless viewers or, in the words of one commentator, a race of people "with eyes as big as grapefruits and no brains, no brains at all."[53] The Italian film director Frederico Fellini once observed that "television isn't art, it's furniture."[54] Mark Fowler, Chairman of the U.S. Federal Communications Commission under Ronald Reagan, once boasted that "TV is a toaster with pictures."[55] But nothing could be further from the truth. Television's power comes precisely from the fact that when we are watching it we are relaxed, unaware of how deeply its messages are penetrating.

And vital information does seep through. As political scientist Morris Fiorina has observed: "[J]ust as exposed portions of skin get tanned by the sun when people walk around out of doors, so people become informed as they go about their daily business."[56]

The key to the kingdom for critical scholars, however, is the conviction that despite the power and subtlety of hegemonic messages, citizens have become experienced and savvy media watchers. This view is directly opposed to the passive view of the audience proposed by advocates of the "democracy without citizens" perspective that we discussed earlier. According to this second position, viewers have the capacity to vigorously oppose, reject or reinterpret messages that strike them as unreal or false. Audiences form "interpretive communities" with the power to "negotiate" meanings and reframe media messages according to their own beliefs and circumstances. They are capable of sifting through the media clutter, actively asserting, actively "constructing" their own meanings. While citizens may know little about the political system and how it operates, they use "shortcuts," "cues," and instinctive "feel" to make judgments about political leaders and the policies that they advocate.

A main tenet of this position is that people pay selective attention to media messages based on their preconceived values and orientations. The power of the media bullet is blunted by all the forces that have gone into the creation of a person's character and world view: family background, religious beliefs, economic circumstances, educational experiences, etc. In the end, people tune out messages that don't fit into their frames of reference or that they find uncomfortable in some way. As Paul Simon put it in his song "The Boxer": "[A] man hears what he wants to hear and disregards the rest."[57] Thus people have an intrinsic capacity to choose and resist.

Moreover, the dominance of elites is never complete. Hegemony is always being contested and challenged; established ideology continually bumps up against and is influenced by populist demands and genuine popular culture. And there are sometimes fissures, sharp disagreements among elites that can be exploited by those below. These divisions allow populist expressions to break through.

John Fiske has pushed the envelope the farthest in terms of seeing the "people" as having autonomous independent power. Fiske sees a continuous battle between established interests that control the "official" media and the will of the people as expressed in popular culture. As Fiske contends: "[P]opular culture is made by the people out of the products of the mass media — it is not imposed upon them by the media and their power-bloc allegiance. The news that the people want, make and circulate among themselves may differ widely from that which the power-bloc wishes to have."[58]

Moreover, optimists would argue that audiences, and hence citizens, are gaining a measure of control over the media. Media organizations that lose touch with their audiences, that don't respond to the popular will or popular tastes, risk falling by the wayside. Newspapers and the main TV networks in both Canada and the United States lost sizeable chunks of their readers and viewers in the 1980s and 1990s precisely because, some would contend, they were unable to tap into, to adapt, to the changing nature of the audience. CBC-TV's audience has hemorrhaged from a 21 per cent share in 1985 to approximately 10 per cent in 1997–98. CTV's audience numbers have nosedived from just over 22 per cent in 1985 to under 15 per cent in 1998.[59] Audiences for the major American networks – ABC, CBS, and NBC – plummeted from 98 per cent in the 1970s to 63 per cent in the late 1990s.[60] Some accounts have audience numbers for the three major U.S. networks collapsing to well below 50 per cent.[61]

While much of this fall-off can be blamed on increased competition from cable stations and from newer networks and stations, media organizations are now desperately scrambling to satisfy their audiences and readers, to be in sync with the drum beats of public opinion.

In fact, some observers now criticize the media for having gone overboard to satisfy mass tastes. They blame the media for collectively lowering public standards, for the new harshness and vulgarity that has entered public life, and for allowing the "tabloidization" of almost all aspects of news. They condemn a media culture that has allowed Jerry Springer, Howard Stern, *South Park*, *The World's Scariest Police Chases*, and the World Wrestling Federation to take centre stage. Carl Bernstein, one of the journalistic heroes of the Watergate scandal, has written with considerable anguish about what he sees as the creation of an "idiot culture," and Pete Hamill, former editor-in-chief of the *New York Daily News*, has denounced some newspapers for having become "brainless printed junk food" and others for being so lacking in conviction and character that their voices "wouldn't frighten a rabbit."[62]

Still, the bottom line is that the public are not helpless victims of hegemonic power. However relentless and inescapable the daily barrage of conservative values, citizens have the capacity to carve out their own niches in the media world and sometimes challenge conventional approaches. While adherents of the critical school celebrate such moments, they also tend to see these triumphs as marginal, as making only a small dent in the power of established interests. It would be a mistake of the highest order, some would argue, to think of the media as servants of the public rather than as the instruments of what writer David Halberstam has described as "the powers that be."[63]

The question of whether the media have conditioned citizens to tolerate only certain conservative points of view, to celebrate only certain cherished values, or whether the media can to some degree be invaded and redirected by opposing tastes and alternative views, is at the heart of the debate.

Election Campaigns and Symbolic Politics

In various works Murray Edelman, a prominent political scientist, has argued that political leaders "construct" publics based on how they use and manipulate symbols.[64] In running for office, political leaders consciously wrap themselves and their parties in symbolic images. They use dramatic visual backdrops and "cue" their audiences through their choice of language, by the issues that they highlight, and by the ways in which they characterize their opponents. In Edelman's "constructionist" perspective, politicians unfurl symbolic flags and voters rally around one of the flags being flown.

If Edelman had analyzed the 1997 Canadian federal election, for instance, he would likely have seen Reform Party leader Preston Manning's campaign as a symbolic construction. He would have noted that Manning's personal appearance was highly choreographed; he had dispensed with his thick glasses and changed his hairstyle, a voice teacher had coached him so that his western twang would be less pronounced, and he would often appear in a blue denim shirt to emphasize his down-home populist politics. Moreover, he was surrounded by props. He sometimes held news conferences using a rustic log building as a backdrop and tossed around a football during campaign breaks (supposedly to contrast his relative youth and physical prowess with that of Prime Minister Jean Chretien). During speeches, Manning used an actual seat from the House of Commons to illustrate his populist message that the seat belonged to the people and not to the Members of Parliament that were elected to sit in them. When he was accused by his opponents of dividing the country, he made a point of appearing in front of a forest of Canadian flags.

But it was his choice of which issue to raise to the top of the campaign flagpole that revealed the most to voters. His main strategic moves during the 1997 federal election were his stand against granting "distinct society" status to Quebec, and the decision to run a TV ad suggesting that Quebec politicians had too much power. The ad showed black-and-white photos of Jean Chretien, then-Conservative leader Jean Charest, Quebec Premier Lucien Bouchard, and Bloc Quebecois leader Gilles Duceppe. These photos were then stamped with a slash mark. The voice-over said: "Not just Quebec politicians." In pressing these hot emotional buttons, Manning sent clear messages to voters. The Reform Party leader, in effect, fashioned a public based on how he chose to construct himself and his party and how voters responded to that "construction."

Jean Chretien's campaign could also be seen as a symbolic construction. TV ads shown during the 1997 federal election depicted the prime minister at home in his living room appearing relaxed and self-assured. Chretien's demeanour was one of comfort and dependability. A ray of sunlight radiated through the room while the prime minister was speaking. The entire election strategy could be seen in two 30-second spots in which the prime minister accused his opponents of proposing reckless budget cuts and jeopardizing medicare. Chretien wanted voters to believe that he represented steady leadership, the tried and the true, the responsible middle ground. Voting for the other parties was risky. Voters would be taking a chance on an uncertain future.

One can similarly view Lucien Bouchard's campaign for the Yes side during the 1995 Quebec referendum as a series of symbolic constructions. Bouchard's main theme was that Quebec's attempts to secure protection for the French language and for its distinct way of life had been continually rejected by English Canada, that every attempt made by Quebec to secure its rights has been met by a harsh rebuff. In Bouchard's view, virtually all of Canadian history was a litany of humiliation for Quebec. An explosive speaker in the tradition of Premiers Maurice Duplessis and Rene Levesque, Bouchard's speeches were emotional appeals to the politics of blood, to feelings of betrayal and injured pride. Moreover, he seemed to be the very symbol, the embodiment of that wounded dignity. Lawrence Martin has described the way in which Bouchard's cane, the cane that he needed to support himself after he had been crippled by a rare disease called necrotizing fasciitis, had become part of his appeal:

> Bouchard lit up the speaking halls with his charges.
> He was a spectacular orator. With the cane as a sort
> of religious symbol, he limped to the microphone,
> so human compared to all the other stiff suits that
> played the game. He started his speeches slowly,
> and gradually, very gradually, intensified the pace.
> The style was authoritative, pounding, theatrical,
> rhythmical. Soon he reached a feverish lather from
> which the vitriol shot like spears. He was in the hot
> zone now, his passion scorching, his mind locked
> in a decades-old time warp where all the old griev-
> ances sat like the great blueberries of Lac Saint-Jean
> ready for the plucking.[65]

Bouchard's was a world of black and white, friends and enemies, victims and victimizers. But it was mostly a world of seething rage.

Bouchard's most effective prop was an oversize copy of the front page of *Le Journal de Quebec* from November 6, 1981 which brandished the headline "Levesque Betrayed by his Allies." The prop reminded his audiences of the famous "night of the long knives" in which the federal government and the other provinces decided to push through a constitutional deal without Quebec's agreement and over its dire protests. Bouchard embellished the event into a metaphor for Canada and conjured up images of Prime Minister Chretien and the other premiers on the phone with each other thinking about ways to outmanoeuvre Quebec, to humiliate her once again.

Of course, politicians are not the only combatants on the political battlefield. Elections (and in Canada referendums as well) are also the Olympics of political reporting. News organizations and journalists believe that their coverage can make or break professional reputations; election coverage embodies their claim to journalistic excellence and their concern for the future of the community. Thus journalists go into elections with their own agendas. Most of all, journalists want hot stories, stories that will garner headlines and grab viewers. This means reporting and highlighting conflicts and disagreements. It means taking their audiences behind the scenes to give them what Joan Didion has called "insider baseball" accounts of the strategies being employed by candidates and political parties.[66] And it often means taking the candidates on by exposing flaws in their policy proposals, and searching for gaffes, miscues, and character flaws. Roger Ailes, chairman and CEO of the Fox News Channel and a former high level political consultant, has described the basic agenda of news reporting this way: "If you have two guys on a stage and one guy says, 'I have a solution to the Middle East Problem,' and the other guy falls in the orchestra pit, who do you think is going to be on the evening news?"[67]

Political scientists such as Larry Sabato have painted a harsh picture of journalistic morality on the campaign trail. In Sabato's account, politicians have to run through a gauntlet of "killer" journalists – journalists who make their own reputations by destroying the reputations of the politicians that they cover. Sabato used the term "feeding frenzy" to describe the ruthless and instinctive biting and clawing, the swarming in packs, that occurs when journalists smell scandal or sense that a politician is in trouble.[68] The shark analogy was not lost on President Bill Clinton's first Labor Secretary, Robert Reich, who was told when he first came to Washington that in dealing with the media, "if you prick a finger, the sharks will bite off your arm."[69] In Joe Klein's best-selling novel, *Primary Colors*, which is apparently based on Bill Clinton's run for the presidency in 1992, Klein refers to journalists as "scorps" – short for scorpions.[70] One deadly strike can leave a candidate gravely wounded or even destroy a political career.

While political leaders attempt to construct a public based on the symbolic packaging in which they wrap themselves and their campaigns, they are well aware that the media have the capacity to construct their own symbolic picture of the candidates and their messages. The symbolic construction created by candidates has to be "filtered" to at least some degree through the refracted lens of news reports. The two campaigns, those of the candidates and those of the reporters who cover them, are often on a collision course. There is almost always an adversarial relationship – as healthy, natural, and inevitable, some would say, as summer rain. Indeed, election campaigns are often pitched battles between candidates and journalists over whose version of reality gets through to the public and which side will set the agenda of public discussion and debate. Politicians possess a formidable arsenal of weapons to ensure that their messages reach the public either through or over the heads of journalists. Senior government officials, even without an election, spend, according to one estimate, at least half of their time managing the media and managing the news.[71] And journalists have their own resources – polls, research teams as well as space and air time – to ensure that their quite sizeable imprint is left on the political landscape. The relationship of conflict and symbiosis that exists between political leaders and journalists sets the tone and conditions for public debate.

The important point in this interpretation is that publics form as a result of the symbolic messages emanating from political leaders and political reporters. Some would contend that for politicians, and indeed for the journalists who cover them, the election campaign never stops. Politicians are always campaigning. But elections are that special moment in the democratic experience when publics form in order to vote. According to this school of thought the public is a responsive force, a swelling of commitment, in reaction to public debate and the political messages that compete for attention on the media landscape. The manipulation of messages by political leaders is simply part of the everyday cloth of political life.

Adversarial Journalism

This fourth perspective sees citizens as having all of the information that they need to make intelligent choices about the world in which they live. This liberal view sees citizens as having a wide variety of sources of information at their disposal. The media marketplace is open to all competing ideas, to all points of view. If anything, people are being inundated and overwhelmed by too much information. They have an endless ocean, a relentless pounding surf of news and information at their fingertips – cable television and the Internet, libraries, museums, bookstores, and newsstands that are brimming with newspapers and magazines from around the world. And we are connected to the vast arteries of communications as never before. According to John Keane, in the space of a single hour, a person at home can "send a fax, be paged, send an e-mail, watch satellite/cable television, channel hop on radio, make a phone call, read a newspaper, open the day's post, even find time for a few minutes' face to face conversation."[72]

Moreover, no topic is too specialized or controversial to have a full airing at least somewhere in the media universe on any given day. TV talk shows showcase the bizarre and the outrageous. The back alleys of cable are filled with channels and programs of every imaginable stripe including an ever-widening circle of all-news channels, and there are web sites and chat lines that deal with every conceivable political philosophy, business venture, professional interest, form of entertainment, medical problem, phobia, obsession, and hobby. Hate groups that deny the existence of the Holocaust peddle their vile messages on web sites, and pornographers have created what is, in effect, their own online red light districts. We get, in short, to use the quote emblazoned on the front page of the *New York Times* – "All the news that's fit to print" – and a lot that isn't.

In addition, journalists are guided, so the argument goes, by professional norms that reward objectivity, balance, and investigative reporting. Robert Hackett and Yuezhi Zhao have written a superb account of what they have called "the politics of objectivity"; how the ethos of objectivity has become the central pillar of journalism and its claims to professionalism.[73] But as part of their objective stance, journalists are expected to bring a healthy dose of suspicion and skepticism to their stories. The Watergate crisis that led to the resignation of President Richard Nixon and the grotesque suffering and miscalculations of the Vietnam War produced a generation of journalists that made their reputations by unmasking the pretensions of the powerful and exposing their weaknesses and flaws. Far from bowing to those in authority, journalists were encouraged to challenge the assumptions and pretensions of political leaders, to ask probing questions, and to expose manipulation and wrongdoing.

Edward Jay Epstein characterized the journalistic ethic that took root during the 1970s in the following way:

> The working hypothesis almost universally shared among correspondents is that politicians are suspect, their public images probably false, their public statements disingenuous, their moral pronouncements hypocritical, their motives self-serving, and their promises ephemeral. Correspondents thus see their jobs to be to expose politicians by unmasking their disguises, debunking their claims and piercing their rhetoric. In short, until proven otherwise, political figures of any party or persuasion are presumed to be deceptive opponents.[74]

Howard Kurtz has described how these very same assumptions guided reporters who covered the White House during the Clinton administration:

> They were focused, almost fixated, on scandal, on the malfeasance and misfeasance and plain old embarrassments that seemed to envelop this administration from the very start. They were interested in

conflict, in drama, in behind-the-scenes maneuvering, in pulling back the curtain and exposing the Oz-like manipulation of the Clinton crowd. It was their job to report what the president said, but increasingly they saw it as their mission to explain why he said it and what seedy political purpose he was trying to accomplish along the way.[75]

While this "adversarial culture" was born in the fires of the American experience, it has been very much in evidence in Canada as well. Indeed Prime Minister Pierre Trudeau once accused the members of the Parliamentary Press Gallery of suffering from "Watergate envy."[76] In Canada, however, there seems to be less taste for exposés about the personal foibles of politicians or for investigations into their financial backgrounds. These stories have often been seen as violating Canadian codes of propriety, and journalists have felt uncomfortable in these roles. But Canadian journalists have chased other kinds of government scandals with extraordinary zeal. The conduct of the Armed Forces in Somalia, the raping of women in the Canadian military, the contamination of the Canadian blood supply, and miscarriages of justice in the Canadian courts have all been exposed to an intense glare of publicity.

The claim made in much of the scholarly literature is that journalists have gone overboard in their criticism of politicians and political institutions. The concern is that the reporting of politics has been so negative and so poisonous that it has severely undermined and devalued not only the credibility of particular leaders and governments but the entire political process. *Boston Globe* columnist Thomas Oliphant has characterized journalists as "the serial killers of democracy" because of their savage no-holds-barred attacks against politicians of all stripes.[77]

Scholars and writers such as Kathleen Hall Jamieson, Thomas Patterson, Larry Sabato, Adam Gopnick, and Jay Rosen have decried the development of an "aggression culture" among journalists, a "cult of machismo" that rewards toughness as a virtue in and of itself, a toughness without restraint or scruples, a toughness based on winning interviews, asking "gotcha" questions and demonstrating their own superiority.[78] It is an aggression that has swung out of control, becoming "a kind of abstract form, practiced in a void of ideas, or even of ordinary sympathy."[79] Some of these critics also contend that when adversarial journalism is taken to an extreme, when it is pushed to its outer limits as it sometimes is, it damages the credibility of journalists just as much as the politicians that they cover. Journalists come to be seen as little more than a bevy of professional cynics and smart alecks.

The persistent and often brutal nature of the adversarial culture that thrives among reporters has been keenly felt by political leaders who believe that they are increasingly under siege. When Ross Perot withdrew from the U.S. presidential race in 1992, he complained that the media coverage given to him had been the "equivalent of the Rodney King beating."[80] Bill Clinton has gone even further, telling strategist Dick Morris that: "The press runs the government. They like to destroy people. That's how they get their rocks off."[81] On another occasion he commented bitterly: "It was crazy. It was sick. I think that it is almost blood lust. I think it is an insatiable desire on the part of the press to build up and tear down. And they think that is their job – and not only that, their divine right."[82]

Canadian leaders have also come to see journalists as deadly opponents and themselves as political abuse victims. Michel Gratton, a former press secretary to Brian Mulroney, recalls how deeply the former prime minister was affected by critical reporting:

> [W]hen they started sticking the knives into him, they did so in a merciless frenzy. Since he attached so much importance to the media, the wounds went all the deeper, and left him with a deep resentment at having been betrayed by people in whom he had invested a portion of his soul. He started to hold them responsible for all his problems ... I can't remember how often he railed against the media.[83]

Former Prime Minister Kim Campbell had a similar tale of woe. After her shattering election defeat in 1993, she accused reporters of having distorted her message and having dwelled on the negative "to the point of gratuitous cruelty."[84]

Joshua Meyrowitz, author of the award-winning book, *No Sense of Place*, has argued that the situation is now the very opposite of the one described by George Orwell in his classic book, *Nineteen Eighty-Four*.[85] In his dark and foreboding portrait of life in the future, Orwell predicted that political authorities would use modern media technology to intrude and spy on ordinary citizens, depriving them of their basic rights and freedoms. But today, it can be argued, it is the politicians that live in a fish bowl. They are the ones held up to constant scrutiny and inspection. They have lost not only their personal freedom but much of their freedom for political manoeuvring. Many politicians probably feel that they are living on *The Truman Show* with the whole world looking in on their lives.

The death of Princess Diana in August 1997 raised important questions about the extent to which her life and that of the Royal Family had been invaded and distorted by the merciless hounding of the paparazzi. At her funeral, her brother, Earl Spencer, described Diana as "the most hunted person of the modern age." She was besieged wherever she went by hordes of photographers equipped with powerful zoom lenses that could take pictures from kilometres away. Every move, every activity, no matter how private, seemed to be exposed to public scrutiny. And while the first reaction in the aftermath of Diana's tragic death was to blame the tabloids for their unscrupulous and bizarre fixation with her, the public could be blamed as well. As Max Hastings, editor of the *London Evening Telegram*, was to describe the situation at the time of Diana's death, "The proven appetite of the public, even the supposedly up-market public, for sensational personality journalism is huge. Every newspaper in Britain … has moved down market, vastly increasing its output of trivia."[86]

It's argued that the Internet has added considerably to the adversary culture among journalists and to what some see as the "race to the bottom" in terms of journalistic ethics and responsibility. Major news organizations could at one time play a "gatekeeping" role by spiking or ignoring stories that contained claims they knew to be unsubstantiated. Today, online hell-raisers such as Matt Drudge have the ability to publicize and thus give a tinge of credibility to what sometimes amounts to little more than gossip. The *Drudge Report* spread both accurate and inaccurate information about the politics of the Clinton/Lewinsky affair for months, if not years. Once a rumour is in circulation, however, it often has a life of its own. Established news organizations then find themselves in the uncomfortable position of having to comment, in effect upping the ante, on stories that they would have ignored in the past.

The end result of this wide open, everything-that's-fit-to-print system is that citizens not only have at their disposal an open market place where many ideas contend but have a place where authority figures, whether they be politicians or members of the Royal Family, are under harsh scrutiny, scrutiny that cannot be endured. Indeed, it can be argued that no political institution or process can withstand the corrosive gaze of the modern media without losing some of their luster, their sense of mystery and authority. The media gaze destroys as much as it creates. As Joshua Meyrowitz describes the dilemma faced by political leaders:

> "Leadership" and "authority" are unlike mere power in that they depend on performance and appeal; one cannot lead or be looked up to if one's presence is unknown. Yet, paradoxically, authority is weakened by excess familiarity. Awe survives through "distant visibility" and "mystified presence." One of the peculiar ironies of our age is that most people who step forward into the television limelight and attempt to gain national visibility become too visible, too exposed, and are thereby demystified.[87]

Of course, critical scholars see the situation differently. They argue that while journalists may appear tough-minded in chasing scandals or in covering the manipulation of politicians, they rarely question the basic assumptions on which the political system rests. According to Robert Hackett and Yuezhi Zhao, "Critical reports tend to be personalized, directed at personal flaws and failings rather than enduring, 'normal' institutional arrangements ... by the time the story runs its course the reports usually return the situation to normal — a cabinet minister or premier may resign, a government is defeated, but the system works. Critical media reports may bring down individual politicians who do not play the game well, but they seldom question the rules of the game itself."[88] Hence the nature and implications of policy choices and the powerful interests that are aligned with the different policy options are rarely discussed. The real "pulling and hauling" of the political system remains, to paraphrase Lippmann, "in the darkness and out of vision."

Moreover, critical scholars would argue that the real power holders — the major corporate empires and owners or executives such as Rupert Murdoch, Warren Buffet, John Cleghorn (Royal Bank of Canada), Paul Demarais (Power Corp.), Peter Monk (TrizecHahn), Matthew Barrett (Bank of Montreal), James Arnett (Molson), Laurent Beaudoin (Bombardier), and Conrad Black — are largely shielded from scrutiny. When reporting on the activities of corporations and their bosses, the "scorps" suddenly lose their sting. The tone is one of respectful distance and admiration. There is also the argument put forward by Anthony Westell that the discrediting of politicians and governments is in keeping with a corporate agenda that wants to see as little government involvement in the economy as possible. By continually attacking politicians and exposing their indiscretions and chicanery, journalists have become either the knowing or unknowing accomplices of those in the business community who wish to corrode and weaken governmental power. A generation of adversarial journalism has produced a widespread cynicism toward government but also a corresponding belief in the value and efficiency of the private sector.

The Dangers Ahead

While each of these perspectives views the relationship between media reporting and the formation of public attitudes differently, there are some common patterns. Worries about the effects that the media have had in diminishing social capital described in the

"democracy without citizens" perspective can be seen as similar to
the effects of the media's corrosive gaze in devaluing the stature and
prestige of political leaders and institutions as presented in the
adversarial journalism position. The view of reporters as being a
part of the establishments that they cover that was portrayed in the
"democracy without citizens" perspective fits nicely into conceptions
of hegemony advocated by critical scholars. None of these perspectives stands alone completely unrelated to other interpretations.
What is most important, however, is that each model warns of some
danger to the future of democracy. Whether the villain is the passivity and fear engendered by television, the power of hegemonic
forces to stifle alternative views, the manipulation of symbols and
the tugs of war between political leaders and the journalists who
cover them, or the corrosive and destructive gaze of an adversarial
culture, there is the keen sense that the success of democracy hinges
on how publics are formed by the media. The sense of alarm that
rings through in this review of the interpretive landscape is that the
balance is shifting in ways that are harmful to citizens and to the
maintenance of our central public squares. Some things, and perhaps many things, are out of kilter, or, to use Thomas Patterson's
phrase, "out of order."[89] There is the disquieting feeling that democracies are now dealing with forces never envisioned in constitutions,
but whose power to shape the public will and change political behaviour needs to be recognized. The next two chapters will deal in
greater detail with the high tides of media change.

THREE

Convergence and the High
Waves of Media Change

Virtually all of the world's media institutions are being shaken
by tumultuous changes. Some observers have likened these
changes to a tsunami – the Japanese term for a giant wave
that can reach ten stories high and descends with such crushing force
that it shatters everything in its path. The tsunami that media pundits are referring to has two very different aspects to it, or rather there
are at least two waves crashing on the barrier reefs at the same time.
The first phenomenon is convergence. Convergence refers to the fact
that technologies, corporations, and cultures are merging at a rapid
pace and on a global scale. Indeed, the convergence wave is so high
that there is a fear that individual media, independent voices, and local and national expressions will be submerged – drowned in a
deadly sea of conformity.

In this chapter I will describe four realms of convergence: the
convergence of technologies, the convergence of corporations, the
convergence of information with entertainment and the convergence of cultures. Each of these phenomena represents an extraordinary change in society, but occurring all at once they are shaking
the very foundations of democratic and national communities. Convergence is being challenged, however, by another simultaneous
development, a countervailing phenomenon, an opposing rhythm,
called fragmentation. The explosion in cable and satellite television
and the development of the World Wide Web has led to a radical
splintering of the audience (read public). Audiences are being broken down into bite-size morsels, into tiny micro-communities. The

media are becoming more customized, more targeted, more tailored to small slices of the market as they identify narrow consumer
needs. Almost every imaginable interest, organization, business,
hobby, or cause has a niche carved out for it somewhere in this
new media world.

This chapter will examine convergence in considerable detail. The
chapter that follows this one, chapter four, will focus on fragmentation. To some degree, convergence and fragmentation contradict and
contest each other. But I will argue that their combined power works
to loosen and lessen identification with the bonds people have with
their own national experience and with their own communities. My
main concern is that countries like Canada are caught in the squeeze,
in the pincer movement, between globalization on one hand and
the hyper-fragmentation of the audience on the other.

These forces, these high waves of change, are only now beginning
to be felt. We are at the toddler stage in terms of the development of
these trends. Whether a strong Canadian identity and democratic
values can survive the full fury of the tsunami remains to be seen.

The Convergence and Collision of Media and Technologies

The changes occurring in media technology are affecting every aspect of contemporary life. Business methods and practices, the nature of work, the culture of teaching and learning, and the worlds
of arts and entertainment are all undergoing profound changes. Even
the medical field is being altered as communication companies experiment with video imaging, so-called telemedicine, and other technologies that will allow doctors to "see" patients or at least make
diagnoses without the patient being there in person.

What is making this revolution possible – the touchstone of
change – is the replacement of analog-based transmission technologies with digitalization. Where once each medium had its own distribution technology – copper wire for telephones, electromagnetic
waves for radio and TV, etc. – digital technology now provides a

common language (the conversion of signals into codes) that can be translated and used in all mediums. Moreover, digitalization and digital transmission allows for faster delivery, higher quality, and greater capacity.

The digital revolution is the key to convergence. But convergence is a complex phenomenon that is occurring at a number of levels simultaneously. First, there is the convergence of technologies – the merging of television, the telephone, the satellite, cable and the computer. As the CBC's Mark Starowicz has observed, "We are witnessing one of the fundamental re-organizations of the world's distribution and storage of knowledge: the hybridization of the computer, the satellite, the visual archive and broadcasting. Its scale parallels the great transformation revolutions of the millennium."[1] People can now watch TV programs on their computer and make long distance calls via the Internet. Phone companies have the capacity to become broadcasters and cable operators are providing long-distance services. As Ray Smith, the President of Bell Atlantic, has described the essence of convergence: "Your computer will speak, your TV will listen, and your telephone will show you pictures."[2] Author Ken Auletta speculates that: "No one knew or knows what will happen as the cable box mates with the computer; the phone with the cable wire; the networks with the studios; the studios with cable; the computer with the studios or with telephone, publishing or electronics companies."[3]

But there is little doubt that the old foundations are crumbling. Writers for *Wired* magazine envision a decentralized and digitized media production system that seems unimaginable today. A world where:

> studios are not studios: feature films are created on desktop computers for less than $1,000. Theatres are not theatres: the cinema experience is being transformed to theme parks and into massive video murals that will forever change our cityscapes. Film is not film: celluloid is going the way of vinyl records as movies are distributed digitally. And Hollywood is not Hollywood: The industry has gone global as

> fibre-optic cables allow simultaneous work on the
> same movie by creatives working from Cannes to
> Calcutta.[4]

These visions may still be only a distant glimmer, but people can already turn to the World Wide Web to learn more about their favorite TV programs, read newspapers from around the world, and get online editions of popular magazines or newsletters. They can use their personal computers to send fax messages, listen to radio programs, and e-mail anyone who has a computer anywhere. Microsoft has taken over WebTV Networks, a company producing devices that allow people to click on to the World Wide Web while sitting comfortably in front of their TV sets.

While critical developments have already taken place, the communications industry is gearing up for the next stage. The future that industry analysts forecast as being just a few years away, or just around the corner, seems, from today's vantage point, to be more dreamscape than reality. They foresee video on demand – the ability to call up any movie or television program or sports event at any time one chooses – as well as the capacity to create an electronic newspaper custom-tailored to one's individual interests and needs. The latest weather reports, sports scores, stock market fluctuations, and political commentary would be no more than a click away. But the key to the kingdom for many in the corporate world would be a new economy based on home shopping or transactions made from the home. One could avoid the crush of people and the hassles of parking by "walking" through the aisles of the local supermarket or department store while sitting comfortably at home in front of the computer/television set. The items chosen would be delivered the next day. Similarly one could "tour" distant holiday resorts, seeing the rooms and roaming the beaches, and then make a reservation simply by pressing a button. Home shopping on television is, of course, already a substantial business – the QVC cable channel in the U.S. averages 100,000 purchases every day.[5] Home banking, bill paying, stock purchases, and charitable giving can now be done electronically, and financial institutions are working hard to ensure that electronic transactions of this kind become a way of life, allowing them to cut costs.

Other experiences are becoming accessible in ways that could not be imagined before. Those interested in the fine arts can "visit" many of the world's great museums, such as the Louvre in Paris or the Prado in Madrid, seeing electronic reproductions of original paintings. It won't be long before these reproductions will be almost as clear as the originals.

Matthew and Joel, my two boys, can now fly over the major cities of the world when they play the computer game *Flight Simulator*. They have flown under the Eiffel Tower in Paris, landed in Calgary at night, crashed (repeatedly) into the Sears Tower in Chicago, and crossed the Mediterranean to land at Ben Gurion Airport in Israel.

Undoubtedly one of the great turning points in the convergence of technologies occurred in July 1997 when an estimated 100 million people around the world viewed television transmissions from the Mars Pathfinder mission via the Internet. The Jet Propulsion Laboratory made the pictures available on the Internet within minutes of having received them from outer space. People at home felt a curious sense of immediacy, as if they themselves were on Mars.

Of course, critics contend that some of these dreams could easily turn into nightmares. If these developments ever come to fruition they would make human interactions more isolated and limited and drastically reduce the quality of community life. The great meeting places that are so much a part of a community – offices, shopping centres, classrooms, banks, check-out counters – would become lifeless tombs. Some people prefer – in fact, relish – the helter-skelter and *mélange* of real shopping, of being there to inspect, to touch and feel fruits and vegetables, bump into neighbours and friends, and exchange pleasantries with the person at the check-out counter. This is part of the zest, the flavour of life. It is also something that couples and families can do together.

Moreover, there is now a great deal of evidence to support the contention that new technologies are devouring jobs at a rapid pace. The jobs crisis of the 1990s, which has produced so much dislocation and personal tragedy, is due to a large degree to the fact that companies are replacing workers with software. Economist Jeremy Rifkin has gone as far as to predict that new technologies will bring the end of work as we now know it.[6] Rifkin's position looks extreme because so many jobs involve intense human supervision and interaction, but the future for the stock keeper, bank teller, gas jockey or check-out clerk may not be bright.

While some experts adhere to the grand vision that there will be a total and absolute convergence of all media, what is currently taking place is a strange and tangled symbiosis; the old media permeate the new even as the new media are beginning to seep into and transform the old.

The old media are reproducing and perpetuating their power through the new media, and to some degree it is through the old media that the new media are achieving their place in the sun. People are accessing the Internet precisely to learn more about people and events that they have read or heard about on radio and TV or in newspapers. They go to the Net to read newspapers and magazines from around the world, find out more about their favorite television shows and stars, buy entertainment-related merchandise, visit museums and libraries, and, of course, connect with other people who share similar interests. They also create their own sites through which they can express their views about their favourite movie stars, sports idols, TV shows, or books. And it is also the case that sites created by large and powerful media organizations to support their shows or products are the ones that are the most effective. These organizations have the money and creative personnel needed to produce the most eye-catching, informative, and professional sites.

There is no doubt, however, that at the same time the very shape of the established media, its very "skin" to use media scholar Derrick De Kerckove's metaphor, is being altered by the new media.[7] We know from history that the development of new mediums – the telegraph, radio, film, and television – has not meant the disappearance of the old. The old mediums find new ways to adjust and survive. They adapt to changing circumstances by transforming themselves into something different. They almost inevitably find new niches, new methods, new audiences and new leases on life.

Magazines and radio adapted to the advent of television by changing the nature of their appeal. Realizing that they couldn't compete

with TV for a mass audience, both mediums became more specialized, targeting particular audience segments or demographic groups
just as cable does now. General-interest magazines such as *Life* and
Look gave way to magazines directed at people with distinctive interests and hence the rise of magazines such as *Fortune, Sports Illustrated, Seventeen,* and my old favourite, *Mad,* the ultimate kids'
magazine that allows children to learn about the absurdities of the
adult world on their own terms. Similarly, the old radio station that
played music that could appeal to everyone, the omnibus station,
was soon swept aside by stations that specialized, that were geared
to audiences of different ages and musical tastes – country and western, classical, hard rock, soul, jazz, talk, etc. In some major American cities, there are now as many as 30 radio stations, each with a
small but often very different slice of the listening audience.

Newspapers are a good example of how different mediums have
had to adjust to survive. The great crisis for newspapers occurred
in the early 1950s when the television era began in earnest. On one
level newspapers responded by becoming more like television – stories became shorter, more visual, more colourful. Newspaper boxes
were even redesigned to look like television sets. But more crucially,
perhaps, newspapers began focusing on doing the things that television couldn't do. Newspapers would be beaten to the punch in
breaking news stories because TV networks could always interrupt
the schedule with news bulletins and 24-hour all-news channels
churn out news like so much sausage. But newspapers could supply
background and context, they could provide an array of opinions,
and they could probe more deeply into stories than could TV news
shows that were more limited by time constraints.

Newspapers also adjusted to television by changing the reading
habits and daily routines of their readers. Where newspapers were
once read mostly in the evenings (and delivered in the late afternoon)
after men came home from work (while women presumably looked
after the children and the dishes), prime-time TV changed the equation. With television dominating the evenings, newspaper reading
was largely transformed into a morning activity. Newspapers were
to be digested in the morning along with toast and coffee.

Today, of course, newspapers are adjusting to the convergence revolution in much the same way that they had to find new ways to adapt to television. Virtually all of the world's major newspapers have web sites, readers can contact most newspaper columnists directly by e-mail, "talkies" (voice messages containing snippets of information or updates about stories or topics that readers are interested in) are offered by most major papers, and papers are inviting their readers to participate in electronic discussion groups. The front pages of some newspapers have even come to look like web sites, with colourful mastheads and short "bullets" that advertise the stories inside. But revamping formats and using the new media as a kind of advertisement – an announcement that the local newspaper is changing and avant garde enough to have a presence in cyberspace – may not be enough to overcome the challenges that lie ahead.

Newspaper owners are aware that online services are ready to challenge their monopoly over classified ads, the bread and butter of their economic survival. They are also aware that Microsoft has pioneered *Sidewalk*, an online guide to restaurants, entertainment, and news about "what's happening" in major U.S. cities. If *Sidewalk* proves to be successful it will rob newspapers of another vital source of revenue, the advertising of local events and entertainment. It will tear another piece of flesh out of the newspaper industry. And as mentioned earlier, the day when customized newspapers tailored to reflect the needs and interests of individual readers are available may not be far off. Readers will be able to order up any combination of articles – news headlines, sports stories, business news, TV listings, or movie reviews – and dispense with the rest of the paper, the stuffing that they don't want and never read.

Newspapers also have to contend with the fact that the Internet is far quicker off the mark than even television in not only being the first to report fast-breaking news stories but in providing instant analysis and background. For instance, when a Korean Airlines 747 crashed in Guam in August 1997, within an hour CNN Interactive, MSNBC, and Yahoo had gleaned and organized substantial amounts of information. The MSNBC site had three news stories, maps, 10 audio clips, background stories on previous crashes, Guam and 747's, a chat room, links to various airlines, and other relevant sites such as those dealing with aircraft safety and an online poll.[8] But it is crucial to note that traditional news agencies provided much of the information that appeared online.

According to some observers, the only way for newspapers to survive is to position themselves as a kind of information air traffic control system, a pathway through the information forest. The job of newspaper journalists, according to media critics like Jon Katz, will be to do the sorting and sifting and lead readers through the onslaught of information that batters them on a daily basis. In Katz's view, newspapers should welcome and not be threatened by the communications revolution:

> It's not bad for you that they're sprouting all over the place. The more of them there are, the more distinctive and valuable you can appear, by providing coherence, rationality and context. Do what they do poorly: investigative reporting, documentaries, special reports, longer interviews, analysis. Sift, provide context, sort through the mess every day; help us decide what we need to pay attention to.[9]

The crisis of identity that now infects the newspaper industry is but one manifestation of a wider media crisis. The convergence revolution has thrown the entire media world into a state of disarray. Every medium is trying to find the formula needed to ensure its own survival, to find its own way through the storm, even as they are adjusting to, being challenged by, and colliding with all of the other mediums. Perhaps the truth is that all of the mediums are merging with each other even as they are trying to retain their distinctive voices.

The Convergence of Corporations

In addition to this first level of convergence – the convergence and collision of mediums and technologies – convergence is occurring at the corporate level. In the last decade, the biggest pieces on the media chess board have changed as a result of a flurry of mergers, acquisitions, and partnerships. Global alliances are being forged to an unprecedented degree. This rearranging of the corporate map has been driven in part by the insatiable appetites and egos of media moguls such as Rupert Murdoch (News Corp.), Michael Eisner (Disney), or the late Steven Ross (Time Warner) who were/are driven to own or control everything that comes within their reach, and by the fact that the up-front costs needed to be a player in the new media game are so enormous. All of the major media conglomerates have sought to reduce risk by creating economies of scale, eliminating competition, and pooling their capital, talent and resources. All of this has both pressured, and been aided by, the vast deregulation of communication industries that has been undertaken by governments throughout the western world.

The developments that have taken place in the worlds of information and entertainment are part of a wider phenomenon. Transnational corporations are becoming ever more gigantic and ever more powerful in every sector of the world economy. In terms of economic influence, these mega-corporations are beginning to tower over countries. According to Sarah Anderson and John Cavanagh: "Of the 100 largest economies in the world, 51 are now corporations. Wal-Mart, No. 12 on the list – Canada ranks No. 8 – is larger than 161 countries, in other words, its gross revenue is greater than the total wealth or gross domestic product (GDP) of any of these 161 countries. General Motors is larger than Denmark, Ford is bigger than South Africa and Toyota surpasses Norway."[10] The great concern with global entertainment empires in particular is that they have become so large, so all-encompassing, that they now have the capacity to submerge national cultures.

Most of the action has taken place only recently, in the mid and late 1990s. Disney took over ABC for a reported $19 billion (U.S.). Time Warner merged with Turner Broadcasting. AT&T bought Tele-Communications Inc. (TCI), the world's largest cable company, for $32 billion (U.S.). Seagram's has taken over MCA with its jewel in the crown, Universal Studios, and PolyGram, the world's largest music company. Westinghouse bought CBS. Rupert Murdoch's News Corporation gobbled up 20th Century Fox, and cable and broadcast giant Viacom's media empire expanded to include Paramount Studios and Blockbuster Video.

Thus a small fistful of conglomerates now exercise vertical as well as horizontal control over much of the world's information and entertainment. Horizontal control means that these corporate behemoths dominate virtually the full length of the media waterfront from films to TV, from cable to music videos. Cross-media ownership on this scale is a relatively new phenomenon. Until the 1980s, the pattern was for a small clutch of companies to dominate a single industry whether that be television, telephones, or book publishing. They seldom spread their wings beyond the confines of their own sectors. Now these media empires span every aspect of the media business. Their fingers are in every pot.

At the same time, these giant corporations exert vertical control. This means that they preside over the entire media food chain from bottom to top. As Benjamin Barber has explained the process of vertical integration in his book *Jihad vs. McWorld*:

> Not only is the corporate proprietor of a conglomerate likely to own a stable of publishers, one of which will publish a given book, but it can also own the agency that sells the book, the magazine that serializes it, the movie studio that buys and films it, the distributor that purveys it, the cinema chain that screens it, the video export firm that brings it to the global market, and perhaps even the satellite pods or wires through which it is broadcast and the television set and VCR on which it is finally screened.[11]

The reality, as author Ken Auletta has put it, is that "every company wants to limit the risk of capitalism by controlling every aspect of its business."[12]

What University of Texas at Austin professor Thomas Schatz has described as the "distribution-exhibition pipeline" usually begins with a movie as its "launch site."[13] The movie is then cross-promoted and pumped by every arm of the corporate empire. For instance, the movie *Jurassic Park*, produced by Seagram-owned Universal Studios, was put through a full turn of the merchandising wheel; there were close to 1,000 licensed products including a video game, a ride at the Universal Studios theme parks, books, comics, toys, a soundtrack on audio disk, pay TV and cable releases, video cassette sales, etc.[14] Similarly, Time-Warner's movie *Space Jam*, starring basketball legend Michael Jordan, was spun into a variety of different products and flogged through media outlets controlled by Time Warner.[15] There was a *Space Jam* soundtrack, a special *Space Jam* edition of *Sports Illustrated for Kids*, a line of toys produced by a Warner Brothers' toy subsidiary, Warner Brothers' TV stations became "Official Space Jam Stations," and the movie was promoted on the Cartoon Network and other Time Warner cable outlets and during Time Warner-owned TBS's coverage of NBA games. There were tie-ins and promotional materials available from corporate sponsors (such as McDonald's and Kraft Foods) with which Time Warner frequently does business. And since Time Warner owns the Atlanta Hawks as well as a slice of NBA broadcasting rights, promoting basketball through *Space Jam* rebounded to its advantage in other ways.

The mammoth scale of what media scholar Todd Gitlin has described as the "conglomeration juggernaut" can best be understood by reviewing the holdings of the seven major power blocs: Time Warner, Disney, the News Corporation, Sony, Seagram, Microsoft, and Viacom.[16] While there are other big players at the global entertainment table such as the German publishing giant Bertelsmann, General Electric (which owns NBC), and AT&T (which controls TCI), the Big Seven play on a different scale. The key for six of them is that in addition to all of their other holdings, they own one or more Hollywood studios. Studios are the booster rockets of cultural production. Without a studio, a corporation cannot produce the motion pictures and TV programs that are still the basic currency of mass entertainment and pop culture.

The biggest of the media giants is the Japanese-owned Sony Corporation, one of the titans of the world economy, with annual revenues exceeding $50 billion (U.S.) in 1998. Sony owns Columbia Pictures, Cineplex Odeon and Loews theatres, electronic games and systems such as Sony Playstation, a major chunk of the world electronic industry (producing TVs, CD players, personal computers, tapes, and cellular phones, among many other products), a sizeable bite of the music business through companies such as Columbia and Epic, and part of a Japanese satellite consortium know as SkyPerfecTV.

With a revenue base of close to $30 billion (U.S.) in 1998, Time Warner-Turner is the world's second largest media empire. It owns a major movie studio, Warner Brothers, which has produced hits such as *L.A. Confidential, U.S. Marshals, Batman, Space Jam,* and the *Lethal Weapon* series and TV programs such as *E.R.* and *Seinfeld* (now in syndication). It owns the MGM/United Artists film library and cable channels such as CNN, Cinemax, and HBO, and it has a substantial grip on cable distribution in the United States. It also owns a bevy of prestigious magazines such as *Time, People, Fortune, Life, Entertainment Weekly,* and *Sports Illustrated* as well as Marvel and D.C. comics and the rights to the pantheon of superheroes that includes Spiderman, Captain America, and the X-Men.

It controls almost one-third of the music recording industry through its ownership of labels such as Elektra, Atlantic, and Warner Bros., is on the front lines of book publishing through Warner Books, and through its amalgamation with Turner has inherited sports franchises such as baseball's Atlanta Braves, the Atlanta Hawks of the NBA, and the NHL expansion Atlanta Thrashers. Time Warner also owns the $245 million (U.S.) theme park-cum-baseball stadium at Turner Field in Atlanta, and a piece of the Six Flags theme parks.

Another of the Big Seven is Disney/ABC with revenues of over $25 billion (U.S.) in 1998. It owns a major Hollywood studio that has dominated animated feature film production for over 50 years (making classics such as *Sleeping Beauty, Snow White and the Seven Dwarfs, Aladdin, The Jungle Book, Pocahontas,* and *The Lion King* among others), a TV network with eight owned and operated stations and 225 affiliates, cable channels such as ESPN, A&E and the Disney Channel, newspapers, magazines, theme parks on three continents, hotels, a cruise line, stores that annually sell approximately $2 billion of products and merchandise based on Disney characters (including exclusive rights to market the Royal Canadian Mounted Police), and sports franchises such as hockey's Anaheim Mighty Ducks and baseball's Anaheim Angels.

With annual revenues exceeding $11 billion (U.S.) annually, Rupert Murdoch's News Corporation is another of the world's major media stakeholders. Murdoch's web of companies includes a film and TV studio, 20th Century Fox and Fox Broadcasting (which have most notably made *Titanic* [with Paramount], *The X-Files, The Simpsons, Mighty Morphin Power Rangers, King of the Hill,* and *South Park*), the Family Channel, a TV network and television stations in New York, Los Angeles, Chicago, Atlanta, Washington, Philadelphia, Boston and 15 other cities, satellite television systems in Europe and Asia, a massive book publishing arm (Harper Collins and J.B. Lippincott among others), the largest newspaper chain in the world (including the *London Times* and the *New York Post*), and a large chunk of the market for preprinted newspaper grocery coupon supplements. Murdoch also owns a host of important magazines and a distribution company that ensures that Murdoch's magazines are displayed prominently at check-out counters and newsstands across the U.S. Murdoch recently launched *Fox News* as a 24-hour all-news channel to rival CNN.

Murdoch has also taken the plunge into professional sports. Indeed, he sees sports as a "battering ram" – the key to attracting subscribers for his satellite and pay-TV operations. He recently bought the Los Angeles Dodgers for $350 million (U.S.) and is a part owner of the NHL's Los Angeles Kings and the Los Angeles Lakers of the NBA. The Fox Sports Net has purchased the regional broadcast rights for 49 professional teams and reaches an audience of 55 million viewers.

Another huge global player is Viacom, owned by Sumner Redstone. Its major launch site is Paramount Pictures (*Forrest Gump, Titanic, Grease,* and *The Truman Show* among others). But perhaps more essential to Viacom's power is that it dominates much of the distribution pipeline through its control of Blockbuster Videos.

Blockbuster has close to 5,000 stores worldwide and is Hollywood's largest revenue source. There are over 70 million Blockbuster members in North America. In addition, Viacom possesses a substantial film library, owns cable channels such as MTV, Nickelodeon, and Showtime, as well as key franchises in the publishing business – Simon & Schuster, Scribner, and Pocket Books.

One of the media giants, Seagram, has at least one foot in Canada. Seagram, made famous for its worldwide domination of the liquor business and for the brusque no-nonsense style of its legendary founder Sam Bronfman, has now expanded into the entertainment industry. While it still maintains a large presence in Canada, Seagram has become one of the most powerful forces in Hollywood. In addition to its global liquor and beverage businesses, Seagram owns Universal Studios, one of the key engines of the film industry. Universal Studios has released blockbuster hits such as *Back to the Future, The Land Before Time, Jurassic Park* and its sequel *The Lost World, Twister,* and *Apollo 13,* and also produces TV shows such as *Hercules: The Legendary Journeys, Xena: Warrior Princess, The Larry Sanders Show, Law and Order,* and *Sally Jessy Raphael* among others. It owns a 50 per cent interest in the USA network, one of the most innovative and aggressive forces in American television. Through PolyGram, Motown, Geffen, MCA, Decca and Deutsche Grammophon, its music holdings currently rank first in market share, and it is adding a new theme park in Japan to the ones that it operates in California and Florida. Seagram recently won a battle with Viacom that will give it a major stake in cable TV.

The last major conglomerate, Microsoft, is an entirely different creature from the others. Unlike the other six, it doesn't have a Hollywood studio as its centre of gravity, as the main spoke of its financial and cultural wheel. Its economic might is based on creating and owning the software, the operating system, that runs most of the world's personal computers. Founded by Bill Gates, the world's wealthiest person with a fortune that is estimated at over $60 billion (U.S.) and who lives in a house valued at over $50 million (U.S.), Microsoft has gone from controlling software to controlling the media message. Its strategy has been nothing less than to invade and subvert the old media either by making some elements of the old media obsolete or by positioning itself as the "toll booth" through which the old media has to pass. Perhaps the best example of the strategy is Microsoft's ownership of a company called Corbis. Corbis maintains the world's largest digital archive of photos and artwork (over 20 million images so far), licensing the right to use these images to newspapers, magazines, film studios, ad agencies, and whoever else might need visual materials. Another potentially decisive move was Microsoft's investment in WebTV, a company that makes the set-top boxes that allow TV viewers to have access to the Internet. One can envision a generation of couch potatoes, lounging in front of their TV sets with beer and chips, clicking effortlessly from TV to the Internet and back.

Yet another possibly lethal challenge to the old media was Microsoft's launch in 1998 of *Sidewalk*, a web site that offers guides to local entertainment, restaurants, and shopping in twelve cities. Until *Sidewalk*'s arrival, newspapers had been the "guide" to the city for most people. Now Microsoft threatens to capture an advertising market and readership that was once the almost-exclusive preserve of local newspapers. The company's travel and investor web sites also have the potential to hurt newspapers and magazines by taking away other sources of advertising. Microsoft has also cleared other new pathways on the information frontier. In 1996, Microsoft joined NBC to establish MSNBC, an all-news cable channel that reaches some 40 million cable subscribers as well as millions of others through its site on the World Wide Web. In 1997, Gates bought a sizable stake in Comcast, the fourth largest cable operator in the U.S. and the owner of the Philadelphia 76ers of the NBA and the NHL's Philadelphia Flyers. Gates also created *Slate*, an online magazine that specializes in politics and current affairs. *Slate* has an estimated 100,000 readers.

While the formation of media conglomerates is hardly a new phenomenon, the sheer size of today's media giants and the cross-media and international nature of their holdings is unique. Although bitter rivalries and grudges sometimes exist (Ted Turner has compared Rupert Murdoch to "the late Fuhrer" because of his authoritarian manner and firm grip over the political message of the newspapers and TV stations that he owns and has reportedly challenged Murdoch to settle their score in a boxing ring), global media ownership has come to resemble a brick of fudge ripple ice cream: all of the major corporate entities blend into and mix with one another. The Big Seven often cooperate with each other, acting as partners in various ventures while remaining rivals at the same time. Some territories are bitterly contested while others are peacefully shared. The reality is that the costs required for and the risks involved in almost any major venture − investing in a picture like *Titanic*, buying into the cable industry, setting up satellite services − are astronomical even for huge corporate behemoths like Disney or Time Warner. Few can go it alone or can go very far without tripping over the interests of their rivals.

When Sony wanted to change a licensing agreement that its TriStar motion picture studios had with Viacom's HBO, a move potentially damaging to Viacom, its executives were invited to visit a Blockbuster video store in order to see how dependent they had become on maintaining good relations with Viacom. They quickly rethought their decision. John Malone, the founder of Tele-Communications Inc., has described the complex relationships of conflict and symbiosis this way: "Virtually everybody who is not on your team or in your company will be both a friend and a competitor. We're partners with Time Warner on a whole bunch of stuff. Yet we are also competitors ... If you have cross-investments, it increases the likelihood that your purposes are aligned."[17] According to Howard Stringer, CEO of Sony Corporation of America, the logic is that: "You're marching off into the unknown, your timetables are very unclear; so in order to offset some of your costs and achieve economies of scale, you need to establish partnerships. This means everybody is forced to talk to each other."[18]

The conglomerates are aware that by combining forces they can wield enormous political clout. While all of the major media organizations have their own full-time lobbyists in Washington, they combine to sponsor the National Association of Broadcasters (NAB) − by some accounts the most powerful lobby organization in the

United States. As House Speaker Newt Gingrich once observed, "The practical fact is, that nobody's going to take on the broadcasters."[19] The key to the NAB's power is not that it gives prodigious amounts of money to political campaigns or that it employs more than 40 lobbyists to monitor legislation and argue its case at all levels of government, although these are significant factors. The key is that politicians believe that the NAB controls the oxygen supply of modern politics, the access that politicians have to have to the airwaves in order to reach voters. Barney Frank, a veteran congressman from Massachusetts, described the NAB's hold in the following way:

> We know (broadcasters) have enormous discretion over what goes on the air each night and what doesn't ... It's not that members of Congress fear out-and-out retribution. It's more subtle. They worry that the station might decide to just ignore the shit out of them. Now I happen to be at the stage of my career where if they never say another word about me, a blessing on their head. But, for a lot of members, it can have a chilling effect.[20]

One example of the raw political muscle of the corporate giants was the lobbying effort they mounted to defeat a provision of the U.S. Telecommunications Act of 1996 that called for an auctioning off of the TV spectrum. Close to $25 billion (U.S.) has already gone to U.S. government coffers as a result of a sell-off of cellular telephone frequencies. This proposal would have forced broadcasters to pay tens of billions of dollars for the space that they now occupy on the airwaves virtually for free. With its interests and perhaps survival directly threatened, the communication industry mobilized a breathtaking campaign, defeating the proposal with relative ease.

Some observers are horrified by the corporate dance that they see developing. They believe that the iron grip of a few powerful conglomerates is strangling creativity, the transmission of new ideas, cultural diversity, and the combative zeal needed for public debate and democratic exchange. They see a deadening uniformity on TV, on radio, and in the movies. They worry that smaller competitors will be swallowed by the larger predators the minute they show signs of success, develop a new concept, or become too aggressive. And they fear that journalists will lose their freedom, that they will not be critical of major corporations with whom their own news organizations are linked. It's not so much that their bosses will give them direct orders about what is "kosher" or not kosher but that a subtle climate of fear will take hold. Those who want to be promoted or who are worried about their jobs (the majority of journalists these days) will know where "the lines in the sand" are drawn in terms of dealing with issues or expressing their opinions. And those lines are rarely crossed.

First, there is the issue of whether large conglomerates smother competition. Canadians have a great deal of experience in this regard because the control of film distribution and movie houses by the big media giants has meant that independent Canadian films or even top foreign films are rarely shown in Canada except on the CBC. Exhibitors can, if they wish, include an off-Hollywood film in the menu of films that they offer their audiences, but the economic incentives are such that they inevitably fill their cineplexes with blockbuster American films.

A similar situation exists in the U.S. cable industry. As one cable programmer described John Malone's (AT&T) stranglehold over cable distribution in the U.S.: "Imagine that you have all these publishing houses but only one book chain ... You can write the book, but what happens if you can't get into the bookstore? John Malone is the bookstore."[21] Microsoft's dominant position in computer software has prompted similar concerns and indeed a spate of lawsuits from the U.S. Justice Department and a half dozen American states. According to one Microsoft official, the corporation operates on a quid pro quo that gives access to companies in a position to do something for Microsoft. His blunt message was that: "There are very, very few people we allow to be in the Windows box. If you want that preferential treatment from us, which is extraordinary treatment, we're going to want something very extraordinary from you."[22] U.S. government lawsuits claim that Microsoft bullied computer manufacturers into installing its Internet Explorer web browser as a condition of being able to use Windows software.

Certainly the huge conglomerates have little trouble elbowing others out of the fast lanes on the information causeway. Rupert Murdoch is said to have offered cable operators $10 (U.S.) per subscriber to carry his Fox News channel.[23] There is simply no way that a would-be competitor will be able to compete against Murdoch unless they have an equally large war chest to dip into. In many cases the choice for smaller companies is either to dance to the tune set by News Corporation, Disney, or Viacom or not dance at all. The fear is that the only way for a fledgling company to prosper is to team up with and come under the protective canopy of one of the giants.

A second question is whether citizens are being given full access to the news and information they need or whether willful owners and corporate imperatives are skewing the message — bending the news and journalism to fit their needs. The greatest controversy seems to surround Rupert Murdoch. In an article that appeared in the *Columbia Journalism Review*, writer Ross Baker accuses Murdoch of being a modern-day Citizen Kane except that his power has a global reach: "He wields his media as instruments of influence with politicians who can aid him, and savages his competitors in his news columns. If ever someone demonstrated the dangers of mass power being concentrated in few hands, it would be Murdoch."[24] According to Baker, Murdoch rewards friendly politicians with hefty book contracts, donates large sums of money to political candidates, ensures that his films and TV shows are "self-promoted" in the magazines and newspapers and on the TV stations that he owns, and encourages the hiring of right-wing columnists and commentators. In fact, Fox News, run by former Bush strategist Roger Ailes, is considered to be little more than a platform for right-of-centre views. Ben Bagdikian, the former Dean of Journalism at the University of California, Berkeley, believes that the Fox News slogan, "We report. You decide," should really be understood to mean: "We decide what news you hear, and you make up your mind based on what we tell you."[25] The reality, according to Bagdikian, is that Murdoch "has never been known for giving balanced news in his newspapers or broadcasts."[26]

TV historian Erik Barnouw believes that journalists now face many agonizing conflicts of interest because of the business interests of their parent companies. The takeover of NBC by General Electric, for instance, placed journalists in a difficult bind. Barnouw's complaint is that: "[O]ne of our major news sources became the property of a company selling military equipment ... and marketing nuclear plants at home and abroad. Every NBC newsman went onto a payroll controlled by GE, and was kept aware of it. From a standpoint of public policy, it's hard to think of a sorrier linkage."[27] In fact, in what was arguably one of the most cowardly acts in modern journalism, NBC apologized to China, a major market for GE, after announcer Bob Costas cited human rights abuses during the opening ceremonies of the Atlanta Olympics.

Prominent media scholar Todd Gitlin asks a similar question about journalists who cover films or TV programs made by the parent companies of the news organizations for whom they work: "Would any reviewer survive in any publishing outlet today who did not gush about a hefty share of Hollywood releases?"[28]

It is interesting to note that soon after Disney took over ABC, *Good Morning America* devoted almost an entire show to commemorating Disney World's 25th anniversary, a show described by one media analyst as being "as close to an infomercial as I have ever seen on network television."[29] Disney also showed that it had little tolerance for any signs of disloyalty or criticism from its own journalists when it fired ABC talk show host Jim Hightower. Although Disney insists that Hightower was fired for low ratings, comments such as "Now I work for a rodent" obviously didn't help his cause.[30]

For some, the issue is not so much whether there are direct marching orders from owners — although such pressures and conflicts of interest seem all too apparent in some cases — as whether there is a subtle censorship that journalists impose on themselves. In Todd Gitlin's view: "It's a close question whether there's more to worry about from top-down censorship ... or from the long chill of a thousand microdecisions made by a thousand personnel about a thousand stories it would seem, well, more trouble than they're worth, to push too far. Self-censorship is probably the greatest danger, and it is rarely expressed; it leaves no smoking memos."[31] Author Ken Auletta describes the self-censorship chill this way: "Today the greater journalistic peril in a large conglomerate comes from self-censorship, by timid and ambitious bureaucrats who want to be recognized. God, if we run this story will it harm our careers? Will we be seen as not team players? Won't our corporate bosses really be pleased if we run this cover story on Bob Woodward's latest book, or Warner Brothers' newest film?"[32]

Is this what the future holds? Journalists holding their fire, pulling their punches, on stories that come too close to the interests of corporate giants, or acting as mouthpieces for the products they create? The stifling of competition so that new ideas or companies can never emerge? Does it mean a relentless conformity, and a narrowing, a choking off, of the economic marketplace and of the marketplace of ideas, the public squares that are essential for a healthy democracy? The assessment of some observers is quite foreboding and gloomy. In Benjamin Barber's view the effects of so much corporate concentration are ominous: "Synergy turns out to be a polite way of saying monopoly. And in the domain of information, monopoly is a polite word for uniformity, which is a polite word for virtual censorship."[33]

Those who favour convergence argue that all of the major technological advances that have transformed the media topography would have been impossible without the financial muscle of large corporate entities. The explosion in cable and satellite TV, the small city of people and resources needed to make a major motion picture, the development and manufacturing of computer software, the massive infrastructure that has been built by phone companies – all require financial investments that are beyond the means of small or even medium-sized companies. Moreover, advocates contend that these developments have given citizens more choices than they have ever had before. Far from information being censored or limited, we are being bombarded by an endless barrage of news and opinion – there are a host of 24-hour all-news channels, a vast expanse of Internet sites with endless chat rooms and discussion groups, the loud and raucous world of talk radio and TV, magazines devoted to every imaginable interest, bookstores that resemble supermarkets, and newspapers that have to include a large menu of subjects and perspectives to appeal to a wide variety of readers and interests in order to be successful.

Supporters of corporate concentration insist that costs are going down and that access to information thoroughfares is being made available to an increasing number of citizens. They argue that the costs of long-distance phone rates, cable TV, and other media products are lower than they once were. Steven Rattner, managing partner in the financial house Lazard Frere, believes that we are now in "the golden age of competition in communication industries."[34] Norman Horowitz, the owner of a TV production company, sees more opportunities for independent producers like himself because of the amorphous, decentralized, and multi-pronged nature of media empires. As Horowitz explains with regard to Time Warner in particular: "Dealing with entities like these is kind of like the difference between shopping at a neighborhood hardware store and Wal-Mart. If there is one set of tastes at one company and they don't like you or your project, it would be over for you. But with the diversity afforded by a decentralized Time/Warner/Turner, you can shop at a variety of stores."[35] Whether one believes that the convergence of corporations is of great benefit or great harm, almost all media observers would agree with the promoters for the movie *Godzilla* that "Size does matter."

The Convergence of News and Entertainment

Convergence is occurring at a third level; there is now a merging, an intertwining, of news and entertainment. It can be argued that more and more of the stories that appear on TV news, especially local news, are either "framed" in an eye-catching, sensational and entertaining way or are about the entertainment industry – celebrities, sports teams, movies, books, etc. The infotainment phenomenon was described with greatest eloquence in a marvelous book entitled *Amusing Ourselves to Death,* written over 15 years ago by Neil Postman of

New York University.[36] The trend that Postman harshly condemned has now, if anything, mushroomed to even more monstrous proportions. We have reached the point where entertainment values and topics are sprinkled like a sugar topping over almost all of the news.

Infotainment stems from three closely related developments. First, when journalists and news organizations cover news stories they carry a "frame" along with them, a frame that they "clamp" over the events that they are covering.[37] The frame constitutes the expectations and requirements brought to the story by journalists. Stories that don't fit the frame – that don't contain the ingredients that journalists are looking for – either tend not to make it onto the news or are downplayed. Those stories that have what news organizations are looking for – high-impact visuals, conflict between two high-profile political leaders, emotional drama, issues that are easily condensed and labelled – become part of the daily news diet. What creates and drives the frame are the perceived demands of the audience, the time, resource and technological demands and constraints of news organizations, and lastly, the personal beliefs and professional judgment of news people.

What this comes down to in most cases are stories that either have some entertainment "juice" to begin with or are "juiced up" by journalists so that their stories (and not others) will impress their managers and make it onto the evening news. Postman's lament was that: "The problem is not that television presents us with entertaining subject matter but that all subject matter is presented as entertaining."[38] Richard Cohen, a former senior producer for the *CBS Evening News*, has put it more graphically and crudely: "Newsroom nonsense always defined the perfect story as anything dealing with pets, tits or tots. There are variations. When our metaphorical news truck pulls into the station for fuel, it pulls up to one of two pumps. One reads, great pictures; the other, high emotion. The news truck takes on all the fuel it can hold."[39] The effects on public policy, and indeed on public debate, while difficult to measure, are enormous. When OJ- or Monica Lewinsky-type news stories dominate the headlines, other kinds of stories don't receive the play that they deserve. The struggles that take place in education and health care, at

City Hall, or in the battle to introduce election campaign reforms don't by their very nature contain the same high-octane news value, the same news kick, as grisly murders, three-alarm fires, and ten-ton trucks overturning on the expressway. And when crucial issues fall off the screen, or in some cases never get on, they fall out of the public's consciousness. "Agenda-setting" studies have shown that there is a direct correlation between the issues that the public sees as important and the issues that are presented as important in the mass media.[40]

Evidence that political issues are no longer central to news reporting, that they are dropping off the screen, comes from a study of U.S. network news programs and newsmagazines conducted by the Project for Excellence in Journalism and the Medill News Service.[41] Based on programs that aired in 1997, the study found that "government" only accounted for 13.3 per cent of all network news items and only 0.6 per cent of the stories that were featured on newsmagazines. Crime stories, consumer and medical news, and lifestyle reporting had become the daily bread of television news coverage.

A second part of the equation is the extent to which news organizations have become advertising agencies for the products of the entertainment conglomerates that they are a part of. When the cover of *Time* or *People* is emblazoned with one of the stars of a Warner Brothers picture or TV show or when a sports story on a Time Warner-owned TV station lauds the triumphs of a Time Warner sports franchise, it is difficult to discern where legitimate news ends and self-promotion begins. While one can always point to such instances, the larger problem is that the news gorges on entertainment topics in general. News and indeed "talk" about celebrities, sports teams, how movies are doing at the box office, the latest from advice and self-help books, the hoopla surrounding rock concerts, and the nice weather in vacation hot spots have become part and parcel of news shows. Although one should not diminish the importance that "soft" news plays as a necessary and enjoyable part of people's lives, it may be no coincidence that the big entertainment conglomerates that own the major news organizations have a major stake in promoting these "products."

A third element is the growing tendency for media organizations to establish "partnerships" with important institutions or events in their communities. Newspapers and TV stations help sponsor sports teams, civic projects, charities, and festivals as a way of raising their own profiles and contributing meaningfully to the communities that they serve. While the intentions are often noble, the result is that events hosted by "partners" usually receive disproportionate and glowing coverage – coverage not enjoyed by other community endeavours. The question is whether readers and audiences are receiving an accurate account of the events being reported on, or whether the reporting dissolves into a form of advertising. The fly in the ointment appears when boosterism and hoopla replace the ability of journalists to make independent and critical judgments.

The Convergence of Cultures

A fourth level at which convergence is taking place is with regard to national cultures. In addition to the convergence of technologies, corporations, news and entertainment, values and cultures are also merging. Technological advances that have reduced time and distance and increasing economic interdependence have produced a new and powerful reality; the globalization of culture. South Koreans and South Africans, Brazilians and Israelis all drink Coke, follow the NBA, watch blockbuster American movies, wear Nike running shoes with the patented swoosh label, listen to hit songs by Bryan Adams, Madonna, Pearl Jam, and Guns and Roses and wear blue jeans.

The emergence of a single shopping centre culture was brought home to me during my stay as a visiting professor at the University of Amsterdam in the Netherlands. The similarities in cultural taste between my Dutch students and the students that I teach in Canada are remarkable. For the most part, students in the two countries listened to the same music, read the same books, wear the same brand-name clothes sold in the same brand-name stores, and inhabit the same video world of TV programs and computer games. A large degree of convergence seemed to exist even in the educational system. Thanks largely to the predominance of English as the language of communication in the scientific and academic community, my Dutch students studied many of the same texts, dealt with many of the same concepts, and covered roughly the same intellectual terrain that they would have had they been in a Canadian university.

I wouldn't want to minimize or belittle some of the substantial differences that exist. The strong belief that the Dutch have in the benefits of the welfare state, the deeply ingrained and harrowing memories that the society as a whole has of Nazi occupation during the Second World War, the perpetual battle with the terrors of the sea, and the historic tolerance and openness of Amsterdam itself make for a different inner world. Dutch literature and painting and popular culture have their own deep resonance and special themes.

Evidence, however, from international surveys suggests that values are beginning to converge, at least in the advanced democracies. Neil Nevitte, a distinguished political scientist at the University of Toronto, found from survey data that citizens in virtually all of the advanced industrial countries have come to share similar values – a deepening cynicism toward and suspicion of governments and political authority, less religious observance, a greater emphasis on individuality and individual rights, and more liberal attitudes about moral and social behaviour than existed a generation ago. According to Nevitte, surveys indicate that there is little to distinguish the values held dear by Canadians from those cherished in other countries.[42]

The most obvious case in point may be Canada and the United States. In an article first published in 1965 and now regarded as something of a classic, the eminent sociologist Seymour Martin Lipset found that important value differences separated Canadians and Americans.[43] According to Lipset, American values were forged in the cauldron of the American Revolution and in the overturning and rejection of British institutions. As a result of this experience, Americans were less deferential to authority, more individualistic, more likely to be members of a religious minority, and more vio-

lent than Canadians (because of the need to raise a militia, the found-
ers of the American Republic had enshrined the right to bear arms
in the constitution). Canada, on the other hand, emerged as a reaction against the American revolution; Canadians rejected American republican values by remaining steadfastly loyal to the monarchy
and to the British way of life. Canadians showed greater deference
to authority, were more law abiding (writer Hugh Dempsey has reported only three gun fights in the history of the Canadian west),
more collectivist, and more willing to allow the state to play an in-
terventionist role in economic and social affairs.[44]

Twenty-five years after the original article was published, Lipset
re-evaluated his original argument in a book entitled *Continental Divide*.[45] He found that although important differences between the
two societies remained, they had moved closer together on almost
every front. Canadians had become far more suspicious of political
authority, far less collectivist, much more individualistic, and much
more tolerant of religious and social differences. Poll results cited
by Lipset showed that differences in values and beliefs between citizens on the two sides of the border were often only marginal – usually in the range of 5 to 10 per cent.[46] The greatest difference seemed
to be in the area of crime and law enforcement where the gap between the two societies remained stark.

Evidence that there is an increasing convergence of values worldwide now seems undeniable. The point is addressed by Benjamin
Barber in his controversial book *Jihad vs. McWorld*. Barber uses the
term "McWorld" to explain the emergence of the new global
economy, an economy based on freer international trade, the har-
monization of economic policies within and between trade blocs
such as the European Union, NAFTA and ASEAN, and a revolution in communication and transportation that have together produced an increasingly borderless world. Barber argues that while
the development of an international shopping centre with branches
in every country, and indeed in every neighbourhood, is still far
from reality (especially in the impoverished third world), a convergence of lifestyles and ways of viewing the world seems to be
underway. As Barber describes the changes that are taking place:

> Music, video, theater, books, and theme parks – the
> new churches of a commercial civilization in which
> malls are the public squares and suburbs the
> neighborless neighborhoods – are all constructed as
> image exports creating a common world taste
> around common logos, advertising slogans, stars,
> songs, brand names, jingles and trademarks. Hard
> power yields to soft, while ideology is transmuted
> into a kind of videology that works through sound
> bites and film clips.[47]

To Canadians there may be no better example of what is taking place than in the world of hockey. Sports has long played an integral role in civic and national identity – inspiring a tribal loyalty among fans that is sometimes fanatical. Popular rivalries and traditions have made sports part of the tissue, part of the sinews, of national distinctiveness. Some Canadians are alarmed by the extent to which the National Hockey League has now become "deCanadianized," a continental and even international enterprise. Teams in Florida, Texas, California, Colorado, and Georgia are populated by Swedes, Russians, Slovaks, Finns, a sprinkling of home-grown American players and sometimes only a few lonely Canadians. In fact, the NHL, directed by an American head office, is modelling itself on the National Basketball Association, which has achieved remarkable success in marketing its products worldwide. The NBA sold nearly half a billion dollars (U.S.) worth of merchandise outside the United States in 1996. Its weekly TV package, *NBA Action Highlights*, is seen literally across the world. Small wonder that a survey of teenagers in 45 countries found that Michael Jordan, basketball's most spectacular magician, had become the world's most recognizable and popular sports star.[48]

While some tend to think of the new international culture as merely the spread of American products and values, there is a degree to which genuine American cultures – the cultures of New England, Chicago, or the South – are also being undermined, submerged, and lost in the vast homogenization that is now taking place. Bill McKibben points out that one rarely hears American regional accents on TV. If we do, "they tend to be country singers or poor people who have been unexpectedly caught in natural disasters."[49] In English Canada, it's only when ordinary people are interviewed from remote places – Newfoundland outports or ranches in southern Alberta – that a noticeable and distinctive twang can be recognized.

McKibben also argues that as international audiences for American films and TV programs have become more lucrative, plots and story lines are geared to appeal to global audiences. He quotes one Hollywood producer as saying: "We have to consider the global market, and we absolutely need more universal stories now. It will be harder to sell a purely American story of an Iowa farmer than something of broader interest."[50] One of the reasons why so many movies try to outdo each other in presenting the most nerve-jarring effects, the most shocking and graphic scenes of violence, horror or disaster, is that blockbuster films travel easily across the globe. They can be understood in any culture. Humour, for instance, tends to resonate and be appreciated only within particular cultures. Comedy doesn't travel as well as violence.

Barber believes that the movement towards McWorld has produced a fierce backlash. Barber uses the term *Jihad* – the Arabic word for holy war – to describe the opposition that has developed to counter international convergence. Those who fear that their cultures will be extinguished by the advance of a uniform global culture have sometimes responded with fanatical intensity. The current surge of religious extremism and strong local nationalism are attempts to protect the old way of life, the old world view, from sweeping and penetrating change. The advent of militant Islamic states such as Iran and Afghanistan and the breakup of the former Soviet Union, Czechoslovakia, and Yugoslavia are examples of the splintering that is taking place at the same time as, and Barber would argue, in response to the advance of a McWorld culture.

Conclusion

Convergence is having an extraordinary impact on almost all aspects of contemporary society. Canada, dependent as it is on a technological and communications infrastructure, is feeling the full force of this crashing sea. In fact, one can argue that few countries are as open and as vulnerable as Canada is to the currents of McWorld. Canada simply does not have the long history, the unity brought by religious or ethnic solidarity, and the deep national roots, the cultural glue, of countries such as France, Japan, Israel, Brazil, or China. It lacks the high protective walls of a strong unified culture. Moreover, its political institutions – the monarchy, Question Period in the House of Commons, the Senate, the electoral system – inspire little loyalty and seem to exacerbate rather than soothe aching regional and linguistic divisions. One of our greatest scholars, Northrop Frye, was fond of pointing out that Canada had taken a long time to sink roots, to explore its vast spaces and its different identities and voices, and to come together as a national community.[51] The near-death experience of the 1995 Quebec referendum (it was at the very least a national nervous breakdown), and the sharp regional and linguistic divisions that have become deeply embedded in Canadian political life are reminders that the country is still fragile, still has to come to terms with its many differences.

In this context the convergence wave has the power to overwhelm a national community such as Canada or at least to dramatically change it. Technological convergence, the pervasive power of the corporate entertainment giants, the merging of news and entertainment and emerging global culture all impinge, define and determine important aspects of the Canadian condition. These forces set the parameters within which our democratic institutions and the popular culture with which they are so vitally linked must function. The challenge is how to maintain or even recreate our public spaces in a world dominated and propelled by convergence.

A cynic might argue that the giant corporations that control the mass media have an interest in having weak national governments, governments without the will or power to provide cultural protection to their citizens. The international media cartels would prefer to be free from regulation, free from any limits on their investments, profits or products. When someone like Rupert Murdoch supports Republican candidates in the U.S. who advocate smaller government and less regulation, through political donations or as some would charge through the views disseminated by his news organizations, his actions may be entirely self-serving.

Yet, as mentioned in the introduction to this chapter, convergence is only one thrust in a media pincer movement that that is encircling countries like Canada. The other thrust is the change created by the explosive effect of audience fragmentation. The next chapter will deal with this equally important phenomenon.

FOUR

Fragmentation Bombs: The New Media and the Erosion of Public Life

T he threat to national communities, and to the preservation of public spaces, also comes from another wave of media change – one that in some respects is the very opposite of convergence. Breakthroughs in cable technology brought by digitalization and the advent of VCRs, satellites and the World Wide Web are splintering the audience into tiny fragments. Convergence is only one end of the pendulum, only one seat on the media teeter-totter. The other is fragmentation. Where the media landscape of 15 or 20 years ago was dominated by highly centralized vehicles of communication, and the ability to bring huge audiences together at a single time and place, the new media have the capacity to splinter the audience into ever smaller slices. And where the organizational structures of the old media were top-down because TV networks dictated schedules, and journalists stood between the audience and the events being covered telling the public what it was seeing, the new media allow audiences to exercise more control and to have experiences that are more direct and "unfiltered."

Fragmentation is to some degree an outgrowth of "narrowcasting" – the propensity of advertisers to tailor their messages to the needs and tastes of small but highly desirable demographic clusters – and of the extent to which cable TV, radio, and the Internet have the capacity to "assemble" these identifiable groups, to create these market niches, for advertisers. Fragmentation is also the result of the autonomy that individuals have gained as organizers and producers of their own media.

Perhaps the first important technological breakthrough of this new era was the videocassette recorder. The VCR ended the monopoly control that TV networks had over scheduling. For the first time, viewers could fit TV watching into their own schedules rather than have schedules imposed on them by the networks. Viewers could sidestep commercials by zipping through them or bypass the parts of movies or TV shows that they didn't want to watch. Hand-held clickers, that symbol of couch potato happiness, brought the freedom to flick from channel to channel so that viewers could watch several programs at the same time. Viewers could effortlessly prowl the TV neighbourhood, constructing their own unique and personalized viewing environment.

This chapter will describe some of the combustible components that fueled the fragmentation explosion – the development of the multi-channel universe created by cable and satellite TV and the Internet revolution. I will also discuss the ways in which the new media are both vapourizing the old public spaces, the old public squares that were the central meeting places of society, and creating new spaces that have the capacity to both enhance public life and do it great damage.

The Cable and Satellite Explosion

Digitalization has changed the topography of cable TV. Under the old analog system the number of signals that could be transmitted was drastically limited by the narrowness of the bandwidth. Digital compression has allowed as many as 10 channels to fit the space once occupied by a single channel, and has the capacity to ignite an explosion in cable channels – the much-heralded 500- or 1000-channel universe. In fact, in the United States there are already cable systems that provide their customers with as many as 150 channels, and Canadians who are fully loaded with all of the basic and pay-TV cable services can now access over 80 channels.

The 500- or 1000-channel universe will offer viewers a bewildering array of choices – a vast horizon of options. There will be a kaleidoscope of all-news channels (we already have four Canadian services: *CBC Newsworld, CTV News 1*, the French-language *RDI*, and *Pulse 24* serving southern Ontario), every major religious denomination is likely to have a channel (modelled perhaps on National Catholic Television in the U.S.), individual sports such as baseball or hockey or leagues like the NBA could have their own broadcasting arms (there already is a Golf Channel), and there are or will be channels for every imaginable interest and hobby – pet channels, gardening channels, fishing channels, carpentry channels, travel channels, military history channels, etc. Political parties are likely to have their own channels (U.S. Republicans already have GOP-TV), government agencies may have them (the National Aeronautics and Space Administration [NASA] already has two), and even large businesses such as General Motors or Microsoft are likely to have their own channels lodged somewhere in the back alleys of cable TV. In addition, there will be a cacophony of home shopping, music, educational, ethnic and movie channels. The 93-channel cable system that Bill McKibben studied in Fairfax, Virginia aired close to 1,000 movies every month, so that the cable box became almost a home video store.[1]

For those who want to keep on top of the action there are split-screen options that allow viewers to monitor twelve or more channels at the same time, and "multiplexing," which permits broadcasters to occupy a number of different channels, airing their regular programs at different times of the day so that viewers can watch their favourite shows at times that they find convenient.

The Canadian Radio-television and Telecommunications Commission (CRTC), which regulates and polices the communications causeway, licensed 43 cable, 6 pay TV, and 5 pay-per-view services in the 1980s and 1990s. Services on the English side include the following: Bravo, a service that provides cultural programming; the all-news channel, CBC Newsworld; CPAC: Cable Public Affairs Channel, which specializes in public affairs programming (run by a consortium of cable companies); CTV News 1, a headline news service; History Television (Alliance Communication together with CTV); Life Network: Home & Garden Television (owned by Atlantis Television Ventures and U.S.-based Scripps Howard Broadcasting); The Women's Television Network (Moffit Communications with CTV as a minority shareholder); Outdoor Life (owned by Baton [CTV], Rogers, and the Outdoor Life Network); Much Music and Much More Music (CHUM Inc.); Pulse 24: a 24-hour regional news channel serving southern Ontario (owned by CHUM and Toronto Sun Publishing Corporation); Report on Business Television (owned by the *Globe and Mail*, Shaw Communications, and Canadian Satellite Communication); Space: The Imagination Station – science fiction programming (owned by CHUM Inc.); The Comedy Channel (CTV, Shaw Communications, and Astral Broadcasting Group); The Discovery Channel, which offers nature and science programming; The Sports Network (TSN); CTV Sportsnet; Teletoon, an animation channel (Family Channel, Shaw Communication); YTV – children's television (owned by Shaw Communications); the Canadian Learning Channel, which airs educational programming; and Vision TV, a service devoted to religious programming (non-profit/ charitable). TV5 is a unique international experiment. It is a service operated by a consortium of French-speaking television networks in various countries that allows Canadian viewers to watch programs being broadcast from Paris or Brussels and Canadian programs to be seen through much of Europe and North Africa.

This is not an exhaustive list. The CRTC, which is now in the process of sifting through another 70 applications, seems unlikely to step on the brake. One of the applications is for an all-aboriginal TV network, Television Northern Canada. The only problem is that as cable operators are not yet fully digitized, a space crunch has made it difficult to accommodate another torrent of new offerings. A complicating factor is that for every two Canadian services that are brought on stream, cable operators are allowed to carry one additional American cable channel. So as the number of Canadian services swell, viewers will also have more American cable channels to choose from. Some of the American channels now carried by Canadian cable operators include CNN, CNBC, The Nashville

Network, Black Entertainment Television, the Food Network, Speedvision, The Learning Channel, Arts and Entertainment (A&E), and so-called superstations such as Time Warner's WTBS (Atlanta), which offers a steady diet of old movies and Atlanta Braves baseball and Atlanta Hawks basketball, and WSBK (Boston), which offers a similar menu except one can watch the Red Sox and the Celtics.

CBC producer Mark Starowicz has described the "atomization" of television that might well occur in the new television universe:

> In this world, nothing restrains a community of interest, or taste, or political conviction, from establishing a channel or service, any more than they're restrained now from starting a magazine or a newspaper or publishing a book. There will be a national gay channel within a short space of time, several channels serving women's interests, regional interest services will spring up, there will be a second explosion of evangelical services ... the list is infinite.[2]

While many of these channels and services have yet to gain their financial sea legs and draw only minuscule audiences, they have collectively, through their combined strength, made a major dent in the position of the main networks. The amount of time spent watching specialty channels rose from 14 per cent of total viewing in English-speaking Canada in 1990 to 19 per cent in 1995 to over 22 per cent in 1998. In Quebec, French-language specialty services attracted almost 30 per cent of the total audience in 1995, up from just 17 per cent in 1990.[3]

It should also be pointed out that audiences for the old lions of Canadian broadcasting, CBC and CTV, have been even further diluted by the emergence of other potent rivals – the Global TV network and a phalanx of so-called independent stations in virtually every major Canadian city. Even cities like Calgary and Edmonton, both with populations of roughly 900,000 people, have four local television stations each. New American networks such as Fox, Warner

Television, and the USA network also cut into the CBC and CTV's viewing pie in some markets. Where the major Canadian and American networks could once be compared to the great cedars of the B.C. coast that towered above everything else, they now find themselves pared down in size and in a thick forest of competition.

Where television viewing once resembled shopping in a large department store, where a single network would provide a wide variety of programming, it now resembles boutique shopping with viewers drawn to a large number of small customized outlets. *Globe and Mail* reporter Doug Saunders believes that the era of "one-size-fits-all TV" has come to an end.[4] Arguing along similar lines, Nicholas Negroponte, the head of the MIT media lab, has declared that the era of "prime-time" television is over. It will be replaced by "my time" TV – TV tailored to small boutique audiences.[5] Rick Salutin, one of Canada's most audacious and far-sighted thinkers about TV and society, has written with some concern about "the unbearable me-ness of the new channel universe."[6]

The biggest push in the development of the 500-channel universe has come from the advertising community. Advertisers have found that in the era of hyper-targeting, the "cineplexing" of the audience works to their advantage. Rather than taking a scattergun approach by advertising in places where only a small fraction of the audience is likely to be in the demographic groups that they have targeted for their products, "narrow-casting" solves the problem for advertisers by handing them the specialized audiences, the market niches, that they desire most. Advertisers aiming their TV ads at children or adolescents need look no further, it can be argued, than YTV. Those targeting young sports fans in order to sell them beer or sports equipment or deodorant will find that The Sports Network (TSN) is where their "primary demographic" is located.

In his book *Breaking Up America,* Joseph Turow, a professor at the Annenberg School of Communication at the University of Pennsylvania, argues that advertisers are the prime movers, the main culprits, in the shift from a "society-making media" to a "segment-making media."[7] Turow believes that virtually all of our public spaces from television to concerts to sports events are now tailored so "that they attract customers who fit narrow profiles demanded by particular sponsors."[8] The important point about cable TV is not the content of the programming on a particular channel but rather its format – its pace, flow, and character. This basic packaging, this "branding," signals to various types of viewers whether a particular channel is where they will feel welcome or whether they should tune in elsewhere. The great danger, according to Turow, is that advertisers are enhancing and deepening social schisms. They are dividing society by creating "different media spheres."[9] Advertisers do damage by discouraging "people from coming into contact with news and entertainment that other parts of society find important."[10] While it may be desirable, for instance, for advertisers to have up-scale consumers turning to Report on Business Television or CNBC for their news, there is a price to be paid when those same viewers, not as consumers but as citizens, are cut off from the news being watched by others in society.

Some observers believe that the 500- or 1000-channel universe is no more than a mirage, an illusion. They argue that most people only have the capacity to deal with between 10 and 20 channels before they feel overloaded and that viewers don't have the time or energy to buzz endlessly through the television cosmos looking for the most desirable channels. Audiences will cling to a small corner of the TV world – a corner in which they are familiar and comfortable. In fact, people turn to television precisely because it is predictable, because the very presence of the same faces and settings is soothing, even tranquilizing. The experts who predict that audiences will be satisfied only if they have a gargantuan list of channels at their disposal may have misunderstood the very nature of TV viewing.

Some predict that with minuscule audiences and low advertising revenues, a number of channels will simply disappear. The CRTC can grant licenses to its heart's content, but the realities of the market are that only a handful of channels, perhaps less than a dozen, will be profitable in the long run.

It soon became clear with the launch of 16 new channels in the fall of 1997 that the CRTC had licensed far more specialty services than the cable companies could offer their subscribers. Wary of a consumer backlash, cable companies concocted what they saw as the most attractive mixes of Canadian and U.S. specialty channels. But a year later, the dust had yet to settle. There were accusations from some broadcasters that the services owned by the most powerful media interests, including in some cases the cable companies themselves, had been given preferential treatment, and there was considerable resentment over the fact that broadcasters had to pay "marketing fees" of $2 million (Can.) in order to be included in the new cable lineup.[11] Not surprisingly, the owners of the new American cable channels didn't have to jostle for position or pay "key money" in order to be placed on the cable spectrum.[12] There was also the suspicion that those services lacking the necessary clout — Vision TV or CPAC, for instance — were relegated to the back of the bus, to the outside tiers of the cable universe where there are presumably fewer viewers. Several of the new Canadian services that were licensed were excluded from cable packages entirely. They never made it on to the playing field.

Some critics argue that there is a monotonous sameness to much of what is offered on cable TV. Few of the channels have budgets to air major productions of their own so they "feed the goat" with endless reruns of old shows, movies, and documentaries. They add to this relatively lifeless TV wallpaper with programs of their own that are little more than shoe-string, bargain basement operations. As media critic Rick Salutin has described the new Canadian cable universe: "[T]here's nothing new or different in the experience of MeTV. It's jammed with reruns. Would you believe Star Trek and Gilligan's Island — again? This is reruns of reruns ... There'll be little new production — mostly cheapo stuff like cooking shows and hosts interviewing guests who are willing to come on for free."[13] Perhaps the one who put it best was rock star Bruce Springsteen, who lamented in one of his hit songs:

> Man came by to hook up my cable TV.
> We settled in for the night, my baby and me.
> We switched 'round and 'round 'til half-past dawn.
> There were fifty-seven channels and nothing on.[14]

There can be little doubt that even if plans for the 1000-channel universe were to implode, a system based on only 60 or 80 channels will dramatically alter the nature of television viewing. The danger is not that few people will watch because the new channels are merely empty boxes filled with reruns and cheap filler, but that there will be "something on" or at least "enough on" to keep a sizeable number of viewers interested. If this is the case, then the effects will be substantial. The major networks that are the main producers of Canadian programming will be weakened, and the large public squares, the central meeting places, created by the ability of those networks to assemble mass audiences, will have been destroyed. Where TV was once a medium that could create and assemble majorities, it will have become a vehicle more suited to both attracting and targeting narrow slivers of the audience or what advertisers call "primary media communities or image tribes."[15] Elihu Katz, a distinguished scholar who has studied the effects that the media have had on nation-building, is astonished at the decision of national leaders to allow the genie of cable TV to escape from the bottle:

> Why are governments contributing to the erosion of nation-states and national cultures? Why don't they see that more leads to less to insignificance ... to endless distraction, to the atomization and evacuation of public space? Why don't they see that national identity and citizen participation are compromised? Why don't they realize that they're contributing directly to the erosion of the enormous potential which television has to enlighten and unite populations into the fold of national cultures?[16]

The advent of satellite-to-home television (direct-to-home or DTH) poses much the same problem. American satellite systems (companies such as DirecTV, EchoStar, PrimeStar, and C-Band) with the capacity to rain down 200 or more channels on homes that own plate-size receiving dishes have been a fact of life in Canada for some time. A small army of over 200,000 Canadians subscribe to these "illegal" American satellite services, satellites that former CRTC

Chairman Keith Spicer once described as "death stars."[17] He used this ominous Star Wars-like term because he believed that these satellites posed a threat to both the main TV networks and national cultures. He also maintained that satellites would render CRTC policies designed to protect Canadian culture ineffective and superfluous because the regulator simply would be unable to prevent a new tidal wave of TV signals from crossing the border. As Spicer expressed his frustration: "The CRTC could become a little bit like King Canute holding back the waves."[18] We would be unable to maintain Canadian-content regulations or stop practices that violate Canadian moral or ethical standards.

In 1997, both Star Choice, 54 per cent owned by Shaw Communications, and Express Vu, run by the giant telecommunications conglomerate BCE, launched home-grown DTH services. By 1998 each service had signed up close to 100,000 subscribers. While these numbers are impressive, satellite systems have yet to approach the dominant position still enjoyed by cable. Canadian cable providers (the big players being Rogers with 29 per cent of households, Shaw with 19 per cent, Videotron with 19 per cent, and Cogeco with 9 per cent) reach 7.7 million Canadians.[19] The CRTC hopes that Canadians will subscribe to these domestic satellite services so that viewers will receive a significant number of Canadian channels along with the cavalcade of American channels that shower down from the heavens.

The Splintering of the Radio Audience

The same brutal segmentation that is occurring along the cable TV frontier is also taking place in the radio industry. While there is less competition in Canadian radio because the CRTC grants licenses to fewer stations in each city than is the case in the U.S., radio's capacity for hyper-fragmentation is startling. Even in the highly regulated Canadian market the number of FM radio stations mushroomed from 296 in 1988 to 517 in 1997.[20] In the United States there are now over 12,000 AM and FM stations.[21] According to Turow, even mid-size American cities can have as many as 30 radio stations, with some able to sustain themselves with audiences of less than 3 per cent of the population.[22] While the great majority of radio listeners cling to just two or three favourite stations, with those stations occupying up to 70 per cent of their listening time, there are enough people with different musical tastes to have produced the current proliferation of radio stations.[23]

Musical preferences are influenced by the age and gender of the listener, ethnic and linguistic backgrounds, and socio-economic status. Each station devises a format that will appeal to a particular segment of the population – country and western aficionados, talk show mavens, or soul brothers – that will signal that this is the sound, and the lifestyle, to appeal to them and to which they most belong. One media consultant has compared radio formats to restaurants: "When you walk in the restaurant you want sights and sounds and you want a waiter with a certain type of attitude."[24]

The key to radio survival is to locate and appeal to a "super core" of ardent listeners: people who will not only listen to the station but identify with the lifestyle and hence the products that it promotes. A radio station, of course, also has to be wide enough in its appeal so that it attracts significant audiences. So stations have to be careful about how they write their signatures, how they establish their brand name, so that they are distinctive and yet inclusive.

The leading sound in the Canadian market in 1996 was adult contemporary/gold music/oldies/rock with country music a strong second. Talk radio was third with 13.2 per cent of the listening audience.[25]

Given the hyper-segmentation of the radio market, CBC radio's appeal to a wide general audience appears to be out of step with the times. Although one could argue that CBC radio has developed its own unique market niche – with listeners who are older, better educated, and more oriented to news and public affairs – its English-speaking listening audiences are at best holding steady with a combined AM and FM audience of approximately 11 per cent (7.8 per cent on the AM side and 3.3 per cent of the FM audience in 1997).[26] While the report of the Mandate Review Committee on the CBC, NFB and Telefilm could wax eloquent about the ability of CBC radio to transport listeners from one end of the country to the other, and from their home towns to the far corners of the universe, through programming that's "informative, intelligent, culturally oriented and overwhelmingly Canadian," CBC radio finds itself in cut-throat competition with hundreds of stations offering their listeners not only distinctive sounds but distinctive identities.[27]

The Helter Skelter World of Internet Democracy

Perhaps the most monumental change to have taken place in mass communications in the last generation is the capacity for transnational communication and hyper-segmentation brought by the Internet, and its major component, the World Wide Web. The Internet provides, in the words of Alan Macdonald, "a delicious anarchy" that some enthusiasts contend is giving citizens important and vital new public spaces.[28] Justin Hall has described the Internet as "the first semi-permanent unlimited worldwide exhibition space," and "a never-ending world's fair."[29] The marvel of the Internet, to push Hall's analogy further, is that it's a world's fair in which everyone can be an exhibitor and everyone can have access to everyone else's exhibit. The Web allows every person to become, in effect, their own broadcaster as well as a member of the audience. The Web's great contribution, according to true believers, is that it has allowed the creation of new public spaces where people from across the neighbourhood and across the globe can meet and exchange ideas or products as equals.

The Internet has been the vehicle for a hyper-fragmentation beyond anything imaginable on radio or cable. There are web sites, news groups, chat lines, and electronic cafés covering every imaginable interest or preoccupation regardless of how narrow or exotic they might be. While the establishment of radio stations and cable channels still involves an expensive infrastructure and regulatory approval, Internet users can create electronic "zines" geared specifically to their individual needs and web sites that reflect their own very particular tastes and passions at little cost and without needing anyone's permission. And while cable and radio transmissions are limited by geography, Internet users can roam the planet visiting sites set up by people who share their interests or sites established by companies, libraries, governments, universities, political campaigns, museums, movie studios, or sports organizations.

First developed by the U.S. Defense Department and then expanded by university researchers to exchange scientific information, the World Wide Web is a network of computer networks. Its special characteristic, its special power, is that it combines instantaneous transmission with the ability to reach and penetrate almost everywhere in the world. But it is much more than a remarkable technological device. It has created a way of life, a culture of its own. According to University of California professor Mark Poster:

> [T]he Internet is more like a social space than a thing; its effects are more like those of Germany than those of hammers. The effects of Germany upon the people within it makes them Germans; the effects of hammers is not to make people hammers, but to force metal spikes into wood. As long as we understand the Internet as a hammer we will fail to discern the way it is like Germany.[30]

Users have the unfettered freedom to exchange views and information and respond immediately to each other in an "unfiltered" way — there are no hosts or editors to blow the whistle, rule people out of order, interrupt, or correct opinions. And the Internet is open to an immense diversity of views. As James Knapp has described the way in which conflicting communities exist together in cyberspace, communities that are often excluded from the central squares created by the old media: "Lesbian discussion groups exist alongside those designated for Christian fundamentalists; discussions aimed at determining obscenity guidelines go on only a few menu headings away from sites containing pornographic pictures, and all of these sites are accessible to all users with relatively minor restrictions."[31]

Many observers see the Internet as having the potential to be an enormous force for good, as fulfilling vital functions for society and even for humanity. In the mid and late 1990s there was a sense of exuberance and even exhilaration as people began to experiment with new ways of connecting. The hope was that the Internet would break down barriers previously imposed by time and distance and produce new and different types of community and interaction. Old friends separated by great distances are able to keep in touch with each other by exchanging jokes or good-natured banter every morning, people who are about to undergo serious medical operations can get advice and encouragement from those who have survived the ordeal, teachers and students can continue their discussions long after the class has ended, and social activists in different countries can meet and share information at little cost. Most moving, perhaps, is that throughout the Internet's endless nooks and crannies there are touching memorials to those who have died – many of them for children. These sites are the post-modern equivalents of the tombstone.

One Talmudic scholar, who studies and discusses the day's reading on the Internet each evening with fellow scholars from all over the world, believes that the Internet is one of God's miracles and serves a divine purpose. It allows people to study and worship together and feel spiritually united.[32]

But the greatest hope is that the Internet will revitalize the democratic experience, that it will open the floodgates to new forms of interaction between citizens and the politicians who govern. The first wave of studies on how the Internet is being used by governments and politicians has generated sparks of optimism. Doris Graber and Brian White, who surveyed what they have called "the cyber-age information bridges" of the major departments and agencies of the U.S. government, concluded that cyber activity has already produced noticeable advantages.[33] Government departments have been able to reduce costs by replacing paper publications with electronic delivery, generate income by marketing and selling government documents, reports, records and data sets, make it easier for citizens to apply for services and respond to inquiries, and give citizens unprecedented access to a vast ocean of government information. The only problems are the sheer volume of what is available on the nearly 4,500 web sites and over 200 electronic bulletin boards maintained by the U.S. government, and the fact that thus far mainly people with specialized backgrounds and interests are attempting to navigating the maze. For many, if not most, citizens the new online culture initiated by governments still seems far removed and impenetrable.

Although a similar study has yet to be conducted in Canada, web sites have been created by the vast majority of federal and provincial government departments. Indications are that these new pathways are yet to be widely used.

In studies of congressional communication on the Internet by John Messmer and by Scott Adler and his colleagues, a similar optimism abounds.[34] Messmer points out that where contact between congressmen and their constituents was until recently limited mainly to appearances in the local media and through mailings whose contents because of costs tended to be very brief, web sites allow congressmen to address a national audience and supply a veritable mountain of information to constituents: speeches, votes, background information on issues, campaign materials, and government or party reports. Most important, perhaps, is that the Web permits politicians to reach voters directly, bypassing the "filter" of journalists.

Canadian politicians have also jumped on the new communications bandwagon. All of the major political parties have web sites as do many constituency organizations.[35] Party sites during the 1997 federal election contained reactions to the events of the day, the latest press releases, campaign schedules, quotes from the leaders, jokes, quizzes, contests, and sales on everything from buttons to T-shirts. More typical of the genre is Alberta Premier Ralph Klein's web site, "Ralph's Log Book." The site contains the Premier's reflections about provincial politics delivered in a folksy, down-home style and the texts of his latest speeches. Albertans are invited to respond to his comments by e-mail.

The real power of the Internet, some would argue, is that it is so decentralized and amorphous that it makes totalitarian regimes impossible. Hitler's Germany or the old Soviet Union under Stalin tried to create totally enclosed societies in which government propaganda machines controlled all aspects of communication from newspapers to films, from books to art. So little light was allowed to permeate through the thick screen of ideological correctness and intimidation that in Arthur Koestler's stark phrase, the society was shrouded in "darkness at noon."[36] Optimists contend that the Internet ensures that the darkness will at least be punctured by some glimmers of light. Attempts, for instance by the People's Republic of China, to erect a "firewall" or "netwall" to prevent international Internet messages from reaching China are proving futile. As part of this firewall, the Chinese recently launched their own self-contained network, China World Web, hoping to control all internal traffic and block unwanted messages from entering the country. But the system can be easily circumvented by almost anyone with a modicum of computer know-how. As one Chinese Internet aficionado explained: "If you really want to find stuff, then you'll get through the wall … and it's easy to get access through sites in northern Europe or Japan. Once you hit upon one, you just take a trip round the neighborhood through links they provide and you've got yourself a gold mine."[37]

For all the excitement and the hype and hoopla – the "superhypeway," as one writer described the frenzy surrounding the Internet – not everyone sees the Internet as delivering a promised land.[38] There are critics who see it as being used predominantly by the wealthy and privileged, as more of a shopping mall than a public square and as not much more than an irrelevant sideshow with little impact on public life or government policies.

These critics note that being online requires a significant financial investment. The costs of a computer, phone line, hard drive, and speakers, software programs and CDs, subscribing to online services, and getting and maintaining the various bells and whistles that are necessary to be fully engaged are beyond the means of many Canadians. Moreover, critics contend that prices are now unlikely to fall very substantially because new and expensive software is continuing to hit the market at a furious pace and price thresholds have already been reached. Surveys reveal that while 36 per cent of Canadian homes had personal computers in 1997, only about 13 per cent were linked to the Internet. And Internet use is largely confined to those who have financial resources; according to one report 57 per cent of households with incomes of over $60,000 (Can.) have access to the Internet.[39] Those who have a university education are also much more likely to have the modems that can connect them to cyberspace.

It's also critical to note that while true believers gush with enthusiasm about the Web's global reach, the vast majority of users are still in the United States. Less than one per cent of the world's adult population currently has access to the Internet.[40]

Moreover, some contend that the Internet's uncontrolled nature has left it open to too many hucksters, scam artists, hate peddlers, rumour mongers and people with dangerous axes to grind. Canadian neo-Nazi Ernst Zundel, who now lives in the United States, has a web site from which he propagates anti-Semitic venom. There is online gambling – "a virtual Las Vegas" – that is untouchable by Canadian authorities because it "broadcasts" from outside Canada's borders, and child pornographers occupy the sinister back streets of the Internet from which they ply their grotesque trade. One observer, Simon Winchester, believes that the Internet has become "an electronic sink of depravity."[41] The most apparent fact, the basic reality, is that those who are chatting, or in some cases pouring their hearts out, to people they have met online, are still talking to strangers. They cannot be sure of the people with whom they are dealing. In the anonymity of cyberspace people can act out their fantasies and obsessions without fear of discovery. One writer has given the following advice to those who are trying to meet romantic partners through the Internet: "Remember that the person you are pouring your heart out to may be married, not of legal age, or not your preferred gender. Anecdotal evidence indicates that fabrication is rampant on the Net, so do what you can not to be duped."[42] During the 1996 U.S. presidential election, millions of voters visited what they believed was Republican candidate Bob Dole's official site when in fact they were visiting an imitation site set up by someone who was either playing a prank or actively trying to sabotage Dole. The site was full of misleading and damaging information about the Republican challenger.

If the Internet is the Wild West then people like Matt Drudge and Harry Knowles are its outlaws. Both Drudge, whose *Drudge Report* site broke the Monica Lewinsky scandal, and Knowles, whose *Ain't It Cool News* site has become a principal source of gossip in the entertainment industry, use their sites to gather and circulate rumours. One writer has described the *Drudge Report* as the "dirty laundry chute of the U.S. political and media elite" not only because the site is visited by journalists and political operatives on the prowl for background information and juicy inside stories, but because these people are also among those who for their own reasons leak the information to Drudge.[43] Thus the *Drudge Report*, which has over 100,000 subscribers, has become a clearinghouse for a whole host of grievances but also for those who want to "legitimize" their own positions by having their version of events aired by Drudge and then picked up by other media. While some of Drudge's tips appear to be valid, others are wildly inaccurate. Harry Knowles operates in a similar subterranean world. His site, which registers 450,000 visitors a day, circulates rumours, tips and inside information from everybody from disgruntled studio executives to the most star-struck fans. Studios now actively court Knowles, taking him on expensive junkets, lavishing him with freebies, and showering him with tickets to movie debuts, all of which Knowles dutifully reports on to his readers. Studio PR people have come to believe that a thumbs-up movie review in *Ain't It Cool News* will translate into increased box office sales. Bob Blakey, the TV writer for the *Calgary Herald* and an astute observer of the industry, has written that: "Studios accustomed to word-of-mouth are learning to deal with word-of-mouse."[44]

Another aspect of the Internet's "underground" culture is that online communication has given a major boost to the sex industry. Or to put it differently and perhaps more accurately, the sex industry has given a major boost to online communication. According to one estimate, sex sites account for at least 10 per cent of all of the retail traffic that occurs on the Web.[45] What author Frank Rose calls the Web's "pornocopia" generated close to $1 billion (U.S.) in revenue in 1996. There are estimated to be close to 30,000 sex sites, about half of which sell products or services of some kind. Rose believes that the ready availability of sex-related materials helps to explain the Web's phenomenal growth: "The Internet is hardly the first new technology whose adoption curve has been driven by sex. Cable TV, pay-per-view, camcorders, videocassettes – most of the home-entertainment innovations of the past 30 years have won acceptance by catering to humans' fixation on the love act in all its variants. The advantage they offered over adult movie theaters, as Pee-wee Herman discovered to his chagrin, was privacy."[46]

One particularly discouraging development is the apparent retreat from Internet democracy by at least some elements in the scientific and scholarly community. Where academics once used the Internet to conduct important exchanges, some scholars are finding its very openness a liability because it brings in the wrong crowd. Some discussions now occur on closed-access list servers, a private rather than a public place.

Still there are those who argue that the Internet will be the saviour of democracy and that new and vital communities are being created. A number of community networks and freenets have used images of a small town in laying out their sites. The intention is to rekindle the spirit of democratic exchange, of warm neighbourliness and civic order that organizers believe once characterized life in a small community. Their efforts may be full of nostalgic longing for a world long vanished and which may be much more narrow and cruel than they imagine, but few can dispute the enterprise and energy behind these projects. Some scholars, however, believe that these "communities" are no more than an arrogant middle-class illusion – a way to escape from rather than embrace others. People can remain in the quiet and secluded comfort of their homes, far away from the unpredictable and gritty helter-skelter of face-to-face human interactions, and from the raw talons, the pulling and hauling, of real politics. Mark Poster uses the term "disembodied politics" to describe the emptiness of communities based on "pixels on screens generated at remote locations by individuals one has never and probably will never meet."[47] This was the view of a scholar who posted the following message after returning from a conference in Austria:

> Talking to colleagues at a recent conference in Graz, I learned that many of them are simply bemused by what they take as the typically American conceit of cyber-communities. And their reaction is understandable when you live in a city that has ample public space with real opportunities and places for people to meet (and publicly-supported) spaces, you are likely to think that celebrations of the "information highway" as a place for meaningful contact between people is more than a little ridiculous.[48]

The distinguished political scientist, Roger Gibbins, sees the situation almost in reverse.[49] He is able through the Web to have meaningful contacts with colleagues all over the planet – exchanging ideas, working on projects, sharing reactions to the developments of the day, but would be hard pressed to say what some of his neighbours did for a living or did in their spare time. When one night an ambulance arrived at his neighbour's house, he had no idea why or for whom.

A main concern is that the Web will become primarily a commercial enterprise, a shopping mall rather than a town hall. Indeed the Internet is already remaking the business environment. The online market totaled over $13 billion (U.S.) in 1997, with over 85 per cent of the business activity occurring in North America.[50] A company called International Commerce Exchange Systems is one of a myriad of companies that are building the new "electronic malls." The company offers those with products to sell access to its web site at a cost of roughly $5,000 a year. Once on site, clients are given the opportunity to connect with 10,000 pre-screened buyers.[51] Amazon.com sold over $16 million (Can.) worth of books in 1997 through its virtual bookstore; Nettrader.hkbc.ca, a discount brokerage house run by the Hong Kong Bank of Canada, accounted for 10 per cent of the Bank's discount trading revenue in 1997; and Auto-

By-Tel Corp sells cars directly to consumers over the Internet.[52] All of these transactions are taking place in an electronic no-man's-land where buyers and sellers rarely meet in person.

But the cyber-marketplace is still very much in its infancy. Online advertising amounted to $300 million (U.S.) in 1996, compared to $38.2 billion (U.S.) and $9.2 billion (U.S.) spent on newspaper and magazine advertising respectively. Estimates are that advertising on the Web will balloon to $3 billion (U.S.) by the year 2000.[53]

Erik Barnouw, a leading media historian, believes that parents who encourage their children to log onto the Internet because they think that they will receive a beneficial educational experience, are terribly naive. They have little idea how commercialized the Internet has become. As Barnouw explains the traps that are set for children:

> The child is welcomed to the website as to a club. There he or she has friends, encounters wondrous creatures, can talk with television heroes and heroines, and becomes a member of something, sharing secret rituals and codes, and may be given special club money, which can be sent in for merchandise or better yet, for a ring or a badge to show you're a member. To get these, you may have to fill out a form explaining who you are, where you live, and all about your family. As a child yields such demographic data, perhaps proudly, it may be caught in a web that blends seamlessly from entertainment to commerce to invasion of privacy.[54]

The enthusiasm of those who once saw the Internet as a tool for enhancing and expressing grassroots sentiments and opinions is also being dampened by the fact that the Internet seems more and more to be an instrument that reflects and reinforces the power of the powerful. Giant corporations such as the entertainment conglomerates described in chapter three have the resources to create and maintain the most enticing and sophisticated web sites and to advertise their presence. These sites are constantly updated, and they can provide what is in effect a multimedia extravaganza. Among the most impressive sites are those that have been constructed by the major political parties and elected politicians. They tend to be attractively designed with striking mastheads, have information laid out so that it engages the visitor, and contain a variety of quizzes, games, chat lines, and souvenir boutiques.

There is also an extent to which the old media still dominates and imposes itself on the new. People go online to continue discussions that began on TV talk shows, visit famous museums or government offices, find out more about their favorite movie or sports stars, read well-known newspapers and magazines, and keep abreast of fast-breaking news stories by visiting sites run by established news organizations like CNN, ABC, or CBC Newsworld.

It is difficult, in this early stage of development, to make conclusive judgments about how the Internet will ultimately evolve. In the 1920s and 1930s, there was considerable excitement about telephone party lines and ham radios as instruments of personal expression and community cohesion before they were swallowed up by larger and more impersonal corporate networks. It is crucial to note, however, that most of the activity that is occurring cuts across territorial boundaries. Whether contacts or discussions are occurring among environmentalists, feminists, evangelical Christians, prospective car buyers, movie buffs, or sports fans, the public spaces that have been created both reach beyond local or national geography and are confined to highly specialized and sometimes exotic topics. The Internet does not necessarily do anything to help in Canadian nation-building, although there are obviously a myriad of sites devoted to Canadian topics and to connecting Canadians to their principal institutions. The simple fact is that it does not assemble a majority of citizens in a single place and at a single time the way television did in its golden age. The great fear is that its radically decentralized and hyper-fragmented character will undercut the creation of vibrant public spaces that will enhance and support national life.

Conclusion

Audience fragmentation raises at least two important issues. The first is the paradoxical question of whether fragmentation produces far less rather than far more diversity. There is a difference between having more media choices and having access to a wide variety of viewpoints. After all, the same conglomerate that owns a movie studio also owns cable channels, radio and TV stations, and a bevy of newspapers and magazines, and has the best Internet sites. The concern is that the same commercial messages and political viewpoints are popping up like a "jack in the box" across a wider spectrum of media choices.

The second question is whether fragmentation might be seen as part of a two-pronged assault on the nation-state. As stated earlier, convergence and fragmentation might be described as huge tidal waves breaking at the same time and with tremendous force. Both, for different and even opposing reasons, threaten to wash away the cement that holds the nation state together. Simply put, the communications system is the spinal cord both of national existence and of a democratic society. If it is severed or disrupted in some way, then a country risks losing touch with its sensory system and citizens risk being disconnected from each other.

Harvard Law Professor Anne-Marie Slaughter believes that the state is not so much disappearing as "disaggregating."[55] In vital areas such as trade and investments, monetary policy, security, and communications, the state is no longer sovereign. At best it shares power with others on a global level. Its power to affect change and to assure its own interests has become marginal. The convergence revolution is part of this larger phenomenon.

Some contend that audience fragmentation also brings a loss of control by the nation state but in a different manner. Cable TV, radio, and the Internet target micro-communities based on particular tastes, interests, or identities. Connections based on the sharing of hobbies or passions both crosscut and perhaps even undercut interest in and loyalty to the local communities where people actually live. A science fiction buff living in Winnipeg or Fredericton may now have far more communication with people in New York or Amsterdam than with the people who live on her or his street, the vast majority of whom she or he will never meet.

At the risk of repetition, it is worth pointing out that in Canada the problem is particularly acute. Canada is not held together by the strong grip of a single language or religion, the collective memory of a historic struggle, dreaded external enemies, or a unique sense of national mission. Moreover, there are few institutions – other than the communication system – that bind the country together. There is no national education system and no national military service, the political system is in disrepute, and virtually all of the country's major institutions are corroded by the acid of public suspicion. The barriers imposed by a vast geography, a bitter climate, and great regional diversity have always been difficult to surmount. It is still often more costly to fly to places within Canada than to fly to Europe. The fear is that fragmentation will add to the disarray, that fragmentation will make it more difficult to maintain significant public spaces, the central public squares that are crucial to the functioning of democracy, in the media society of the future.

For much of this century, broadcasting has been a central strand in the maintenance of a national identity. How the forces of convergence and fragmentation have affected Canadian broadcasting, and particularly the role played by the CBC, will be examined in the next chapter.

FIVE

Chilled to the Bone:
The Crisis of
Public Broadcasting

I n a country that spans a quarter of the world's time zones and
has a population thinly spread across the waistband of a
continent, broadcasting is nothing less than the central public
place, the village square, of Canadian life. The publicly financed
Canadian Broadcasting Corporation (CBC) has been not only the
major chronicler of Canadian life but one of its defining features.
Its influence can be compared to the other great nation-building
exercises of the nineteenth and twentieth centuries – the National
Program of 1879, which fastened the West to Central Canada through
tariffs, immigration and railways; the welfare and medicare programs
of the post-war era, which established not only a social safety net
but became the great symbols of social equality; and the Charter of
Rights and Freedoms of 1982, which constitutionalized citizen and
group rights.

The Canada that we know today was formed by the fur trade
and the old trade routes that connected and interlaced the northern half of the continent. But transactions based on the canoe, the
voyageur, and the European demand for furs were uncertain and
fragile. The country really came into existence in the late nineteenth
century when railways and the telegraph imposed a standard clock
and made a constant traffic of people and information possible. People became connected by being exposed to the same newspapers,
magazines, and catalogues. Broadcasting added muscle to the sinews

of national life by linking individuals more directly and immediately than ever before. Broadcasting reordered people's external gyroscopes so that the country came to mean something to them beyond the confines of their immediate vicinities and circumstances, their towns, or their provinces.

This chapter will describe the CBC's earlier years and the concerns and pressures that led to the creation of a public broadcaster. It will also examine the political wars that have been fought between politicians and the CBC over the nature of CBC programming – wars that left the CBC weakened and bloodied. This chapter focuses on three major episodes in the history of the CBC – the controversies that surrounded *Preview Commentary*, *This Hour Has Seven Days*, and *The Valour and the Horror*. Each of these shows pushed the boundaries of political acceptability and provoked sharp conflicts among political leaders, CBC executives, and working journalists. These brutal struggles were to produce a "chill" whose cold sting can still be felt in the village squares of Canadian journalism.

Constructing the Village Square

From its very inception, political leaders realized that broadcasting would be a potent and galvanizing force in Canadian life. Prime Minister Mackenzie King, who was to establish the CBC in 1936 (after the failure of a first experiment, the Canadian Radio Broadcasting Commission created in 1932) was spellbound by the possibilities presented by radio. After his first radio address from Parliament Hill in 1927, King pronounced that:

> It is doubtful if ever before ... those in authority were brought into such immediate and sympathetic personal touch with those from whom their authority derived ... All of Canada ... became a single assemblage swayed by a common emotion ... As a result of this ... there will be aroused a more general interest in public affairs and an increased devotion of the individual citizen to the common weal.[1]

But creating a national broadcasting system was not going to be easy. By 1930 American broadcasters had set up shop in Canada, and the vast majority of Canadians could listen to U.S. programs. To Graham Spry, Canadians faced a brutal choice: either "the state or the United States." Either the government intervened to establish a publicly financed broadcasting system – "a single, glowing spirit of nationality" in Spry's words – or Canadian broadcasting would become part of the American commercial system.[2] There was also the realization that great distances and a sparse population made it unlikely that private radio could do the job. Although private stations could operate profitably in major centres like Montreal and Toronto, many areas of the country could not be reached by private broadcasters without incurring considerable costs.

The 1930s were also a time of fierce ideological struggle. Bolshevism had triumphed in Russia, socialist governments had been elected in France and Britain, and fascist governments had come to power in Germany, Italy, and Spain. All of these governments were ideologically committed "in the name of the people" to some form of state control over broadcasting. But there was also the American "free enterprise" model that allowed private companies such as RCA, Westinghouse, and CBS to operate radio stations "in the public convenience, interest and necessity."[3] Whether the airwaves would be controlled by a handful of wealthy individuals or corporations or managed as a "public trust" became a central focus of debate. A CBC white paper expressed the prevailing view in Canada about the dangers of having the airwaves controlled by a few wealthy individuals. The paper stated that there was a need above all "to prevent the air from falling under the control of wealth or any other power ... The air belongs to the people and the constant aim of the CBC is to have the principal points of view on questions of importance heard by the people as a whole."[4]

It should also be remembered that at the time, Canadians were still very much under British influence. Indeed, British values and ways of doing things were almost universally admired, and so the British example of the publicly financed BBC weighed heavily in the Canadian decision-making process about how the airwaves should be governed.

To some extent Canada's choices in broadcasting were to mirror the influences that prevailed at different periods of time. When Canada was firmly within Britain's orbit, as was the case before World War II, the British broadcasting model prevailed. With the emergence of the United States as a cultural superpower, Canadian broadcasting tilted toward private broadcasting, although it maintained the public broadcasting tradition to a much larger degree than was ever the case in the United States.

The Purpose of the Broadcasting System

Those who first envisioned a public broadcasting system had at least three objectives in mind. The basic premise was to replace what Davidson Dunton, a one-time chairman of the CBC Board of Governors, called "the ordinary commercial arithmetic" with the "the arithmetic of patriotism."[5] In this calculation the primary goal was to counter the cultural influence of the United States. It should be remembered that this was an era in which radio and film were seen by communication scholars, and by most media observers, as "magic bullets" capable of hitting individuals with devastating effect and transforming values on a mass scale.[6] As mentioned previously, Canada was already falling within the orbit of American broadcasting and the fear was that unless the country took dramatic action it would lose its distinct identity – its cultural and perhaps even its political independence. A former president of the CBC, A.W. Johnson, expressed the concern that has always motivated supporters of the CBC: Canadians who are exposed to American broadcasting are "absorbing American interpretations of events ... soaking up the value system of the United States ... coming to expect Canadian traditions and institutions to look and behave as if they were American traditions and institutions."[7] Because erecting a cultural fortress – the cultural equivalent of a Great Wall of China – was impossible given the sheer magnitude and attractiveness of American culture, Canada had to produce a dynamic alternative that would attract a mass audience. The challenge was to counter American influence by creating a distinctly Canadian mass media culture, one that would generate its own stars, its own memorable and popular programs, and its own allegiances.

Public broadcasting had the capacity to conserve Canadian culture in two concrete ways. First, it could transmit historical memory and traditions and Canadian artistic achievements and sensibilities to future generations. Public broadcasting became in this sense a school yard for cultural learning. Second, it could create and maintain a reservoir of skilled and experienced professionals and state-of-the-art facilities so that Canadian programming could be competitive.

A second strategic objective was to unify the country by bridging the enormous gap that existed between French- and English-speaking Canadians and between the different regions of the country. The problem was that, in order to succeed, broadcasting had to overcome the very divisions, the very wounds, that it was attempting to heal. Attempts to build a single broadcasting system where air time would be shared equally by both language groups collapsed almost immediately. By 1934, two separate systems, one aimed at English Canada and the other based largely in Quebec but reaching out to francophones across the country, were already in place. As Marc Raboy, a distinguished professor of communications at the University of Montreal, has described the policy that has allowed two solitudes to exist within the CBC for close to 70 years: "Canadian public broadcasting served two audiences, two markets, and two publics with one policy, one mandate, and one institution."[8] Even modest attempts to construct crosswalks between the two broadcasting systems – the CBC and its French-language arm, Radio-Canada – were often bitterly resisted and contested by people in both language communities. Andre Laurendeau, the legendary publisher of *Le Devoir*, offered the following scornful response to the 1949 Massey Commission's prescription for a broadcasting system whose purpose was to staunch the flood tide of American cultural domination: "What dike can be built to defend against this irresistible tidal wave? Only that of a Canadian national culture – that is to say, a myth, a phantom, the shadow of a shadow. There is not one Canadian national culture. There are two: one English and one French."[9]

One of the great ironies of Canadian history is that a broadcasting system originally designed to create mutual understanding and sympathy helped to fuel the fires of Quebec nationalism. For there can be little doubt that Radio-Canada, in creating its own distinct programming style, in marching to a particular Quebec beat, and in serving the needs of a Quebec audience, contributed to the emergence of the intense nationalism and pride of the Quiet Revolution. According to historian Paul Rutherford:

> Radio-Canada offered to the Quebecois a concrete, visible expression of their own unique places, past and present, and ways. "Television in Quebec," Susan Mann Trifimenkoff has observed, "magnified the tiny world of a Laurentian village, a lower town Quebec, or a local hockey arena into a provincial possession." Its newscasts and its public affairs shows plus the many, many features and documentaries swiftly created a novel means of focusing attention on the activities and concerns of the province ... This drama didn't so much create as perpetuate and update a cluster of symbols that gave definition and meaning to the community.[10]

The claim is not that Radio-Canada undermined the Canadian dream by airing bitter and subversive messages against Ottawa or cultivated a journalism that harped endlessly on Quebec's frustration, but that the creation of an exclusive Quebec public square in broadcasting could not help but have stirred nationalist sentiments.

The third objective in the new arithmetic of patriotism was the hope that a public broadcasting system would promote citizenship and community values. The notion was that the CBC would treat the airwaves as a public trust – a property owned by the people as a whole and not by a small bevy of powerful businessmen or advertisers. The audience would be seen primarily as citizens and not as consumers, and the broadcasting system would be open to and reflect minorities that are usually ignored by private broadcasters because they lack the numbers or characteristics normally desired by advertisers. This meant that commercial imperatives took a back seat to other values. Where commercial networks would try to maximize audiences and advertising dollars by catering to audience demands for pleasure and sensationalism, the CBC would offer a broad range of programs including programs that attracted smaller audiences. Popular entertainment would be important but it wouldn't become a main focus or obsession. Room had to be made for educational and cultural programs and for programs that viewers might find challenging and even deeply disturbing. While during its early years the CBC was careful not to use shocking language or report crimes in ways that would upset audiences, a documentary tradition established at an early date emphasized "reality" programming.

Today the CBC has reports or documentaries almost on a daily basis that might not be aired on many if not most private stations because they deal with subjects that touch raw nerve endings, that are often grim and harrowing, and that lack the sugar coating – the cotton candy wrapping preferred by private TV. Canada's tainted blood supply, the fate of burn victims, the condition of Canada's natives, life in the country's prisons, the horror of Rwanda, the struggles of children with attention deficit disorder, the painful twists and turns of Canada's struggle for national unity, have all been treated to lengthy examinations by CBC radio and television.

In its 1996 report, the Mandate Review Committee on the CBC, NFB and Telefilm reiterated, as had many earlier reports on the CBC, the mission that was central to public broadcasting – that it be the main window for Canadian programming. In the report's view:

> Canadian programming ... should be based on a profound curiosity about things Canadian , as well as about the rest of the world. An understanding of the world, however, starts with an understanding of ourselves, of those near and dear to us, of our neighbours and compatriots. A vast country like ours desperately needs a medium of communication like CBC radio and television to enrich its citizens – not only as individual citizens but also as members of a community, a region, a province, a country. No other institution could do more to promote understanding and sharing among Canadians than the CBC.[11]

In its first decades, the CBC succeeded in creating a new public gathering place and a sense of belonging and identification that hadn't existed before in quite the same way. Perhaps the first great "nationalizing" event to be covered by CBC radio was the Royal Tour of 1939. The CBC hopscotched across the country, reporting from every major stop during the King's month-long tour. There were 91 broadcasts in all. It can be argued that radio coverage not only generated massive turnouts but helped cement a loyalty to Britain in the months preceding the outbreak of the Second World War.

The CBC was particularly instrumental in creating a national sports culture. It is not too much to say that without the airing of *Hockey Night in Canada* on radio and then later on TV, the NHL would never have emerged as such a popular and almost folkloric force in Canadian life. As David Whitson of the University of Alberta has described the phenomenon: "Yet it was the magic of radio that would take the live drama of sports into homes across North America, making men like Babe Ruth and Red Grange into larger-than-life characters, making the major league seasons into ubiquitous features of popular life and conversation, and making their annual championships – the World Series, the Stanley Cup playoffs, and so on – into national events."[12] By the early 1940s, *Hockey Night in Canada* was attracting audiences of well over two million listeners. Allegiances to teams and stars, the beginnings of large-scale sports merchandising (the selling of sticks and pads and team jerseys – and, of course, hockey cards), and the incentive for millions of young boys to play the game, often in sub-zero temperatures on outdoor rinks, were the direct products of broadcasting.

One extraordinary example of how radio created new meeting places, new public squares, was *The National Farm Radio Forum*, which began broadcasting in 1941. It was the first attempt ever made in Canada to involve the audience in a significant way. The Farm Forum was interactive media long before anyone had ever heard about talk radio or the Internet. Every Monday night at 8:30, hundreds of thousands of people would gather to hear a discussion of a contemporary issue on the radio, with many listeners forming groups (at its height there were 1,600 groups) to discuss the issue after the show was over. Discussion was aided by the fact that discussion guides were available to these groups before the shows. Notes of the points made in group discussions were then reported to the CBC's Farm Forum office, and would sometimes be summarized in the weekly Farm Forum newspaper.

Before radio, and certainly before television, Canadian political life was for most citizens a distant and mysterious phenomenon. Few people ever heard or saw the party leaders directly, although a greater percentage of people came out to rallies, debates, and picnics than is the case today. Most people had to rely on newspaper accounts that, because of the highly partisan nature of political reporting at the time, either venerated party leaders or tore them to shreds. For the vast majority of citizens, knowledge about leaders and party positions could only be gained second-hand, filtered through the often coloured glass of newspaper reporting.

CBC radio transformed the relationship between citizens and those who governed. For the first time, millions of people could hear the speeches of political leaders – and could judge leaders not only by their words but by the timbre of their voices and the confidence with which they spoke. Firebrand speakers such as Quebec Premier Maurice Duplessis and Alberta's William Aberhart were catapulted to power based in part on their ability to stir their audiences via radio. In the United States, President Franklin Roosevelt's famous "Fireside Chats" delivered during the gloomiest days of the Depression inspired trust that had been lacking before in the presidency and in government policies. Radio was the vehicle of communication and power for a president who, as someone who had been crippled by polio and could only walk with the aid of heavy braces, was especially limited in his ability to meet voters. Prime Minister R.B. Bennett's dry and uninspiring speeches during the Depression helped to seal his political fate – a shattering defeat at the polls during the 1935 federal election. That election was the first time that election night results were broadcast by radio, the first time that Canadians were able to experience the drama of an election night together.

The Second World War was a great watershed for the CBC. With loved ones serving overseas, radio was a vital link not only to the wider landscape of battle but to the fates of those caught in the whirlwind. From the sounds of aerial dogfights over the English Channel to Matthew Halton's dramatic account of a Canadian artillery barrage of German soldiers at Normandy to the joy of the Allied liberation of Paris, radio provided an immediacy, a sense of direct experience, that newspapers couldn't rival. But those at the top of the CBC pyramid were also aware of the propaganda role that radio played as an instrument of the war effort. General Leo LaFleche, who as Minister of National War Services was responsible for the CBC, believed that radio was "a war machine, a war weapon. With it one can play upon the minds and hearts of men. It can be used to strengthen the moral fibre of a people at war or it can be used to demoralize ... In a war where everything that we have is at stake ... it is to be remembered that the radio is essential."[13] Lafleche ensured, for instance, that the anti-conscription campaign that created such turmoil in Quebec received little coverage.

During the period from the 1930s to the 1960s the CBC was without rival as the main engine of Canadian cultural life. It provided Canadians with their most fundamental grounding, their basic education, about the country in which they lived. Former CBC president A.W. Johnson recalled his own experiences as a young man growing up on the prairies: "It was the CBC that introduced me to Canada. The CBC was Canada. Without it, for me, Canada would only have been Saskatchewan. It was our Canadian theatre and newsmagazine and music hall. We loved it and we needed it."[14]

In his superb chronicle of the early years of Canadian television, entitled *When Television Was Young*, historian Paul Rutherford quotes popular author Pierre Berton as describing CBC radio in 1950 as being "a curious brew of corn, culture and Canadianism" mixed with dashes of British and American influence.[15] Rutherford believes that in the first decade of television, CBC television's offerings were made up of roughly the same ingredients. While Rutherford takes issue with the view that television transformed the culture, he does credit TV with helping to preserve "a separate national identity and a distinctive civic ethic."[16]

William Thorsell, editor-in-chief of the *Globe and Mail*, expressed a view that is probably shared by a large number of Canadians when he complimented CBC radio in particular for raising the standard of public consciousness and debate because of its exceptional "commitment to the life of the mind." The very existence of public broad-casting at this level had made the Canadian experience unique. As Thorsell wrote:

> CBC Radio's main daily fare ... provides a consist-ently nourishing menu of information and provo-cation for the mind. A large proportion of Canada's thinking population shares the broadening experi-ence of CBC every day. As a country, we are much better educated and thoughtful as a result. It sim-ply wouldn't happen without CBC Radio, as any-one who has spent any time in the United States can woefully attest.[17]

Today, the CBC consists of a phalanx of networks and services: the main English- and French-language TV channels; Radio One (AM) and Radio Two (FM) in both languages; Newsworld, its 24-hour English-language all-news network, and Newsworld Interna-tional, which broadcasts outside of Canada's borders; the Reseau de L'information (RDI), which is the French-language all-news net-work; northern services that broadcast in part in native languages; and Radio Canada International. The corporation's mandate is ex-tremely broad and ambitious, some would say too broad and am-bitious. Under the Broadcasting Act of 1991, the public broadcaster is expected to cover an entire waterfront of public needs. The CBC's programs must be uniquely Canadian; they must "contribute to shared national consciousness and identity"; and they must give expression to regional and linguistic differences as well as reflect the country's multicultural and multiracial makeup. In addition, the public broadcaster must offer a wide range of programming that "informs, enlightens and entertains."

Among its other tasks the CBC is expected to give major cover-age to the landmark events on the Canadian political calendar – the opening of Parliament, the bringing down of the federal budget, fed-eral and provincial elections, Canada Day celebrations on Parliament Hill, Remembrance Day services from the Cenotaph in Ottawa, etc. Although these events are important in binding the country together, in broadcast terms they are often expensive money losers. In 1995, the CBC covered the many celebrations that marked the 50th anniversary of VE Day – the end of the Second World War in Europe – so extensively that some commentators referred to it as being a second invasion. In 1997, the corporation devoted three hours of uninterrupted commercial-free coverage to the festivities surrounding the 500th anniversary of John Cabot's voyage to Newfoundland. Michael Valpy of the *Globe and Mail,* who watched the CBC's broadcast with all its pageantry but also its discussion of historic controversies such as the fate of Newfoundland's native populations, wrote: "I don't know how much it cost the CBC to do all this. I know there are stories to be told about a national society's life where the market is not appropriate and shouldn't be welcome. I hope there were schools across the country that let their students watch."[18]

The CBC is also expected to provide more thorough coverage of public affairs than that provided by private networks and stations. Indeed, roughly 70 per cent of CBC television's total schedule can be described as news or current affairs programming. With the public mood about politics and politicians often wavering between ho-hum boredom and bitter cynicism, extensive political coverage has sometimes pushed the CBC into a ratings graveyard. During the battles over the Meech Lake and Charlottetown Accords, for instance, the CBC had to contend with a public that had reached the saturation point, not to mention the boiling point, with regard to constitutional issues. The network was caught in a proverbial Catch-22 situation. The more it reported on the crisis, the more its audience would drift away. Again from a dollars and cents, audience- and advertiser-driven, perspective it is more lucrative to report on lifestyles and crime, scandals and celebrities, the "news lite" approach taken by many private stations.

Although proponents of public television may see the differences between public and private broadcasting in black and white terms – service versus profits, citizens versus consumers, Canadian patriotism versus Hollywood – the CBC is far from being a "pure" public broadcaster. The Mandate Review Committee has described the CBC as a "hybrid" – an institution that is a mishmash of public and private enterprises. While the CBC depends on an annual grant from Parliament for approximately 75 per cent of its funding ($854 million [Can.] in 1996–97), advertising and sales added $250 million (Can.) to its coffers in 1996–97. It should be noted that while CBC radio still doesn't carry ads, CBC television has become increasingly dependent on them. By one account ad revenue provides roughly 50 per cent of the TV budget, with ads even appearing during *The National.* Moreover, the CBC contains within its family of 47 TV stations approximately 30 privately-owned affiliates. These stations must carry approximately 37 hours of network programming each week but are free to air other shows as they see fit. This means that many CBC programs are replaced or rescheduled to make way for big-ticket American programs. In addition, the CBC rarely produces a dramatic series by itself. It usually has at least one major Canadian or foreign production house as a partner. Indeed, the driving engine both financially and creatively for many productions is often from the private sector.

Political Pressures and Journalistic Freedom

While the CBC has throughout its history always been under attack from some quarter, its enemies now appear to be stronger, more numerous, and more fervent than ever before. During the 1990s the corporation's budget was slashed, its audiences lured away by the explosion of competition from private stations and cable services, and its mandate and programs placed under intense scrutiny.

The corporation's defenders believe that if the CBC has been bent out of shape, it is because of a failure of will by governments and by citizens who no longer see the value of having central meeting places, central public squares, in which Canadians can gather. They claim that harsh political pressures and the power exerted by the private sector have not only drastically changed the climate in which the CBC operates but endangered the future of public broadcasting. A number of observers even predict that the CBC's days are numbered, that it will not survive the shocks that are bound to come in this new turbulent era. The remainder of this chapter will focus on the assault against the CBC that has come from political leaders, who in order to gain political advantage or because of private vanity have sought to use the CBC for their own ends. As is apparent in this chapter, politicians sometimes succeeded in creating "chills" that penetrated into the corporation's very bones. They have been able to set boundaries, lines in the political sand, beyond which the CBC has been prevented from going. In a later chapter I will argue that disgruntled politicians have also created conditions that give private broadcasters the upper hand.

The politics of public broadcasting have undoubtedly influenced the reporting of politics, and this has on occasion drastically limited and narrowed the journalistic enterprise within the CBC. What is most disturbing, as the distinguished American scholar James Carey has pointed out, is that "journalism and politics mutually form one another" and "that democracy and journalism are names for the same thing."[19]

In former CBC news anchor Knowlton Nash's excellent history of the CBC, *The Microphone Wars*, Nash chronicles the virtually endless barrage of attacks and threats that have been made against the CBC by leading politicians literally from its very first days on the air. The battles that took place between politicians and the public broadcaster reflected the basic contours of Canada's post-war history. From anticommunist witch hunts in the 1950s, to concerns about separatists at Radio-Canada in the 1970s, from the cancellation of *This Hour Has Seven Days* in 1966 because politicians had come to fear critical exposés of their characters and policies, to the controversy that surrounded its coverage of the 1995 Quebec referendum, the CBC has always been a convenient target for enraged politicians.

There are two major fault lines in the politics of Canadian broadcasting: attempts by politicians to interfere with programming or with journalistic freedom and the controversy that surrounds the CBC's coverage of national unity. Both of these issues have pockmarked the CBC's relationship with its political masters for at least 40 years.

The willingness of elected politicians to endure criticism from the mass media is one of the essential tests of a healthy democracy. Politicians with bruised egos and policy proposals that have been shot through with holes by journalists are almost naturally tempted to use their power to punish those in the press whom they have come to see as their "enemies." But the well-understood rules of democratic politics dictate that attack and counterattack on policy issues are necessary in a free society and that a certain level of antagonism between politicians and the press is, in fact, healthy. While political leaders try to manipulate the press almost on a daily basis, their weapons are, for the most part, used with subtlety and moderation. The use, however, of coercion to shut down opponents or silence critics is considered a brutal and dangerous misuse of power – a drastic overstepping of moral and political authority.

There have been at least three occasions, apart from the controversies involving national unity, in which journalistic freedom at the CBC was threatened by the machinations of politicians. The first was the Diefenbaker government's attempt to cancel CBC radio's *Preview Commentary* in 1959. During John Diefenbaker's tenure as prime minister, his suspicion of the CBC reached monumental Richard Nixon-like proportions. In Diefenbaker's mind the journalistic world was neatly and brutally divided between friends and enemies. The small coterie of reporters whom he considered to be loyal were lavished with invitations to dinner, were allowed to accompany him on trips, were given scoops and inside information, and usually reciprocated with stories that put the prime minister and his government in a favourable light. But stories that were critical of Diefenbaker would provoke towering rages, public temper tantrums, and implacable hostility.

The prime minister had had a number of unfortunate run-ins with the CBC before his showdown with the network over *Preview Commentary*. Perhaps the most famous incident was when a teleprompter broke down just before the prime minister was to speak to the country. Despite the fact that the teleprompter was repaired on time, Diefenbaker exploded uncontrollably after the broadcast. He screamed at Alphonse Quimet, the CBC president, for close to ten minutes, threatened to fire the technicians, and accused the corporation of plotting against him. But there was little about the CBC that could ever satisfy the prime minister. He would make frequent phone calls to George Nowlan, the minister responsible for the CBC, accusing the corporation of having perpetrated various sins. In public, he claimed, in the style of Senator Joe McCarthy, that Radio-Canada had been infiltrated by "left-wing communists," and denounced the corporation for being a "mass propaganda agency."[20] The public broadcaster had also, in his view, subverted public morality by preaching "the gospel that wrong is right, that decency is dirty, that observing the law of the land is lunacy."[21] At one point, he told his cabinet that there needed to be "a cleaning up at the CBC."[22]

Preview Commentary was a four-minute segment aired each morning on CBC radio in which members of the Parliamentary Press Gallery expressed their opinions on the news stories of the day. Diefenbaker was convinced that the show's producers were deliberately trying to undermine his credibility. CBC executives soon learned through the Ottawa grapevine that their jobs would be on the line unless something was done about the show. Buckling under the pressure, Ernie Bushnell, the CBC's acting president, cancelled the program. The reaction among front-line CBC journalists was almost immediate. A petition was drawn up and mass resignations were threatened. There were also expressions of outrage from the public and "a hailstorm of headlines and accusations" in the other media.[23]

Fearing a public relations disaster, wholesale rebellion from its journalists, and an unacceptable loss of face and credibility for the corporation as a whole, the CBC's Board of Directors reversed Bushnell's decision to cancel the show. While CBC executives who appeared in front of a parliamentary committee were to deny that political pressure had been brought to bear by the government, the putrid smell of political interference was not hard to detect. Frank Peers, the supervisor of talks and public affairs, testified that Bushnell had told him that the government had given the CBC president two alternatives: either take the program off the air or face actions that would endanger the corporation as a whole.

Although Diefenbaker's move against *Preview Commentary* had been blocked, "the Chief" as he was affectionately known to his followers, had other ways of getting even with the corporation. He kept CBC president Alphonse Quimet's salary frozen for years, and there is evidence that the prime minister "had had a role" in securing a TV license for his friend and political ally John Bassett, the publisher of the *Toronto Telegram*. Bassett and John Eaton, whose family controlled the Eaton's department stores, had formed Baton Broadcasting. They soon used their valuable Toronto TV license, CFTO, as the launching pad for a new network based on an alliance of different ownership groups. The new Canadian Television Network (CTV) began broadcasting in 1961 and became the CBC's principal rival.

No sooner had the CBC weathered the Diefenbaker storm than new clouds began to gather. A new program, *This Hour Has Seven Days*, would shake the foundations of conventional television journalism and embroil the CBC and the government of Lester Pearson in prolonged controversy. The show, which aired on Sunday nights and ran from 1964 to 1966, was a radical departure from anything that had been seen before on Canadian television. *Seven Days'* approach was to illuminate the issues of the day and the people who made the news by using shock tactics and turning journalism into theatre. It sought not only to tell a story but also to become the story – that is, its producers wanted the program to set the political agenda, to be the centre of attention.

Politicians and other prominent guests would be put in a "hot seat" where they would be subjected to an inquisition-style grilling. Its journalists would often engage in guerrilla tactics such as ambushing prominent individuals outside their homes or offices or bringing a surprise guest on the show in the middle of an interview. Political leaders were viciously lampooned in songs and skits. The show was always pushing the edge of what was seen as acceptable, hitting an issue or a personality over the head with a sledge-hammer. *Seven Days* was television with an "attitude." Paul Rutherford has described the values that underlay the hijinks, the values that made *Seven Days* tick: "*Seven Days* very often assumed a pose of moral arrogance from which it could condemn or praise. It presented not only that there was a 'right' and a 'wrong' way of doing things, but that social betterment was indeed a real possibility. The task was to reveal abuses, uncover hypocrisy, and educate the public."[24]

While today's audiences, hardened by exposure to the likes of Jerry Springer, Kids in the Hall, Howard Stern, and *Saturday Night Live*, would probably not be shocked by anything that they saw on *Seven Days*, the Canada of the mid-1960s was scandalized. And audiences mushroomed. By the end of its run in spring 1966, the show was attracting an average of over three million viewers, a mega-hit by the standards of its day.

But for all of its popularity with the public, and no doubt because of it, the show deeply unnerved politicians and CBC executives. Prime Minister Lester Pearson received bags full of mail from outraged viewers and no doubt had to swallow hard when he saw his government skewered and roasted on almost every show. He eventually forbade cabinet ministers from appearing on the program. While there is no evidence – no smoking gun – to suggest that Pearson took any direct action against the show, the cancellation of *Seven Days* and the uproar that followed took place on Pearson's "watch."

The crisis began when the CBC decided not to renew the contracts of hosts Patrick Watson and Laurier Lapierre. What ensued was a bare-knuckled fight for survival by the *Seven Days* team. Watson, Lapierre, and producer Douglas Leiterman held a press conference to denounce what they claimed was an attempt to strangle the program. Prominent academics, writers, artists, and MPs formed a national "Save Seven Days" committee, and CBC offices were picketed by *Seven Days* supporters. Seven thousand calls were made to CBC switchboards during the weekend following the dismissals. With the temperature rising, the prime minister stepped into the fray. He ordered the parliamentary broadcasting committee to undertake its own investigation and briefly attempted to mediate the dispute. He then summoned Stuart Keate, the publisher of the *Vancouver Sun*, to conduct a special investigation under the auspices of the Prime Minister's Office.

At the parliamentary committee's hearings the CBC came under intense scrutiny. The major figures in what was now a national political drama all appeared in order to give their own versions of the truth and vilify their enemies. In effect, the public broadcaster was sliced open and put on display. Alphonse Quimet blamed Pearson for enflaming the situation by creating the spectacle of public hearings, hearings that he saw as giving legitimacy and publicity to attacks against the CBC. According to Quimet: "The effect was to encourage the rebels to prolong ... their mutiny ... To lead power-hungry young men, already on an ego trip, to believe their goal was within reach ... To have irremediably biased public opinion ... (and) to have done all this without contributing one iota to the solution of the conflict."[25]

In effect, Pearson, a seasoned political pro if there ever was one, was playing both sides of the street. He gave the appearance of being concerned with the shoddy treatment that Watson and his colleagues were receiving, and yet was benefiting from the fact that the CBC had chosen to cancel the show. The simple fact was that the prime minister had chosen to meddle in the affairs of the public broadcaster — in this case allowing the corporation to become a political football.

The struggle over *The Valour and the Horror* was to strike even deeper nerve endings. This series of three documentaries about Canadian involvement in the Second World War was broadcast on consecutive Sunday nights on the CBC's main channels in January and on CBC Newsworld in March and April 1992. Viewed by an estimated 6 million Canadians, the series retold the story of three epic battles — the Japanese capture of the Canadian garrison in Hong Kong, the Battle of Normandy, and the air war over Germany waged by Bomber Command. But instead of lauding Canadian efforts, the series focused on mismanagement by the General Staff, the lack of even elemental training and preparedness, and the blunders, fiascoes, and needless suffering that the series claimed characterized each of those battles. Ordinary soldiers and airmen were portrayed both as courageous heroes who faced often insurmountable odds and victims of the arrogance and incompetence of their commanders.

Revisionist history was packaged as gripping melodrama. The production used stark film footage and paintings, followed teary-eyed veterans as they revisited the old battlefields, employed actors to represent the wartime fighters so that younger viewers could empathize with their fears and doubts, and utilized somber music to help create an eerie mood. The intention of the *Valour*'s producers, Brian and Terry McKenna and Galafilm, was to question and perhaps even overturn conventional and official history — to debunk war myths that they believed had been perpetuated for too long.

The controversy exploded almost immediately after the airing of the second episode, "Death by Moonlight: Bomber Command." The episode provoked a strong outcry from veterans' organizations and a hailstorm of protests from almost every direction. "Death by Moonlight" depicted the bombing campaign against Germany as a merciless assault on civilian populations. It also claimed that the High Command had little regard for the lives of their own men – lives that they squandered needlessly – and that the campaign was a strategic failure. The most shocking moment occurred at the very end of the documentary when writer Freeman Dyson was quoted as saying that: "The German night fighters ended the war morally undefeated ... We had given them, at the end of the war, the only thing they lacked at the beginning, a clean cause to fight for." To add insult to injury, the episode showed Canadian veterans appearing to apologize to victims of the bombing for the destruction that they had caused. The McKennas had reversed the presumed moral order – the Germans were the victims, Canadians servicemen were the villains.

In response to the uproar, the CRTC, the Senate subcommittee on veterans' affairs, and the CBC Ombudsman launched investigations into the series. The hinge on which the Senate investigation rested was that the series had received financial support from the public through the CBC, Telefilm, and the National Film Board. The Senate subcommittee became a forum for attacking and discrediting the documentary. What took place was a kind of "counter spectacle" in which senators, veterans, and historians fiercely attacked and attempted to discredit the version of history presented by the McKennas. Witness after witness tore into their arguments and pointed out flaws in their thinking. Aside from trial by ridicule that the Senate committee had orchestrated, the committee also wanted to have the documentary banned and new rules for documentaries imposed on the CBC.

The hearings were denounced by critics as being "literally an inquisition," as a "kangaroo court," a "witch hunt," and a "Shakespearean crowd scene" in which the producers were placed at the mercy of the mob.[26] Brian McKenna thought that the inquiry was "designed to shelter a politically correct view of history and to put a chill in the creative air."[27]

The controversy over *The Valour and the Horror* took place against a wider political backdrop. In fact, it couldn't have come at a worse time for the CBC. Prime Minister Brian Mulroney, continually up-set by the coverage that he was receiving from the CBC, appar-ently wanted to teach the corporation a lesson. Patrick Watson (the very same Patrick Watson who had been dismissed during the *Seven Days* affair), who was chairman of the CBC's Board of Directors, remembers phone calls from Mulroney that ranged from "angry protestations to subtle suggestions."[28] Mulroney's most overt action was to stack the Board of Directors with fellow Conservatives, some of whom believed that the corporation had to be scrutinized for signs of liberal bias. One appointee, John Crispo, had described the CBC as "Radio Baghdad" because of what he saw as its anti-American stance during the Gulf War.[29] Crispo once suggested that cuts to the CBC's budget that had been made in 1991–92 were "a down payment and a warning."[30]

In reality the chill that affects the CBC is a budgetary chill. There is always the fear that in angering politicians the CBC will not have friends at the table when its budgets are being decided.

Under pressure from the veterans and from an activist board of directors, the CBC began to distance itself from the McKennas. Eventually Gerard Veilleux, the CBC president, issued a statement expressing his "sincere regret" for the hurt that the programs had caused, and accepting full responsibility "to the extent that these programs fell below acceptable standards."[31] In addition, Trina McQueen, then Head of News and Current Affairs, was demoted. Some believed that McQueen was being made an example of, that she had "taken the bullet," as one CBC informant put it, to satisfy the board's desire for tighter control over CBC journalism. One sen-ior journalist described the CBC's retreat this way:

> The fact is that they could have done a documen-tary on the history of beer in Canada and had Molson jump on their face. They would have run to the nearest sanctuary. I think the corporation ba-sically lost its nerve, it lost its spine … There is no-body outside of a handful of people at head office … who believe justice was done. In the end, that was the incandescent moment of Trina McQueen's

career. That was it. She was gone. She was toast long
before everything else fell into place where she was
demoted, vilified and removed.[32]

The CBC president now faced open rebellion from the corporation's journalists. Union representatives condemned what they saw
as the betrayal of the McKennas and the all too easy and brutal use
of journalists as scapegoats. A petition, signed by over 1,000 CBC
employees, stated that CBC journalists had "confidence in the professionalism and integrity of this documentary team" and were "profoundly disturbed" by the "secret and arbitrary" process employed
by the broadcaster. The petition expressed the fear that "a chill"
was now in the air that threatened "controversial documentary production and journalism in general."[33] At a meeting between Veilleux
and 185 journalists, the journalists told the president that morale
had hit bottom and that *Valour* should be rebroadcast in its original
form in order to demonstrate that the corporation was not about to
crumble under pressure from the government.

The CBC's retreat in the face of what many believed was government intimidation sparked a wave of protests and indignation
from the journalistic and arts communities. An editorial in the *Globe
and Mail* didn't mince words: "The CBC's journalistic reputation
lies in pieces today, slit wide and deboned like a fresh-caught fish."
The fault lay with "the craven efforts of the corporation's senior executives to appease the programme's enemies in Parliament."[34]
Popular author Pierre Berton believed that "the CBC has crawled
on its belly."[35] Timothy Findley, author of the much-celebrated
novel, *The Wars*, accused the Mulroney government of staging "a
coup" within the CBC. His view was that: "They have reached ...
where the government has no business reaching."[36]

Perhaps the most poignant criticism came from historian Michael
Bliss who was concerned about the how the power of Parliament
was being used to suppress controversial points of view and a version of history that made people feel uncomfortable. He addressed
the following remarks to the Senate subcommittee:

My understanding of a free society is one in which
there is no such thing as historical and political

correctness. There are points of view, some better and more sophisticated and more responsible and nearer the truth than others; some also more troubling, more likely to disturb or give offence than others. We are all accountable for the points of view we express to the people who listen to us, to the people we work for and, above all to our consciences and our sense of professionalism ... When you exceed your mandate and hold an inquisition, when you become a vehicle which the disgruntled and troubled and offended can use to lash out at and destroy the reputations of those who disgruntle and trouble and offend them, when you become a captive of special interest groups ... then I believe the Canadian people can properly ask about your own sense of accountability and your use of our money.[37]

In the end, two concrete results emerged out of the storm that raged around *The Valour and the Horror*. First, *The Valour* has not been, and may never be, shown again on Canadian television. This was a clear victory for the Senate subcommittee and for the veterans. Presumably this also meant some financial loss for the documentary's producers, the McKennas and Galafilm. Second, the CBC made changes to its policy on "point of view" documentaries to ensure that an opposing point of view would have a chance to be heard during or immediately after a broadcast.

Conclusion

The cumulative impact of the three crises may not be directly apparent or observable. This is because the "lessons" that were learned may well be lodged below the surface, deeply embedded in the CBC's organizational memory and psyche. These three crises may also have had an impact on the culture of Canadian journalism generally. One can argue that these events represented a kind of

Watergate in reverse. They taught journalists not to stick their necks out too far, not to rile governments or question the accepted versions of the truth. They demonstrated that violating norms and upsetting politicians or the public could exact a heavy price. There were clearly lines in the sand that could not be crossed without endangering careers, subjecting journalists to inspection and ridicule, and tarnishing the reputation of the CBC as a whole.

Still, those who watch the CBC will rightfully argue that the CBC's sword has not been blunted on many of the stories that it has pursued. Its exposés on the Canadian blood supply, on the grotesque actions of members of the Canadian Armed Forces in Somalia, and on child poverty seemed to have left few stones unturned. CBC news and current affairs teams forage into many nooks and crannies of Canadian life with great tenacity. And programs such as *This Hour Has 22 Minutes* and *The Royal Canadian Air Farce* mercilessly satirize Canadian politicians. In fact, *22 Minutes* has reinvented the political ambush: Preston Manning, Paul Martin, Jean Charest, Ralph Klein, and Mike Harris have all been recent victims of various gags and set-ups. The CBC's dramatic lineup has also had an "unafraid" quality. Movies and docu-dramas such as *The Boys of Saint Vincent*, *Giant Mine*, and *The Arrow* and programs such as *The Newsroom*, *Urgence*, and *Réseaux* have been eloquent and searing commentaries on Canadian events and institutions.

The CBC's supporters would argue that the public broadcaster is still the village square that Canadians come to in order to express themselves and to laugh and cry at their own difficulties and experiences. Still others see the CBC as a battlefield and believe that the corporation has learned to watch its step, to tread softly, when it comes too close to sensitive political toes. The next chapter on the bitter struggle over broadcasting and national unity examines the difficulty that the CBC has faced when national survival has been at stake.

SIX

The Worst Assignment: Reporting National Unity

Public broadcasting organizations were created to insulate national societies from the power of multinational media conglomerates and the imperatives that drive commercial broadcasters. Public broadcasters are designed to be the alternate media – the guarantee that a society will have a place within the broadcasting community where its problems and prospects can be fully explored. But public broadcasters are often put in difficult, if not impossible, situations. There are constraints – red lines – beyond which public broadcasters cannot go, that sometimes impair their ability to cover stories in the depth and with the perseverance that they would like.

Perhaps the most dangerous fault line in the politics of Canadian broadcasting has been the issue of national unity. The reporting of national unity issues has been an open sore constantly picked at by politicians on both sides of the political barricades. Virtually every major combatant in the national unity wars has levelled accusations of bias against the CBC at one time or other. The pressure brought to bear on the corporation and on journalists has often been extraordinary. Moreover, the reporting of Canada's struggle for national unity represents a unique case in the history of public broadcasting worldwide. While public broadcasters in France, Britain, Germany, or Sweden, for instance, face political pressures of one kind or another, they have never had to cover the potential breakup of their countries. They have, arguably, never had to cover events where the stakes were so high. And they have never had to face the intense scru-

tiny and the painful journalistic dilemmas or walk the political tight-
ropes that the CBC has been forced to walk on for years.

The problem is that while Canadians sometimes seem blasé about
or tired of the endless wrangles over national unity, when emotions
do surface they are often at the boiling point. It doesn't take much
for accusations of bias to be hurled at both the messages and the mes-
sengers. Even Pierre Trudeau, who arguably was the staunchest sup-
porter of freedom of expression and civil liberties of any prime
minister, could barely resist the temptation to intervene when he
heard pro-separatist views being expressed on Radio-Canada. In fact,
soon after becoming prime minister, Trudeau threatened to close the
CBC because he thought the French-language Radio-Canada was
being contaminated by separatist propaganda and by "a sickness of
the spirit."[1] Speaking at a Liberal party function in 1969, Trudeau
conjured up an image of what would happen to the CBC if it didn't
move to stanch the separatist menace that was supposedly lurking
within the corporation: "[W]e will put a lid on the place ... we will
close up the shop. Let them not think we won't do it. If need be, we
can produce programs, and if not, we will show people Chinese or
Japanese vases instead of the nonsense they dish out. That would be
of some cultural benefit."[2] While Knowlton Nash argues that Trudeau
might have been playfully and cleverly goading the corporation in
order to make a point, others saw Trudeau's threat as anything but
playful. One has to remember that a number of French-speaking journalists were arrested and that some forms of censorship was imposed
on news organizations during the FLQ crisis of October 1970.
Trudeau did not shrink from using the War Measures Act and the
power of the state when he believed that it was necessary to do so.

The problem for the CBC is not only that the national unity issue
touches raw nerve endings because of the enormous stakes and deep
passions involved but that the struggle has been exceedingly difficult
to cover journalistically. Indeed, the national unity question intro-
duces structural problems that are unique in Canadian journalism.
First, during the struggles over the Meech Lake and Charlottetown
Accords, media coverage both intruded on and organized much of
the political battle. It was the stage on which the drama itself took
place. To use another analogy, the media could be compared to the

walls of a squash court (although media scholars might argue that the walls were themselves in motion); bargaining positions would have to be hit against the media walls to keep them in play, test reactions, and give them legitimacy. The instant nature of modern communications and the extent to which political leaders used television to convey messages, not only to their respective publics but to each other, created uncharted terrain into which journalists were venturing for the first time. To make matters worse, the issues were often exceedingly difficult to explain to the public. Amending formulas, the use of the notwithstanding clause, powers of veto, Supreme Court decisions and interpretations, and formulas for a revised Triple E Senate made reporting the news seem like a senior graduate seminar in political science. It was difficult to keep audiences riveted when the temptation of so many viewers was to reach for their clickers. Given all of these factors, the CBC could do little to prevent being caught in the undertow of events, struggling to keep its head — its integrity and reputation for excellence and impartiality — above water.

A second problem is that journalists in Quebec and in English Canada, including CBC journalists, tend to view national unity issues through an entirely different lens. Journalists in Quebec are aware that their audience is divided almost evenly between sovereigntists and federalists. They know that their credibility depends on giving weight to both sides of the independence question and on reporting what many Quebeckers see as their province's special position and grievances. Anglophone journalists, on the other hand, have to gauge their reports to audiences that are overwhelmingly pro-federalist. For this reason news coverage is "indexed" differently in Quebec than it is in English Canada.[3] These constraints and expectations are not always understood by political leaders, whose first instinct is often to lash out when they feel that journalists are giving too much play, too much ice time, to the other side. Chantal Hebert, the Ottawa bureau chief for *La Presse,* described the pressures that Francophone journalists were under during the 1995 Quebec referendum campaign:

> It's one thing to cover a referendum and come from
> Winnipeg and cover it in Quebec if you don't speak
> French and tell people who watch television every

night that they should get very worried or that they can go to sleep safely ... In a way it's like covering a foreign country. If you cover the campaign for a Quebec paper, you're covering it with your friends voting, your family, people you see on the street, it's a different proposition all together. You're not just bringing somebody news from the front, you're on the front here ... and what people think about this is worth just as much as what you think.[4]

An anglophone journalist and the media reporter for the *Ottawa Citizen*, Chris Cobb, described the difficulties in this way:

In the referendum campaign, the hope for fairness and balance was a vain one. The coverage was generally one-sided on both sides of the linguistic fence. Outside of Quebec the English-language media have an audience that is 99.9 per cent on one side of the argument. If any great effort had been made to tell the separatist side of the story, as we would with any other assignment, there would have been a risk of alienating our audiences. The separation issue is unique in that sense. It's deeply emotional – about the breaking up of our country. Anglophone journalists are like every other anglophone in that regard. We don't want to see it happen. But every day, we cover the Bloc Quebecois in Parliament and give their views a public airing. That's either remarkably mature or ill-considered but the separatist view is not shut out.[5]

This chapter will describe the political and journalistic controversies that plagued the CBC's coverage of national unity issues from the Meech Lake drama of 1987–1990 to the 1995 Quebec referendum. The examination is based in part on interviews conducted with reporters who covered these events for the CBC and other news organizations. The main argument is that the public broadcaster has been placed under an intense scrutiny that has prevented it from aggressively reporting critical national issues. Reporters have to be free to report the truth as they see it even if this means offending powerful politicians or interests. This chapter also emphasizes the degree to which a country such as Canada that lives on a knife's edge of political survival needs "hard" news, informed opinions, and high professional standards in its journalistic community. These are not frills but necessities. It is in order to maintain these principles that a public broadcasting system exists in the first place.

The CBC and the Agony of Meech Lake and Charlottetown

One of the most difficult periods in the history of CBC journalism was the controversy that erupted over its coverage of the last-gasp attempts by the country's first ministers (the prime minister and the 10 provincial premiers) to save the Meech Lake Accord in June 1990. Indeed, the Meech Lake drama represented one of the worst moments in the corporation's history and a dividing line in the history of Canadian journalism. As was the case during the *Seven Days* and the *Valour* affairs, the CBC came under the intense glare of a parliamentary inquiry, undertook an internal investigation of its reporting practices, and faced threats of resignation from some of its leading journalists. What was particularly perplexing was that the public broadcaster was first accused of having undermined the Mulroney government's constitutional initiatives, and then later, in *Toronto Sun* columnist Bob Fife's words, of "being in bed with the government."[6]

The first charge stemmed from a speech made in Calgary in 1988 by CBC-TV's Ottawa bureau chief Elly Alboim, an almost legendary figure within the CBC. Alboim had covered virtually all of the major events in Canadian politics for almost 20 years, was well connected to the major players in the political game, and knew where the bodies were buried (figuratively speaking). He ruled the roost in the Ottawa newsroom by a combination of his powerful intellect and a fear among journalists of the verbal chastisement that would await them if they failed to live up to Alboim's high standards.

In his Calgary speech, Alboim described what he saw as the political motivations and forces that had produced the Meech Lake

Accord during the summer of 1987. The Ottawa bureau chief claimed that Mulroney's "sole motivation" for pursuing the accord was "to establish that he could do in Quebec what Pierre Trudeau could not."[7] He also observed that with the prime minister, the ten provincial premiers, and the leaders of the major political parties all supporting the accord, it was difficult in the first weeks after the agreement had been signed to find interested parties who were prepared to criticize what had been negotiated. He believed, however, that his role as a journalist was to seek out opposing voices so that the public could get a balanced assessment of whether the agreement was workable.

In the fall of 1990, with the dust from the failure of the Meech Lake initiative still hanging over the country, Alboim came under withering attack from John Meisel, a former chairman of the CRTC, and a much respected and even venerated figure in Canada's academic community. Meisel accused the CBC in general and Alboim in particular of having "contributed to the process that ultimately scuppered constitutional reform by seeking out and encouraging attacks against the Meech Lake project by people who could be expected to attract a lot of public attention."[8]

Meisel's tough denunciation of Alboim's methods set off a chain reaction. In a witch's brew of news stories and columns, journalists either unsheathed their knifes to attack Alboim or leapt to his defence. According to reports, CBC president Gerard Veilleux, under pressure from the Board of Directors, attempted to dismiss Alboim. He eventually backed down when faced with a potential rebellion by CBC journalists, including Peter Mansbridge and David Halton, who threatened to resign if Alboim was fired. The CBC president then ordered an internal investigation to determine whether Alboim had deliberately manipulated coverage in order to present the constitutional deal in a negative light. While Alboim was cleared of the charges, a climate of uncertainty swept through CBC newsrooms. Journalists were fearful that their ability to exercise independent judgment in deciding how news stories would be covered would be curtailed, and that their professional integrity was being compromised for political expediency.

But the Alboim affair was only one ripple in a larger lake. During the waning days of the struggle over the Meech Lake Accord, accusations against the CBC were suddenly to come from a completely different direction. Critics now claimed that the corporation had become the handmaiden of the Mulroney government. The charge was that the CBC's decision to provide extensive coverage to attempts by the First Ministers to salvage the accord in early June 1990 bolstered and legitimized Mulroney's claim that the country would break up if the Meech Lake Agreement were scuttled. Critics contend that by bringing anchor Peter Mansbridge on location, providing blanket coverage that pre-empted the prime-time schedule (882 minutes of live coverage), and assigning a small army of 25 reporters to cover the story, the CBC had bought into and was promoting the government's doomsday strategy. The broadcaster had, in effect, become part of Mulroney's famous "roll of the dice." It wasn't only the decision to treat the Meech Lake negotiations as an extraordinary news event that was in dispute but the dramatic all-or-nothing tone of the coverage that raised hackles. The CBC was accused of fomenting crisis, of placing the country on the edge of an abyss.

While some will argue that CBC journalists fell into a trap set for them by shrewd federal negotiators, the reality is that they were again confronted, as they had been during the first days of the accord, with a difficult decision. Jason Moscovitz, now the chief political correspondent for CBC-TV, recalled the problem that the CBC faced: "You have a prime minister who keeps saying it's the end of the world if this thing doesn't go through. I think that the Prime Minister deserves to be covered."[9] Of course, not giving Mulroney the stage that he required would also have been seen as unfair. It was a case of CBC journalists being damned if they did and damned if they didn't.

In Professor Gadi Wolfsfeld's analysis of press coverage of the Oslo peace process that led to Israel's withdrawal from Gaza and Jericho and to the establishment of a Palestinian authority, he suggests that news reporting has the capacity to both alter the dynamic of the negotiations and exacerbate conflict.[10] His argument is that once negotiations are placed under a news frame that focuses on conflict, demands immediate solutions, and declares winners and losers, and that "news" is then fed back into the negotiating process, a different set of reactions and circumstances is created – one that can be harmful to the negotiations. The CBC's problem was that the very existence of the news spotlight, the very presence of its microphones and cameras, altered the Meech Lake and Charlottetown negotiations. This happened in a number of ways:

1. The major political actors would play to the cameras. They would use television interviews to appeal to their own publics, put their own positions in the best possible light, or send messages to other leaders. Media interviews became, as the German military strategist Clausewitz might have put it, the continuation of the negotiating process by other means. Threats, charges and countercharges, expressions of frustration, and appeals for popular support all took place in the arena that had been created by television.

2. Journalists employed the time-honoured "strategy frame," covering political events as if they were a horse race. They reported on who was ahead and who was behind rather than on the substance of the issues. They became obsessed with declaring winners and losers. Journalists often portrayed a willingness to compromise as a failure, an act of weakness. Consequently political leaders could not retreat from positions that they had taken without losing face, and face-saving compromises were exceedingly difficult and perhaps even impossible to achieve under the searing heat of exposure.

3. As every government or societal group could see what every other constituency had achieved in the negotiations, they were all under pressure to match the gains that the others had won, to in effect see their perfect reflection in the constitution. In this case, Natives, women's groups, Senate reformers, language rights advocates, and provincial governments that wanted greater powers from Ottawa were all pushing their own causes and interests. Exposure and publicity had created a "bandwagon" effect so that the negotiations soon became overloaded with too many interests having to be accommodated within too short a period of time. The accord collapsed, one can argue, because of the sheer weight of the demands and interests that had been placed on the negotiating table.

While Wolfsfeld believes that the turbulence of media reporting cannot prevent a sturdy plane from reaching its destination, the media's presence means that the negotiating parties "will be much tougher about things than they would without spotlights" and that "it's much easier to do it secretly and quietly."[11]

Although the CBC was venturing into new and dangerous terrain, it had little choice but to push ahead. In fact, the CBC's defenders would argue that the decision to provide what was, in effect, wall-to-wall coverage during the fateful week of meetings in early June 1990 to save the Meech Lake Accord was in fact what public broadcasting is all about. Far from having to apologize for reporting that became part of the negotiating process or that angered or discomforted viewers, the CBC was depicting the reality of the Canadian constitution-making process with all of its complexities and blemishes. In any case the Meech Lake bullet was not something that, given its mandate, the CBC could duck.

On the French-language side the issues were, if anything, even more toxic. There were claims that Quebec journalists had a nationalist bias and had become powerful participants in the political process. Keith Spicer, a former chairman of the CRTC and the head of a commission on Canadian unity that was struck in the aftermath of the Meech Lake debacle, went as far as to charge that media "ayatollahs" had manipulated coverage in order to discredit efforts to bring constitutional change.[12] Laurier Lapierre, no stranger to controversy as the former host of *This Hour Has Seven Days*, believed that Quebec was dominated by a coterie of "notables," a journalistic and intellectual elite that is unable to accept the "goodwill, the passage of time and the usual trade-offs that make for a democratic political process."[13] Ovide Mercredi, the Grand Chief of the Assembly of First Nations, at one point accused all francophone reporters in the Parliamentary Press Gallery of being separatists.[14]

Susan Delacourt, the veteran *Globe and Mail* reporter, contends that francophone journalists reported events through the looking glass of "rejection, acceptance or humiliation" with virtually all actions or statements by political leaders judged against these yardsticks.[15] This standard, one can argue, made Quebec journalists especially susceptible to the appeals of a politician like Lucien Bouchard, who finds evidence of Ottawa's betrayal and Quebec's humiliation at every turn in the road.

Although bashing the Quebec media and Radio-Canada for sins real and imagined had become a cottage industry during the country's national unity battles, there is no question that reporting by Quebec journalists altered the political landscape substantially during the Meech Lake and Charlottetown constitutional rounds. Although one could hardly suggest that media coverage created Quebec's grievances or the long-standing desire for some form of political autonomy felt by many in Quebec – both of these realities being deeply embedded in Quebec's collective experience and psyche – media reporting was able to transform some events into potent symbols. One such event was the notorious Brockville incident. At the height of the battle over the Meech Lake Accord, some TV stations in Quebec gave what some saw as extraordinary play to footage of English-language extremists trampling on and burning the Quebec flag. The implication was that these extremists represented English-Canadian attitudes toward Quebec. Since opposition to the Meech Lake Accord with its provisions for recognizing Quebec as a "distinct society" was being interpreted by many in the Quebec media as a humiliating rejection of Quebec by English Canada, the Brockville incident soon took on a life of its own. Another hot visual that became a symbol of sorts in Quebec occurred during the Charlottetown round. Footage of an Inuit leader holding up a map of Quebec that showed huge portions of the province as belonging to the Natives received wide coverage.

A classic example of agenda-setting by Quebec reporters was the famous "ambush at Bourassa Pass" that took place in September 1991. When it appeared that Quebec Premier Robert Bourassa might be willing to forfeit a Quebec veto over future constitutional change, a major compromise, he found himself surrounded in a scrum by journalists who according to one observer had "literally ganged up on him."[16] Unable to escape, the Premier was battered relentlessly with accusations that he was betraying Quebec's interests. Wilting under the journalistic pressure cooker, Bourassa soon reversed his position.

Another example that illustrates Wolfsfeld's claim that intensive media scrutiny makes it difficult for political leaders to compromise occurred during the Charlottetown Referendum campaign in 1992. A taped conversation between Diane Wilhelmy, Quebec's Deputy Minister of Intergovernmental Affairs, and an unidentified civil servant in which Robert Bourassa was criticized for having "settled for so little" was leaked to reporters. Quebec journalists and indeed the national media had a field day with the Wilhelmy tapes. While one can argue that the tapes were a time bomb cleverly planted by opponents of the Charlottetown Accord to detonate at a decisive moment during the campaign, the explosions would not have taken place without reporters who were willing to, in effect, pull the trigger. Instead of being "framed" by journalists as a strong leader willing to make sacrifices for the common good, Bourassa was pilloried for being weak.

Fallout from the controversy over the reporting of the Meech Lake drama took two forms. First, strenuous efforts were made to ensure that the CBC was more "accountable" to its political masters. After the collapse of the Meech Lake deal, CBC executives were paraded before the House of Commons Standing Committee on Communications and Culture to answer questions from angry MPs about why the CBC hadn't done more for national unity. The CBC's Board of Directors, filled with Mulroney appointees, was anxious to exercise a greater measure of control. They wanted and succeeded in getting a new regime of monitoring procedures (some would describe it as a system of journalistic surveillance) put into place. Although there had been periodic in-house monitoring of news coverage since 1980, this new system, which was put in place prior to the 1992 Charlottetown referendum campaign and then altered somewhat for the 1995 Quebec referendum, was of a different order of magnitude. There was now a Vice-President for Media Accountability; an oversight group was established within the corporation to monitor coverage of important political events; a daily logging system was set up to document whether coverage of these events was balanced in terms of the amount of time allocated to various party leaders, political parties, or sides in referendums; and

Erin Research, an outside consulting firm, was hired to do its own surveys of CBC's coverage. In addition, polls were commissioned to determine public perceptions of whether the CBC's reporting had been fair, and academics were asked to evaluate some of the findings and provide overviews of the situation. All of these steps were formalized within an Office of Media Accountability and through an Ombudsman's Office.

As part of this new effort, when the Charlottetown Round began in September 1991 guidelines were issued to CBC journalists restating the basic rules that should normally dictate political reporting. Reporters were reminded of some of the principles that they may have overlooked during the frenzy and turmoil of covering the Meech Lake extravaganza. Those interviewees who advocated partisan positions had to be clearly identified as such to viewers, and reporters were instructed that a full range of views had to be reflected in network coverage. At least one of the new rules, however, caused considerable consternation among Radio-Canada reporters in Quebec. The guidelines instructed journalists "to reflect Canada as a nation and evoke the social, economic, cultural and political benefits of nationhood" and to "explore as well the costs and consequences of the changes being proposed." Some reporters felt that they were being given pro-federalist marching orders, that they were being asked to be partisan soldiers in the upcoming political wars.

A second change in direction was that a much more concerted effort was made to connect with public opinion. While during the Meech Lake drama CBC news had reported on virtually every pronouncement made by the first ministers in almost microscopic detail, the public broadcaster had failed to notice the sharp turn that public opinion had taken against the accord. In the heartland beyond the narrow confines of the world inhabited by reporters and politicians, populist anger and a deep cynicism towards politicians had taken hold. The sense that the CBC news machine was out of touch with the concerns of ordinary viewers coincided with another development that was occurring throughout the television world at the very same time. As discussed in the first chapter, a populist wave was sweeping through the U.S. television networks during the early 1990s: news and news magazine formats were being revamped in order to recapture audiences that had been fleeing to cable, new networks such as Fox, and independent stations. The networks were attempting to connect more directly with viewers and to mirror their interests.

What was being asked of the CBC was nothing less than a fundamental change in psychology. For decades the CBC adhered to a top-down civil service/professional model of news reporting. According to James Curran, a British scholar who has written about the British Broadcasting Corporation, this is a "mandarin-like conception in which the electorate, the rulers of democracy, are briefed by intelligent and responsible public servants rather than merely entertained by market spectacle."[17] With Meech Lake this entire edifice seemed to come crashing down. Journalists had to seem to be more directly connected to the public or risk losing their credibility.

At the CBC a number of populist experiments were undertaken. One of the most controversial experiments was the "Town Hall" meeting. The idea was to recreate the down-home surroundings and atmosphere of a local town hall, a gathering in which citizens and political leaders could exchange ideas in a direct and straightforward manner. The CBC Town Halls, usually a special edition of *The National*'s magazine segment, allow viewers (chosen because they represent widely held opinions or concerns) to question prominent politicians or government leaders. Town Halls, including Town Hall meetings with the prime minister, had until 1997 become one of the standard rituals of Canadian political life – a new, more egalitarian, and more accessible form of Question Period, if you like. Politicians including Prime Minister Jean Chretien, however, view them with some wariness, even dread, because they fear that they may be walking unprotected into a political firestorm. Prime Minister Chretien's inept performance during a December 1996 Town Hall meeting was an example of the dangers that await politicians who aren't prepared to face tough questioning. Chretien seemed to be dazzled by some of the questions that were asked, appeared strangely disconnected, and fumbled his answers. Politicians suspect that questioners are chosen because they have particular axes to grind and will supply the emotional fuel, the combustible material, needed for good television. They also think that the hosts sometimes add fuel to the fire by goading politicians into admitting failures and "egging-on" or cheerleading those members of the audience who ask embarrassing or aggressive questions. The CBC has insisted that participants are carefully chosen to reflect public concerns and that little of what takes place during the Town Halls is either orchestrated or rehearsed.

The CBC's newfound populism would take other forms as well. *The National* established a "Your Turn" segment; viewers are encouraged to contact shows through fax, 1-800 numbers, e-mail, or voice mail; and every major program has a World Wide Web home page that allows viewers to register opinions or participate in discussions. During the 1995 Quebec referendum the CBC was inundated by between two and three thousand e-mail messages a day from viewers.[18] According to David Bazay, the CBC's Ombudsman, these attempts to connect with viewers and listeners had a very significant effect on programming: "There is absolutely no question that we used to sit in splendid isolation and sketch out and plan our coverage. Now when you get into computers and the Internet and 1-800 numbers you encounter an electronic universe of people who have suggestions on how coverage should be improved. While you are still dealing with some kind of elite, there are a wide variety of messages that come in."[19]

Although the crises that exploded during the struggle over the Meech Lake Accord caused the CBC to institute new systems for monitoring coverage and to shift into a more populist mode, it was not yet out of the woods in term of pleasing its political masters. It wasn't long before the CBC was again knee-deep in controversy. This time the stakes were to be much higher than ever before – the 1995 Quebec referendum shook the country to its very core.

Where Journalists Feared To Tread: Covering the 1995 Quebec Referendum

One can reasonably argue that the 1995 Quebec referendum brought the country to the edge of an abyss. The result of the vote was excruciatingly close with the No and Yes sides separated by only a whisker – the federalist No campaign won by only 54,288 votes. The No forces had 50.58 per cent to 49.4 per cent for the Yes side. Quebec Premier Jacques Parizeau has already admitted that had there been a victory by the Yes side, in this case a shift of a relatively small number of votes, he would have used the vote to declare some form of sovereignty for Quebec. On the eve of the referendum vote, Quebec's Deputy Premier Bernard Landry notified foreign embassies in Ottawa that: "When the Quebec National Assembly will have proclaimed the sovereignty of the new state the moment will have come to recognize it, without putting in peril relations with the rest of Canada."[20] With these actions, the Canadian dream in Quebec, to use Laval University professor Guy Laforest's apt phrase, would very likely have come to an end.[21] At the very least, a Yes vote would have shattered the constitutional framework that now exists.

A number of veteran CBC journalists have described the high-voltage political pressure that was exerted on them during the referendum campaign. According to Jeffrey Dvorkin, who was managing editor of CBC Radio News during the Quebec referendum and is now with National Public Radio in the U.S.:

> When the polls started to slip for the federalist side, we started hearing pressure from the politicians, from the Board of Directors, which never filtered down to the journalists. That's what this office is for. This is a firewall between them and them. Once Bouchard took over from Parizeau and once the panic really set in in the Liberal caucus – that filtered down right to this office. Interviews with Monique Simard, the Parti Quebecois vice-president, on *Morningside* were objected to. I have never seen it like this ... there was the impression that there were too many separatists on the radio and on television and that the CBC as a crown corporation had a duty to support the federal system at all levels. At the end of the campaign a member of the CBC Board of Directors stated that there were doubts about whether our journalism was appropri-

ate. The Erin Report [an outside content analysis of CBC's reporting] would decide if we had been fair. The Erin Report exonerated us. Had it been otherwise I think people would have resigned.

Let's face it. The Liberal caucus had a near death experience and instead of looking at their strategy and tactics they looked at ours. If the vote had gone the other way, if the Yes side had won, I think there would have been dark days for the CBC.[22]

Peter Mansbridge, the chief correspondent of the CBC National News and anchor of *The National*, had learned to roll with the punches:

To put it bluntly, I didn't feel the pressures as much this time as I had in the past. It's part of the process. I've got my own superiors, the CBC Board of Directors, federal cabinet ministers, provincial cabinet ministers, universities, the CRTC, television critics. They're all watching – for words, for eyebrows, for all that. If you really let that get to you, you would really be a basket case. I mean, it got pretty bad during Meech and the hits that we took during Meech were never that far from my mind in Charlottetown ... But I got over those things ... You know they are out there watching everything you do. But you would go nuts worrying about it."[23]

As one might expect, the Quebec referendum produced a flurry of charges and counter-charges against the CBC. Predictably there were accusations from sovereigntists that the CBC was little more than a stalking horse for the federalist side. Quebec Premier Jacques Parizeau demanded that CBC President Anthony Manera resign after Manera met with Quebec MPs to answer questions about the CBC's plans for covering the referendum campaign. The Premier thought it was no coincidence that Manera's meeting with MPs had taken place at the same time that the CBC's budget was being reviewed by Parliament. The leader of the Yes forces, Lucien Bouchard, found Radio-Canada reporters so hostile that his press secretary told Radio-Canada's Michel Cormier that it "would be a sunny day in May" – apparently sometime in the new millennium – before Bouchard would again agree to do an interview for Radio-Canada's flagship news program *Le Point*.[24] After the CBC refused to air an advertisement submitted by the Yes committee until the Yes side was able to substantiate claims it made in the ad, both Bouchard and Parizeau charged that Radio-Canada "was taking its orders from the federal government in Ottawa."[25] The ad had flashed the words "Nous voulons un Quebec français" ("We want a French Quebec") across the screen and then showed several prominent federalist politicians saying "No." Other broadcasters had accepted the ad.

Sovereigntists also charged that the CBC showed its true federalist colours by giving extraordinary play to a pro-federalist rally that took place in Montreal on October 27, the Friday before the vote. It should be noted, however, that estimates of the size of the crowd varied considerably between the corporation's English- and French-language networks; CBC Newsworld estimated the crowd at 150,000, while RDI reported that only 30 or 40 thousand people had attended the rally. And sovereigntists also complained that the broadcasting, in both English and French, of a special "Messages to Quebec" magazine show, which featured sometimes impassioned pleas from citizens across the country imploring Quebeckers to stay in Canada, was virtually a campaign ad for the federalist side. Coverage of the Montreal rally and "Messages to Quebec" made for powerful television. Viewers were treated to heart-rending scenes – a montage of people's faces, the swirl of Canadian flags, fervent displays of emotion and stem-winding rhetorical flourishes. There is no question that they were a unique and moving testimony to the spirit and passion of those in the federalist camp.

Interestingly, a study conducted by the Fraser Institute's National Media Archive claimed that both the English-language CBC-TV and CTV had favoured the federalist side; the number of statements that were quoted from the No camp outnumbered those from the Yes campaign by a margin of two to one.[26] This meant that viewers heard more about the arguments for federalism than they did about the case for Quebec independence. An independent study conducted for this book by media researcher Mark Simpson showed a similar tilt when qualitative factors were considered. In assessing whether stories had a positive, negative, or neutral slant, Simpson found that although most stories on CBC's *The National* were judged to be neutral in tone, the No side received almost twice the percentage of positive stories as the Yes campaign.

Federalists took an entirely different view of the CBC's coverage. Michel Cormier, the parliamentary reporter for Radio-Canada's *Le Point*, reports that at a meeting which took place in Ottawa several days before the vote, federal liberals "vowed privately" to close what they called the "boîte à séparatistes" – the separatist nest, i.e., Radio-Canada. After the vote, these same Liberals blamed Radio-Canada for their near defeat in the referendum, claiming that the broadcaster did not allow federalist messages to "be properly transmitted" to the Quebec electorate.[27] Bitterness was not confined only to the troops in the field. The general himself, Prime Minister Jean Chretien, griped openly about what he saw as the pro-sovereigntist slant on Radio-Canada. He complained that Lucien Bouchard received "kid glove" treatment from Radio-Canada reporters who never challenged the sovereigntist leader's harsh indictment of Canada's recent constitutional history, an interpretation that distorted the truth, vilified Chretien, and painted English Canada as an oppressor. The prime minister also accused the network of ignoring at least one of his major speeches and of downplaying his other pronouncements. As Chretien expressed his frustrations about the coverage given to a speech he made at the United Nations during the campaign: "I think I made a good speech, and I was the seventh item just before the sports. When the people were already asleep, probably they put my item in."[28] In fact, Radio-Canada's *Le Téléjournal* did carry Chretien's speech as the seventh item in its news lineup. The speech, however, did rate a higher billing on CBC's *The National*, where it was the third item in the newscast. Reporters claim that when he was scrummed in New York, Chretien refused to answer questions about statements that had been made by Quebec Liberal Party Leader Daniel Johnson; so that it was the prime minister who refused the coverage that was offered to him. It should also be noted that on another occasion RDI interrupted its regularly scheduled program, *Capital Actions*, to broadcast a speech that the prime minister was making on behalf of the No side in Shawinigan.

Nevill Nakivell, publisher of *The Financial Post*, found Radio-Canada's involvement almost "Orwellian" – overestimating the size of crowds at sovereigntist rallies while underreporting those at federalist events. Nakivell quoted Ottawa pollster Conrad Winn as saying that "a one-way war of attrition" launched well before the referendum campaign "was a major reason the separatists came so close to victory."[29]

The mystery for many English Canadians is why so many Quebeckers failed to understand that a Yes vote would mean a fundamental and irrevocable break with the rest of Canada. Or to put it differently, why so many in Quebec didn't seem to appreciate that the temperature level in English Canada had reached the boiling point, that if Quebec chose to secede from Canada it would not be allowed to keep much of the furniture or anything else. Chris Cobb blames the media in Quebec for preventing these messages from getting through, for being a one-way mirror:

> There was a fundamental misreading of the attitude toward Quebec. Even though it had been stated and restated countless times, the message did not get through to Quebec voters. Quebeckers went to the polls thinking that even if Quebec separated they would continue to use Canadian passports, the Canadian dollar, and continue the economic relationship as if nothing had happened. Those three points were pounded away at during the campaign but, for some reason, Quebeckers got a totally different story. This would suggest the francophone media were not comprehensively reporting what was being said outside Quebec in the English-language media. There is still a gulf misunderstanding. My impression is that Quebeckers haven't a clue of how vociferous and emotional people outside Quebec will be if there is ever a Yes vote.[30]

One poll found that over 20 per cent of Yes voters believed that Quebec would continue to be a province in Canada after Quebec declared sovereignty.[31] Another poll showed that as many as one out of three Quebeckers thought that they would continue to hold Canadian passports and send MPs to Ottawa.[32]

While political leaders fumed about the CBC's coverage, the public seemed relatively satisfied. A public opinion poll taken in Quebec found that 46 per cent of respondents thought that Radio-Canada's coverage was fair and balanced as against 16 per cent who thought it was slanted in some way. Of those who thought that bias existed, 11 per cent believed that coverage had leaned toward the No side (the federalist camp), while only 3 per cent thought that the broadcaster sympathized with the Yes side.[33] The complaints about coverage received by Radio-Canada's ombudsman were almost equally divided between those who thought that coverage was too pro-federalist and those who thought that it leaned too heavily toward the sovereigntist position.[34]

Moreover, a study of referendum coverage on Quebec's two main French-language television networks – Radio-Canada and TVA – undertaken by Denis Moniere, a political scientist at the University of Montreal, gave Radio-Canada a clean bill of health. Its television reports had featured 285 Yes supporters as against 284 sources from the No camp.[35]

In evaluating bias, one has to remember the supercharged, almost pyrotechnic, atmosphere that surrounded the reporting of the referendum. Certainly in the last ten days when the Yes side began to lead in the polls, it dawned on journalists that the country, much like Humpty Dumpty, could fall off the wall and never be put back together again. Reporters began to sense that they were living through what could be a historic event that could transform their lives and that the old tried and true journalistic rules seemed difficult to apply. As Michel Cormier has described the situation:

> CTV's Mike Duffy could wear a tie emblazoned with the Maple Leaf, he could wish Sheila Copps good luck in the campaign, he could try to convince Mario Dumont to vote "No" without jeopardizing

his journalistic integrity. A CBC producer felt free to join the march for a united Canada in Montreal without fear of reprisal. Rosemary Speirs was able to write in the *Toronto Star* that "we get to breathe a shaky sigh of relief" at the result of the referendum without being branded partisan. Such behavior on controversial issues like abortion would be unthinkable. But when the survival of Canada is the issue, it seems normal rules and standards don't apply; public displays of patriotism by journalists are accepted.[36]

For francophone journalists the political environment was structured much differently and in a much more complex manner. André Picard of the *Globe and Mail* explained the fundamental predicament this way: "I think people fail to make the distinction between sovereigntists and nationalists. I think French reporters are very nationalistic in that they really defend the French language and the French culture. Some people confuse this defence of culture and language with a political viewpoint. It's definitely a bias but I'm not using that word too negatively. It's a bias equivalent to the one held by Parliament Hill reporters whom I call Team Canada. They always rah rah Canada. Whatever the issue. It doesn't matter. Sovereigntists are always wrong."[37] Of course, the nationalist position covers a wide spectrum of beliefs: from those who want greater powers for Quebec, or a radically decentralized and much more loosely arranged federal system, to those who support some form of independence. In this context it's sometimes easy to confuse those who believe that the current federal system, Canada as it is now constituted, no longer works in Quebec's best interests with those who want outright independence.

It was especially difficult for reporters who are used to stuffing the stories that they cover into a black versus white, pro versus con, heroes versus villains, federalists versus separatists "box" to capture the nuances and ambivalence – the complex currents of Quebec public opinion. The problem is that many Quebeckers have a divided heart. They remain proud of their Canadian roots and continue to see Canada as a good country even as they identify strongly and fervently with Quebec. They remain loyal to Canada at some level even as they harbour resentments against perceived injustices or want much greater autonomy and more power for the Quebec government. A survey taken during the referendum campaign discovered that two-thirds of Quebeckers still felt "deeply attached to Canada." And these attachments, these bonds of the heart, could be found even among supporters for the Yes side. Another survey, taken four months later when a majority of those who were questioned indicated that they would vote Yes if another referendum were held, showed an astonishing 85 per cent agreeing that "Canada is a country where it is good to live."[38]

Some reporters, such as the CBC's Quebec City correspondent, Tom Kennedy, tried to capture the ironies that were to be found everywhere in Quebec. He remembered covering one women who after much soul-searching had finally decided to vote No. When she was watching the results come in, however, she found herself instinctively cheering for the Yes side to win.[39] Most reporters had few occasions to report on these nuances as they focused on the leaders, the campaigns, and the events of the day. To some degree they missed the main story.

Rhéal Séguin, the Quebec correspondent for the *Globe and Mail*, was angry with English journalists outside of Quebec who ignored the possibilities for change or compromise:

> There is this conscientious effort here of the media, of the Francophone media especially, to give both sides balanced coverage. You don't get that from the English media in the rest of the country. The more you condemn the sovereigntists the better you are. The more that you can defend Canadian unity, whatever model you may be proposing, the better it is. No one is saying, wait a minute. Let's take a look at this thing. What are they proposing? Maybe there is some form of accommodation.[40]

Clearly, debris from the battle over partisan and biased reporting still litters the journalistic landscape. Journalists felt this was the worst assignment because their devotion to professional standards often clashed with the feelings that they had as proud Canadians or Quebeckers and the messages that their audiences wanted to see and hear. But even if one accepts the special difficulties inherent in this kind of battlefield reporting, there are at least two painful and agonizing questions about the CBC's referendum coverage that have to be addressed – questions that will remain open sores.

The first is whether the CBC adequately prepared the country for the possibility of a Yes vote. Or to put the question differently – did coverage lull the country into a false sense of security, into a dreamy and misleading optimism about how well the federalist side was doing? The other question is whether Lucien Bouchard's harsh rendition of Canadian constitutional history – his constant drumbeat of charges and accusations, in which he portrayed Quebec as having been continually betrayed and humiliated by English Canada – was effectively challenged, even questioned, by CBC journalists. Was Bouchard's version of the past with its invented ghosts and nightmares allowed to stand as the truth, at least on CBC television?

Having been accused during the Meech Lake drama of having created a false sense of crisis, the CBC may have been guilty during the referendum of leaning too far in the opposite direction – of not ringing the alarm bells sooner and more loudly. A study conducted by the Fraser Institute suggests that during the campaign's first weeks, English-language TV coverage did not prepare Canadians for the possibility that the sovereigntists could win.[41] News reports focused on infighting among the leaders of the Yes side and poll results showing the federalist forces cruising to an easy victory. The public was given little sense that Quebec opinion was volatile, that there were potential storm clouds on the horizon. Even reporters who had watched Bouchard's brilliant oratorical flourishes for years, who knew that he had the power to bring audiences literally to tears, failed to alert viewers to the possibility that the dynamic might change dramatically when at mid-campaign Bouchard took control of the Yes side. If this were indeed the case then society's faithful watchdogs had fallen asleep.

For instance, CBC's *The National* devoted very little attention to the referendum question even though the question was, to say the least, highly contrived and confusing. To some observers it was an outright set-up, a obvious trap. The question suggested that Quebec sovereignty would not proceed unless Quebec made a proposal to Canada for an unspecified form of partnership. This twisted formula was likely to leave at least some Quebeckers with the hazy impression that a Yes vote did not mean independence or separation from Canada. The strategy of the Yes campaign was to ease the insecurities of "soft" nationalists by suggesting that a Yes vote would not be a dramatic step into the political unknown because some form of partnership with Canada was virtually guaranteed. Needless to say, federalist politicians immediately pounced on the referendum question, arguing that it was little more than a charade or a Trojan horse.

Although the question was dealt with in a news story on *The National* (September 7) and on two occasions by *The National*'s magazine segment, including one quite extensive discussion (October 2), CBC-TV seemed to let the issue drop.[42] The logic on the referendum desk was probably that with the No side far ahead in the polls and with the result of the referendum appearing to be little more that a *fait accompli*, there was little to be gained by inflating the referendum wording into a major news story.

In fact, some would argue that in the first weeks the tone of the coverage was decidedly low-key. Peter Mansbridge has described the difficulty that the CBC faced, the difficulty of trying to awaken viewers to the gravity of the situation when they were apparently not yet prepared to digest the information being given to them:

> There is a similarity between the referendum and every major campaign of the last ten years. During the federal election campaigns, Meech Lake, free trade, and Charlottetown people didn't show interest in the story until the last few weeks. Now is this a failure of the media for not informing the people or the failure of the people for not wanting to know about the issues? It's like a carbon copy of the free trade debate. We spent a year covering Free Trade, all the ins and outs, the arguments over this section

or that section. We got laughed at by the papers and the editorial cartoons. Then came the 1988 federal election and after the debate people were phoning demanding that we do more. Why have you never told us about this?

We could have reported the referendum differently but I'm not sure anybody would have been watching. They didn't feel they were on the edge of a precipice and it sure as hell wasn't our job to come on and tell them that a month from now you may be about to lose your country because there was no reason to say that. There was no evidence to say that. And if we would have gone on heavy with night after night of this kind of stuff in the first half of the campaign we would have been accused of doing exactly what we were accused of doing in Meech — that we were torquing the issue, that we were playing to one side's agenda.[43]

Cynthia Kinch, a senior producer at *The National,* believes that CBC television did the best it could given the unpredictable sea of emotions and factors at play during the referendum. Kinch asks: "Is that our job to prepare people for what the results are? I think we prepared them for the fact that it was going to be a close race. I don't think anyone could have prepared them for it being that close. Who was to know?"[44] Joan Bryden, an Ottawa reporter for Southam, contends that the referendum result shook the confidence of almost everyone in Canadian journalism. As Bryden described the situation: "Everybody was shocked because it went beyond everybody's assumption. Reporters' confidence was shaken in their ability to be pundits and understand what's going on. It's like 'Holy shit did we misread that one' ... now you sort of second guess your assumptions and on the other hand who knows. It's required a huge rethinking."[45]

At least as serious as the charge that the CBC was, in effect, fiddling while Rome was burning is the accusation that CBC journalists never challenged Bouchard's one-sided, distorted, and inflammatory version of Quebec's political history. Much of

Bouchard's campaign rhetoric harped on the supposed betrayal of Quebec's interests during the making of the Constitution Act of 1982 and during the battles over the Meech Lake and Charlottetown Accords. In Bouchard's version of events, the constitution of 1982 was imposed on Quebec against its will, English-Canadian leaders had never bargained with Quebec in good faith, and Quebec was the perpetual victim — the whipping boy of Confederation. Canada had always said no to Quebec's demands. Yet he also claimed that Canada had little choice but to enter into a partnership with Quebec, that a partnership could be taken for granted. In a reply to Bouchard's claims published on February 3, 1996, former prime minister Pierre Trudeau accused the leader of the Yes forces of "demagogic rhetoric" and a "preaching of contempt" that "went beyond the limits of honest and democratic debate." He described Bouchard as an "illusionist."[46]

An independent study conducted for this volume by Mark Simpson found that there were only seven news stories on *The National* and *Sunday Report* that could be described as "challenging" or "adversarial" during the entire length of the referendum. These were stories in which journalists attempted to refute the claims made by political leaders. There were no stories that zeroed in explicitly on Bouchard's "Canada as demon" view of Quebec's history.

The problem for CBC journalists was that they felt they had to wait for the response to Bouchard to come from federalist leaders. It was deemed far more appropriate for the corporation's journalists to cover what the politicians were saying about each other than to be the ones initiating a debate or leading an attack. Past experience had taught CBC journalists about the dangers of even the appearance of partisanship. But virtually no one in the federalist camp rose to the occasion. Federalist leaders may have been wary of taking on Bouchard, given his mounting popularity, or they may have felt that attacking his version of Quebec history would have given his claims greater publicity and hence credibility. In any case the federalist guns were largely silent.

The issue is whether it was now up to the journalistic community to "take on" the leader of the Yes side or allow Bouchard to have what would be, in effect, a free ride. In a scathing indictment, one of Canada's great literary lions, Mordechai Richler, blasted *The National*'s Hana Gartner for an interview that she conducted with Bouchard at the height of the campaign. According to Richler, when "Bouchard went on to say that French Canadians are a people and that it is therefore natural for them to have a country, I waited for Gartner to inquire if Bouchard also favoured nationhood for the Cree, who are also a people. Instead at any moment, it seemed the adoring Gartner would ask Bouchard what his favorite flower was, and had he given Audrey chocolates for Valentine's day."[47] Even more astonishing to some observers was the special documentary on Bouchard hosted by Francine Pelletier. Pelletier's documentary, which appeared on *The National*'s magazine segment, set out to capture 48 hours in the life of the sovereigntist leader. The documentary was filled with bucolic pictures of Bouchard at home in Lac St. Jean and glad-handing on the campaign trail. It's charged that Pelletier never scratched below the surface, asked tough questions, or challenged Bouchard's essential logic and arguments, that she never really took the gloves off. Pelletier admits that she was sympathetic to and fascinated by Bouchard, but claims that she resisted falling under his spell, succumbing to his charm, and that she asked the tough questions.

> I asked him the questions that I thought English Canada wanted to ask him which a Quebecois reporter would not (Why are you such a fickle friend? Why do you think Quebec can have its cake and eat it too? Why do you think that you can hold Canada hostage?). At the same time I asked it with the understanding that I knew that there was more than just a traitor there. I knew the magic he worked and I wanted the rest of Canada to understand that as well. But once someone is the devil incarnate no person, no one documentary, can possibly change that impression. And I didn't.[48]

Joan Bryden believes that it was difficult for reporters to refute Bouchard's claims because of the sheer magnitude of the falsehoods that were being perpetuated by the sovereigntist leader:

Reporters did this fawning coverage. Here's Bouchard. He's exciting and people like him and so that becomes the story. I think we created this St. Lucien business. Lucien did things that should have been challenged by journalists. When Bouchard says something like to hell with the studies on the costs of separation. They don't matter any more. And I'm telling you you'll have a magic wand and poof, there's no cost. It's pretty astonishing that someone gets away with that.

One of the reasons the separatists have been so successful is because they repeat the litany of humiliations and grievances all the time. And you cannot in every story go back and correct the record or try and put balance to the record. You can't do it. It would take up so much blinking space. So they end up getting away with it.[49]

The argument, in effect, was that journalists could never hope to catch up with the sheer torrent of claims made by Bouchard or untangle the many elements that, sewn together, constituted the basis of his position.

But it may also be that after all the controversy and agony that the CBC had been through since the Meech Lake crisis, the reflex reaction of reporters was to avoid doing or saying anything that might be perceived as interfering in the campaign – with the result that the public broadcaster may have become overly cautious, too tied up in knots and inhibitions, too afraid to offend political sensibilities, too afraid to ask tough questions or refute the charges that were being made by either side. If this was the case, then one wonders whether the regime of monitoring, of studies and polls and number counting, of journalists feeling that they were under constant scrutiny, had proved counterproductive. The issue, perhaps, is whether political pressures had finally taken the starch out of CBC journalism. The question is whether all the instances in which the CBC had been treated as a political football, as a political pawn, had finally taken a toll – dampening and inhibiting the public broadcaster at a time when the country needed a strong and courageous voice.

Conclusion

Public broadcasters in virtually every western country have at one time or another come under intense pressure from their political masters. The BBC in Britain, PBS in the United States, France-Television, RAI in Italy, and ARD in Germany, among others, have had to contend with the wrath of politicians who also control their purse strings. Politicians know that their survival often depends on how their actions and policies are reported in the media and particularly on television. For political leaders to have any hope of success they must learn to play the media game. But there is always the temptation, especially when things are going poorly, to use blunter instruments of power and coercion. In most cases political leaders resist this temptation, knowing that there are lines that cannot be crossed without violating the public trust, damaging journalistic freedom, and interfering with the vital ebb and flow of democratic debate.

Canadian leaders have sometimes been unable to live with the media criticism and scrutiny that is the normal traffic of political life. They have resorted to threats and fear tactics, exacting their revenge on those who stir public inquiry and debate. Public denunciation, phone calls to CBC presidents, appointments to the CBC board, the spectacle of parliamentary inquiries, the canceling of programs, and threats of budget cuts have all been used as weapons against the CBC at one time or another. In addition, a system of news monitoring has been put in place to ensure "accountability."

The national unity struggle has been by any measure an extraordinarily difficult story to cover. Journalists are caught between many contending forces. The complexity of the journalistic issues and the many traps that they can easily fall into, their own deeply held emotions and convictions, the expectations of their audiences, the demands of political leaders and pressures within news organizations have all conspired to make national unity the worst assignment for reporters. While the CBC contributed enormously to public debate and understanding during the country's tortuous march from Meech Lake to the 1995 Quebec referendum (and much of its programming was truly excellent), there were instances in which the public broadcaster lost its footing. During the Quebec referendum the question was whether the corporation had become too cautious, too wary in approaching issues that are seen as overly complex or politically sensitive. Questions remain about whether the public was properly prepared for what might well have been a full-scale national catastrophe and why Lucien Bouchard's one-sided and misleading interpretation of Quebec's history was never adequately challenged. One is forced to ask whether, amid all the pressures and uncertainties, the corporation had abandoned the critical guardianship and trusteeship roles so fundamental to journalism and democracy. The whole purpose of public broadcasting, after all, is to allow a society to freely and openly address the nagging and unpleasant problems that it has to deal with if it is to survive.

The CBC, whatever its faults, remains a vital element in national life. It airs more news and documentaries, is more committed to "hard" news, and does more in-depth reporting than any of its rivals. To the extent that attempts have been made to "de-fang" the lion, or at least to make it more timid, the media system as a whole is damaged and weakened. Having a public broadcaster means giving its journalists the freedom to push boundaries, to take unpopular positions, and to challenge the power of the powerful if there are legitimate and compelling reasons to do so.

SEVEN

Bringing You Hollywood: Private Broadcasters and the Public Interest

I n a famous description of the television business, the renegade American journalist and pop hero, Hunter S. Thompson, wrote: "The TV business is a cruel and shallow money trench, a long plastic hallway where thieves and pimps run free and good men die like dogs."[1] When Thompson wrote this piece of "wisdom," there were very few women in television's executive suites — one can presume that they too now die like dogs. What Thompson was portraying was a cutthroat world in which only the most loathsome creatures — the most hardened, cynical and cunning operators — emerge on top of the heap. Those who try to do good, who believe in things, who represent common decency end up in the trash can, figuratively speaking. While Thompson's claim is no doubt overblown, he is not alone in his indictment of TV executives. Writer Peggy Noonan has described TV executives who are responsible for the current crop of children's TV shows as "moral retards." Media critic Michael Medved has described Hollywood's television producers as suffering from "a sickness in the soul" and of working in "a poison factory."[2]

Although harsh criticisms of American television fare are hardly new, what is interesting is the degree to which commercial broadcasters in Canada, the principal importers of American TV shows, have gained the upper hand in the debate over the future of broadcasting. The moral high ground, and the intellectual and political atmosphere, has now shifted so dramatically that private broadcast-ers rarely have to account for any of their actions. Virtually all of the debate swirls around the CBC and the question of whether pub-lic broadcasting has a future. Private networks and stations, which often contribute very little to political debate or national understand-ing, have captured the offensive to the point where the broadcast-ing system seems to be run largely for their benefit.

My contention in this chapter is that private networks are mainly in the business of importing Hollywood hits and do relatively little to keep the public squares of Canadian culture, identity, and politi-cal debate open. And although these broadcasters describe them-selves as "private" they are the beneficiaries of a culture of government subsidies, without which they would likely produce very little Canadian programming at all. As it is they do the minimum. Canadian broadcasting is a prime example of how what appears on one level to be greater competition, because of the continued licensing of new channels and the explosion of cable services, may be producing fewer real choices and less diversity. The weakening of the CBC and the triumph of private broadcasters has meant that it is more difficult to find quality Canadian programming in the media universe. As we devour greater and greater quantities of cul-tural fast food prepared by the Hollywood studios and served to us by private broadcasters, we are less likely to be able to tell our own stories or even after a while to appreciate them or want to see them.

I will begin the chapter by reviewing the arguments being made by those who believe that we no longer need the CBC. The CBC's critics believe that in the fast-changing media cosmos, the CBC rep-resents the broadcasting of a bygone age. Overblown, weighted down by bureaucracy, highly centralized, lacking in the ability to adapt quickly to new situations, and unable to find a new younger audience, the CBC is seen as a muscle-bound dim-witted Neander-thal lurching from one crisis to the next. Eventually, the critics con-tend, the CBC will die a natural death as it slowly loses its audience and as its ability to fulfill its mandate gradually diminishes or falls to others. Why not, they argue, give the old soldier a merciful death and save the taxpayers much needed money?

My goal in this chapter is also to turn the tables by questioning the role played by private broadcasters. My contention is that the economics of broadcasting and the lax standards maintained by the Canadian Radio-television and Telecommunications Commission (CRTC) have conspired to create a broadcasting system that is more Americanized and less unique and original than was the case a generation ago. Private broadcasters such as Can-West Global and CTV reap sizeable profits through the double-barreled strategy of buying big-ticket programs off the shelf in Hollywood while producing poor quality Canadian programs at bargain basement prices. The first guarantees substantial audiences and advertising revenues and the second satisfies, with relatively little effort or expenditure, Canadian content requirements that have been set by the CRTC. To make the game even easier to play, Canadian productions are bolstered by infusions of government grants and subsidies. For the most part, private broadcasters are essentially conservative middlemen – more re-broadcasters and brokers – than true creators or risk-takers. In the end their profits are made by meeting the needs of audiences as consumers rather than as citizens. Unfortunately, if the broadcasting system is to succeed it has to do both.

Private Broadcasters and the War Against the CBC

The CBC's opponents contend that in a time of severe budgetary restraint when hospitals are being closed, medicare is slowly being eroded, and the scandalous level of child poverty has become a national shame and scourge, the CBC is a "frill," an "add-on" that can no longer be justified. While the CBC's budget was reduced by approximately one-third during the 1990s, critics contend that the roughly $854 million allocated by Parliament to the CBC in 1997 is money that could be better spent elsewhere. To some right-wingers, of course, all public institutions are suspect. They believe that the public sector is awash in mismanagement and red tape, and that government agencies by their very nature lack the energy, the

174 · POWER AND BETRAYAL IN THE CANADIAN MEDIA

creative juices and spark, needed for success. The old joke is that the only thing worse than buying a car made by General Motors is buying one made by the government.

The great irony, perhaps, is that the CBC, which has been viewed with such suspicion by politicians of literally every stripe, has come to be seen as a symbol of government bureaucracy and officialdom. The fault may lie with the approach taken by programs such as *The National,* which may come across to some viewers as having a superior and pontificating tone. Although a superb journalist by any standard, Peter Mansbridge, sitting behind his large desk, can sometimes look like the very epitome of distant and unreachable authority. While the CBC has tried to be more user-friendly, more populist, more open, it still has a starchy – even stodgy – image. It has made little headway with younger viewers and listeners, for instance, who may want a more laid-back, funkier approach. One can argue that the CBC succeeds best when it sheds its grave demeanor and becomes zany, warm, irreverent, off the wall, and over the edge. When Mary Walsh of *This Hour Has 22 Minutes* dressed up as Xena, Warrior Princess, to ambush Ontario Premier Mike Harris during a scrum, she was breaking the mold in more ways than one. Her madcap antics represented the view from the bottom up rather from the top down. They reversed the image that many viewers have of the CBC. Similarly Ken Finkelman's *The Newsroom* and *More Tears* showed that the CBC could both laugh at itself and offer viewers a searing critique of the news business. Hockey analyst Don Cherry ("the Prime Minister of Saturday Night," as he's been described by some of his academic critics) also reveals a different side to the corporation. Cherry's "take no prisoners" style appeals to those who prefer their hockey with sharp elbows and blood on the ice.

But even these steps have made it difficult for the CBC to shed its "official" image. To some of its critics the corporation is simply broken beyond repair. The solution is to dismantle the organization, to melt the CBC down to its component parts – perhaps keeping CBC Radio, CBC Newsworld, and a handful of national TV news and current affairs programs, while selling off the rest. Private ownership groups would pick up the pieces, breathing life back into the rotted structures. The result would be a boon for taxpayers and a boon for private industry. Other critics, not so generous, would sell the CBC lock, stock, and barrel.

Commercial broadcasters have complained for years that the CBC takes advertising revenue away from the private sector. Not only is the audience and advertising pie smaller but the CBC provides unfair competition. Private stations are handicapped in having to compete against stations that don't have to meet the bottom line in quite the same way.

The heart of the argument made by the CBC's critics is that the private sector can not only do everything that the CBC can do but it can do it better. Commercial broadcasters have displaced the CBC from the role that it once played as booster rocket of the entire broadcasting system. They point out that Canada is now the second largest exporter of TV programs in the world after the United States.[3] Revenue from Canadian TV and film productions, including foreign location shooting, skyrocketed from $1.4 billion to $2.8 billion (Can.) between 1991 and 1997.[4] Canada has a thriving and dynamic independent film and TV production industry with tentacles that reach across the globe. Productions such as *Road to Avonlea, Traders, Due South, Fashion TV, Care Bears,* and *Babar,* which have been spearheaded by independent producers such as the newly amalgamated Alliance Atlantis productions, have earned worldwide audiences. For instance, *Road to Avonlea,* produced by Sullivan Films, is seen in 122 countries. *Care Bears* and *Babar,* produced by Nelvana, are shown in 145 countries. Moreover, the country's commercial TV networks, principally CanWest Global and CTV, are now able to play in the big leagues and flex real muscles. Global TV's parent company, CanWest Global Communications, generates revenues of close to $1 billion (Can.) annually and CTV's annual revenue approaches $600 million (Can.).[5]

In responding to these arguments, the CBC's defenders argue that the CBC has suffered more than its share of budget cuts compared to many other government agencies and that a decade of downsizing has sapped energies and morale, destroyed careers and production units, and drastically weakened the corporation. Of course the CBC's experience with "learning to live with less" was similar to what was experienced in many other corporations and institutions during the late 1980s and 1990s. But the pain and disfigurement were no less real. As many as 4,000 employees have been let go since 1990, local newsrooms have been either axed or cut back to little more than bare-bones operations, and program budgets have been decimated. The corporation found that with so little "up-front" money to invest in dramatic shows it was simply no longer in the same league with expensive, high-gloss Hollywood shows such as *Frasier*, *ER*, or *Friends*, whose budgets are in the range of $3 million (U.S.) per episode. The CBC has been forced to mount fewer specials, often repeats episodes, and has had to shelve ambitious projects. Indeed, it has had to make a virtue out of necessity by airing marquee programs such as *This Hour Has 22 Minutes* twice a week and *The National* at both 10 and 11 p.m.

Since it cannot compete against blockbuster American hits, the CBC has been forced to retreat into several low-cost programming ghettos. One of them is comedy. Relatively low-budget ensemble productions such as *Royal Canadian Air Farce*, *Sketchcom*, *Broad Side*, and *This Hour Has 22 Minutes* have become the staple of English-language TV. Another and somewhat peculiar twist is that sports has become, in the words of the Mandate Review Committee, "the cornerstone of the English schedule."[6] Indeed, critics complain that the CBC has become a kind of shadow TSN or CTV Sportsnet with sports coverage accounting for over 35 per cent of its prime time audience. Coverage of the NHL playoffs is draped across the schedule literally for months, pre-empting all other programming including *The National*. While wall-to-wall hockey coverage brings in some viewers, others are lost. Viewers who are unable to find their favorite shows in their usual time slots are forced to migrate to other networks. The Mandate Review Committee observed that even the U.S. networks, which tend to put a premium on sports, limit their coverage of the NBA playoffs (for which there is a large and rabid following) only to weekend games. They do not turn their schedules inside-out or perform scheduling contortion acts to nearly the same extent that the CBC does.

To argue that the CBC does a poor job simply because it is a crown corporation dependent on funding from Parliament ignores some important realities. First, it ignores the extraordinary contributions that the CBC has made and continues to make to Canadian life. According to the Mandate Review Committee, "With all its shortcomings, the CBC talks to more Canadians about Canada than any other medium."[7] It remains the central sphere of Canadian public life, providing more in-depth coverage of news and public affairs than any other broadcaster. It is the window through which Canadians witness virtually all of the significant events of national life, whether broadcasting those events is profitable or not. It is also the main stage for Canadian films, music, and comedy. And its programs have sometimes "scaled artistic heights ... that set them apart from any other Canadian broadcaster, and perhaps from any American broadcaster for that matter."[8] A mini-series like *The Arrow,* about the legendary Canadian jet fighter, films such as *Giant Mine,* which depicts the pain and turmoil surrounding a strike at a Yellowknife mine, and *The Boys of St. Vincent,* a harrowing portrayal of abuse at a clergy-run orphanage, and a documentary such as *Dawn of the Eye,* a brilliant history of television news, all reveal disturbing truths that probably wouldn't be told if the CBC didn't exist. For all of its frailty, the CBC was able to launch six new Canadian shows in prime time in January 1998 and another seven in the fall of 1998. The shows covered a wide swath of Canadian experiences. One was a sitcom set in inner Toronto. Another was a comedy about a TV and film producer trying to make it in the big time. There was a crime series featuring an alcoholic Vancouver coroner, a comedy series portraying women throughout history, and a show about the rugged life of B.C. cowboys in the 1940s. There were documentaries about the rough-and-tumble world of NHL hockey, the part that the Mounties have played in Canadian popular culture, the underside of the public relations business, and gang warfare in a poor Toronto neighbourhood.

Some would argue that home-grown indigenous programming is one of the ways in which a society can heal, can put soothing lotions, on its social wounds. As one prominent CBC producer has put it, "Without our own Newharts, our own mystery programs, without our continuing serials, without our own made-for-TV movies, we lose much more than identity. We need comedy and drama to mediate our social problems and to reflect the changing character of our society, to ascertain our values." It's also important to note that the cultural space created by television affects the other cultural spaces in society. For instance, Canadian booksellers know full well that after a book is reviewed on Oprah's Book Club, sales can shoot up dramatically. The problem is that Oprah's tastes run to American regional literature. Canadian books never make it on to the book club despite Oprah's sizeable Canadian audience. The CBC, particularly CBC Radio, is perhaps the only broadcasting institution that attempts to fill this gap.

Second, these arguments ignore the fact that the CBC is an amalgam, a blend, of public and private spending and interests. The corporation has been a key engine for independent TV and film production in Canada, teaming up with independent producers to make and air programs. The CBC provides a vital showcase for Canadian-made feature films, documentaries, and TV series that might never be seen by a large audience if it wasn't for the CBC. But it is also a lifeline for countless independent writers, producers, and other creative people. Having the CBC as a financial and creative partner has often made the difference between success and failure for many independent production companies. In 1997, the CBC also had 30 affiliates that were privately owned and operated. These stations are run as businesses, with the eyes of their owners constantly on the bottom line. And most importantly, the CBC depends on advertising for its survival. In 1996–97, the corporation attracted slightly over $250 million in advertising revenue.

Third, the anti-CBC position presumes that a society doesn't need the things that government spending can provide – investments in basic human services such as schools, hospitals, roads, and what is at least as important, a communication system that links the country together. Even veteran conservatives such as Hugh Segal believe that hatred of government, the blaming of government for all of society's evils, has reached outrageous proportions in certain quarters. He contends that private greed is the prime motivation for those who want to save tax dollars by privatizing, downsizing, and discrediting any activity that involves the use of public funds. According to Segal, what they are asking for is the equivalent of wanting to reduce the costs of a hockey team by eliminating the goalie and thinking that they can still win the game.[9]

It should also be noted that Canada now spends less per capita on public broadcasting than any Western country with the exception of the United States. Where Sweden spends $116, the United Kingdom $60, France $40, and Australia $33, Canada only spent $19 (all figures quoted in Canadian dollars) per capita in 1996.[10]

W.T. Stanbury, a professor in the Faculty of Commerce and Business Administration at the University of British Columbia, claims with regard to Canadian content regulations that viewers are being made to pay for "something that they do not want."[11] The same argument is used with regard to the CBC. People who are not regular CBC viewers, and their number is growing, may feel that their tax dollars are being wasted on something that gives them little if anything in return. The same argument, of course, can be applied to expenditures on any public enterprise – the armed forces, hospitals, schools, highways, etc. Those who believe that we will never have to go to war, who never get sick, who don't have children in school, or who don't benefit when roads are built in another part of the city resent the "waste" of money. Experience in the United States shows that propositions put on the ballot asking for new moneys for schools or police are continually defeated: citizens can be very mean-spirited about paying for any service from which they do not benefit personally. Needless to say, such logic is rooted in ruthless selfishness and is ultimately destructive to the society as a whole.

Perhaps the most important argument in favour of public broadcasting is the increasing power of the huge corporate empires described in chapter three. International news and entertainment moguls such as Rupert Murdoch, Ted Turner, Edgar Bronfman Jr., and Bill Gates have gained a stranglehold over much of what Canadians see, read, and hear. The problem is that if commercial TV networks are primarily pipelines for the delivery of Hollywood products then who in the end will tell Canadian stories, cover Canadian issues and controversies, and deliver Canadian perspectives on the events that shape our lives? Some will argue that only a public broadcaster has the ability to address the needs of Canadians as citizens desirous of information about their country and their lives rather than as customers in a global shopping centre. For many the CBC remains the alternative voice – the only broadcaster that will ruffle feathers, disturb audiences, and probe deeply into issues that affect Canadians. Seventy per cent of its programming is news and current affairs and close to ninety per cent of its prime-time programming is Canadian. The CBC is the national insurance policy against a cultural tsunami, the giant waves of American and international media dominance.

Those who champion the CBC argue that commercial broadcasters cannot be trusted with this responsibility because they are inexorably linked to and dependent on the global giants. They are not interested in bucking trends, committing resources to anything that will not have a financial payback, or offending the interests of other powerful media players.

Critics of the CBC claim that the corporation has already lost the high ground in terms of being the defender of Canadian culture. *The CTV Evening News* attracts larger audiences than CBC's *The National,* programs such as *Canada AM* and *W5* do as good a job as any of CBC's stable of current affairs shows, and CTV stations dominate the local news market. Opponents would also charge that CBC shows have lost their edge and that most of their audiences long ago departed to greener TV pastures. CBC's share of the prime-time English TV audience dipped below 10 per cent in 1998, and CBC radio only captured 7.8 per cent of the AM radio audience and 3.3 percent of the FM listeners.[12] The game has moved elsewhere and the CBC is no longer the main player.

A further criticism is that the CBC is being put to rout at the local level where broadcasting, one can argue, counts the most. In deciding to gut the "regions" in order to preserve resources at the centre, CBC management may have made a drastic miscalculation. Local morning and afternoon drive-time radio shows and supperhour TV news programs took much of the brunt of budget cuts and have not in most cases been able to regain their audiences. In cutting off its regional nose, the corporation may have hurt its national face by not meeting the needs of audiences where those audiences live. The local CBC, from programs such as *Land and Sea* in Newfoundland to *The Eye Opener* in Calgary, is where the heartbeat of cities and provinces and even the country can be heard. The question is whether the CBC still reflects that heartbeat.

There is another, perhaps even more delicate, issue that surrounds regional programming. Some observers would claim that in some locations the CBC is the only news outlet where liberal or even centralist views can be heard. In Alberta, for instance, some analysts claim that almost all of the main news organizations have a right-wing tilt and support the policies of the Klein government. Premier Ralph Klein is protected by high media walls over which his opponents cannot leap. Newspapers are either owned by Conrad Black or belong to the *Sun* chain, both of which do little to hide their strong conservative orientations; talk radio is unabashedly right-wing as is the principal magazine, the crusading and evangelical *Alberta Report*. Private television stations are largely apolitical, focusing on crime, activities around town, weather, sports, and civic boosterism. News operations tend to be low-budget and there is hardly any serious investigative reporting. Coverage of the 1997 Alberta provincial election was so light at one private TV station in Calgary that it spent less than one-quarter of the amount of time covering the election than did local CBC television.[13] In this environment the CBC's role is critical. It is one of the only sources that Albertans can turn to for a different perspective and more in-depth coverage and, indeed, where critics of the Klein government have their turn at the plate. Friends of the CBC contend that if the corporation were taken out of the equation, if it were to suddenly drop off the TV and radio map, there would be an enormous information vacuum, not only in Alberta but in cities and regions across the country.

The existence of the CBC is also of enormous benefit to journalists working for other news organizations. Although journalists have been amongst the keenest cheerleaders for various schemes to dismantle the CBC, they reap tangible rewards from having a competitor "across the street" that can keep their own organizations from drifting into lethargy, scaling back salaries, and lowering journalistic standards. If nothing else, the presence of another news organization acts as a safety net, allowing journalists who feel that their careers or their views are being stifled another option, another place to go. Journalists can only gain, some would contend, if the ocean of Canadian journalism is larger rather than smaller.

It is also important to note that a survey taken in 1995 by Angus Reid found that CBC news and current affairs shows were seen as having a considerably higher level of journalistic credibility than either private or U.S. networks.[14] Another survey taken in 1996 by Louis Harris Canada gave the corporation high marks for "good" news coverage, for fairness, and for covering issues and topics not covered by commercial broadcasters.[15] It may be a strange paradox of the Canadian condition that people want to know that the public broadcaster is there, and they support its values even if they don't regularly watch or listen to the CBC themselves.

Fragmentation Bombs and Canadian Broadcasting

The CBC's opponents claim that it is fruitless to keep propping up the CBC when, like Humpty Dumpty, it is about to fall in any case. The reality is that the corporation will be unable to withstand the competition that will come from the 500-channel universe and the torrent of other new media. Although the CBC still has the obligation to fulfill the broad mandate given to it under the Broadcasting Act of 1991, there are now specialty services devoted exclusively to subjects and viewing audiences that were once the corporation's almost exclusive preserve. The CBC's tasks have been effectively downloaded to or are at least duplicated by other broadcasters perched along the chain-link fence of cable TV. Cable channels now compete against the CBC in areas such as children's television, the fine arts, news and current affairs, documentaries, ethnic programming, sports, science, music, and religious programming. The CBC not only faces stiff competition everywhere that it turns but that competition eats into audiences that were once its own.

Hockey is a prime example of what has happened in the new television universe. The CBC's long reign as the host broadcaster of NHL hockey has, over the period of the last ten years, been jeopardized by the emergence of other outlets. While the CBC, together with Labatt's, has signed a four-year deal with the NHL that will allow it to be the principal Canadian broadcaster until the year 2002, games will also be broadcast on local TV stations, TSN, CTV Sportsnet, and ABC. The result is a veritable feast of coverage for hungry hockey fans. But with the market saturated, audience numbers for the CBC's *Hockey Night in Canada* have declined.

The same can be said of news and current affairs coverage, once a cornerstone of the CBC's mission and identity. Instead of allowing CBC Newsworld to have a distinctive pride of place in the cable strip mall which, one can argue, it well deserved, the CRTC opened the door to a bevy of competitors – CTV N1, CNN, CNBC, PBS, Pulse 24, CPAC, ROBTV, Now TV, etc. News junkies can revel in an endless news cycle, but Newsworld's potential audience has been cut into smaller slivers than it otherwise would have been.

The most painful reality is that the CBC suffers what is in effect a double whammy. Not only is its audience diminished by so much competition but the explosion of cable channels cuts into the CBC's prime audience: educated, middle-class Canadians. Those who subscribe to cable channels or satellite services, and also those who are connected to the World Wide Web, tend to be upscale, wealthier, better informed, and more inclined toward high-brow interests – precisely the constituency that the CBC once counted as its own. Where viewers interested in quality news and current affairs programs were once wedded to the CBC and its flotilla of information programs, they now have a cornucopia of choices from CNBC to PBS to the Discovery Channel to Vision TV. Meanwhile audiences for hit U.S. shows like *Frasier, ER,* or *NYPD Blue,* the main diet of private networks and stations, tend to remain steady.

The problem for the CBC is that the tidal wave of media change is only beginning to be felt. While cable only accounted for approximately 22 per cent of English-language TV viewing in 1998, its share of the audience pie is likely to increase as more and more channels become available.[16] Moreover, as television becomes integrated with the World Wide Web and other media, there will be further shocks to the system. Some observers contend that it is time to shut down the CBC, since investments can only bring diminishing returns, and redeploy resources, talent, and energy along the new frontier of cable services. In this way the Canadian presence on the TV spectrum can be expanded to dozens of channels. The CBC represents a 1950s' model of television broadcasting – the department store. What is now needed is a new decentralized approach based on niche marketing, a realization that there has to be a strong Canadian presence in a variety of TV pockets. It's time the cards were laid out differently.

The CBC's defenders assert that the much-vaunted 500-channel universe, and predictions of a wired world where everyone will be in effect their own broadcaster, is little more than a mirage, an illusion. While a great deal of shifting and sorting still has to occur before we really know how the TV universe will unfold, as stated in chapter four some observers believe that most viewers are only able to cope with a limited number of channels, perhaps 10 to 20, and that stretching the range of choices beyond that point is counterproductive. What propels expansion, of course, is that each person has a different 10 or 20 channels that captivate his or her interest. But at some point the continued expansion of the number of channels and services will mean diminishing returns as the audience is cut into slices that are too small to reap benefits to advertisers. Some cable services are already attracting audiences that are almost negligible, that barely register on the audience Richter scale. Their survival, let alone the survival of a 500-channel universe, is hardly guaranteed.

Izzy Asper, the founder and driving force behind CanWest Global, is banking on the notion that audiences will not want a dizzying array of channels. "What people really want," according to

Asper, "is something simple – one channel that you get to program yourself. Say you want to watch the first episode of *Seinfeld.* You could do that with video-on-demand."[17] Asper holds one of the licenses for a video-on-demand service. His gamble, and it is a gamble, is that people who have trouble programming their VCRs will suddenly have the wherewithal to be able to navigate the labyrinth of a mammoth digital entertainment library with relative ease.

Some observers also question the survival prospects of many of the sites currently on the World Wide Web. Some sites have been able to attract advertising and wide followings – *ESPN's SportsZone,* *E! OnLine,* or MSNBC, for instance. But others, including sites operated by a number of major publications, have had to abandon subscription fees and are searching desperately for advertisers. These sites remain in place as a kind of advertisement for the publication, a billboard in cyberspace, but they do little to engage or attract audiences. It is difficult to imagine these sites rivaling TV as a gathering place for a national community any time soon.

Supporters of public broadcasting believe that the backbone of a strong Canadian broadcasting system is quality programming. They contend that scattering resources, energies, and talent in 20 or 40 or 100 different directions will only weaken the capacity of Canadians to compete, to have any voice at all in the new multi-channel chorus. The old strategy of creating a significant infrastructure, of amassing collective strength in three or four or six channels, is perhaps the only guarantee that important Canadian programs will ever be produced and a Canadian public space maintained. CBC producer Mark Starowicz has argued that now is precisely the time when investing in public broadcasting will count the most. As he has written:

> ... the smart policy is not to dismember or fragment whatever television industries or corporations a country has. It is smarter to double their size and assure that you have global class industrial units. Had the British fragmented the BBC, and flooded their own market ... it would have been the equivalent of dismembering an aircraft industry at the

threshold of the jet travel era. Now they will reap the benefits of nurturing their public sector investment.[18]

James Curran, a British scholar, has documented the ways in which public broadcasters in Britain, Germany, Spain, and Italy have been able to retain their dominant positions. First, there was a conscious decision by regulators not to expand the TV spectrum to the point where it would endanger public service broadcasting. Then the very centrality of the broadcasters to the system allowed them to gather even greater strength. Large revenues and economies of scale permitted public broadcasters to maintain quality and hence their audiences.[19]

The contention is that producing quality television will not only bring Canadian viewers back "home" but make Canadian programs more competitive in the global marketplace. Investing in core networks and stations is not just the better part of valour in terms of securing and protecting Canadian public places, but it's also a good economic bet for the country.

The Failure of Canadian Broadcasting Policy

Canadian broadcasting policy during the 1980s and 1990s was built on the notion that if everything is done to ensure that commercial networks and stations can make sizeable profits, then broadcasters will have more money to invest in Canadian programming. This has led to a fascinating if bizarre twist in logic – that Canadian TV will be Canadianized by first being Americanized. Indeed, the entire broadcasting system is tilted in this direction. The simple economics of television dictate that it is far cheaper to buy a program off the shelf in Hollywood than to produce a program of the same quality in Canada. Commercial broadcasters can buy the rights to a top-tier Hollywood show for between one-fifth and one-tenth of the costs of production. Such discounts are possible because American TV producers have the advantage of a huge domestic market: whatever sales they make overseas become icing on the cake.

The advantage of going Hollywood for Canadian broadcasters is that American shows are a magnet for audiences and advertisers. In fact, broadcasters speak openly about "opportunity cost" – the amount of money that they lose every time a Canadian program is aired in prime time. According to communication scholar Liss Jeffrey, CTV calculates that even a low-rated American series will bring in roughly $2 in revenue for every dollar of cost, while a Canadian show will make only make 62 cents for every dollar expended.[20] CanWest Global estimated that the replacement of a single hour of U.S. programming in prime time by a Canadian show would cost the network close to $3 million a year.[21]

Commercial networks clearly spend as little on Canadian programming as the CRTC will allow them to get away with. CanWest Global spent a measly 18 per cent of its revenue, $67 million, on Canadian programming in 1997. CTV spent $147 million, roughly one-third of its revenue. By contrast, English-language CBC television spent $208 million.[22]

Producing a Canadian TV series involves not only the costs of production and promotion but the shouldering of risks and uncertainties. The series may not be popular with Canadian audiences and may not find the niches in the U.S. and global marketplaces that will ultimately determine its financial success. High-octane American shows such as *Frasier, The X-Files, ER,* or *Ally McBeal* already have high audience ratings, the promotion for the shows leaks across the border from the U.S. networks, and advertisers flock to programs that they see as proven winners. While the networks charge advertisers roughly $15,000 for a 30-second commercial on an average prime-time show, a smash hit can bring three times that amount.

These economic realities have meant that CTV, CanWest Global, and independent stations are primarily rebroadcasters rather than broadcasters. They make their money selling Hollywood TV hits in the Canadian market. In fact, virtually all of the most-watched TV programs in Canada in any given season are American shows. During the 1994–95 season, for instance, only one of the top 20 shows watched in Canada could be considered Canadian. And even this was stretching the point, since NHL hockey, which ranked 20th, can really no longer be considered exclusively Canadian. The top 20 programs in the Toronto market in spring 1998, all American, were the following:

1. *Seinfeld* (CanWest Global)
2. *X-Files* (CanWest Global)
3. *E.R.* (CTV)
4. *Friends* (CanWest Global)
5. *Frasier* (Tuesdays; CanWest Global)
6. *The Simpsons* (CanWest Global)
7. *Frasier* (Thursdays; CanWest Global)
8. *Law & Order* (CTV)
9. *Jeopardy* (CTV)
10. *King of the Hill* (CanWest Global)
11. *60 Minutes* (CanWest Global)
12. *Party of Five* (CanWest Global)
13. *Ally McBeal* (CTV)
14. *Melrose Place* (CTV)
15. *Wheel of Fortune* (CTV)
16. *Beverly Hills 90210* (CanWest Global)
17. *Third Rock From the Sun* (CanWest Global)
18. *The Young & the Restless* (CanWest Global)
19. *NYPD Blue* (CanWest Global)
20. *Dharma & Greg* (CanWest Global)[23]

Canadian content accounts for less than 25 per cent of viewing on English-language television during the crucial 7 to 11 p.m. time period.[24]

The CRTC seems to do everything possible to ensure that U.S. programs enjoy a right of entry into Canadian homes. Canadian content regulations, the heart and soul of the Canadian regulatory system, are less stringent for private broadcasters than for the CBC. Although all broadcasters are obliged to ensure that 60 per cent of all programs are Canadian during the broadcast day, commercial broadcasters are allowed to reduce their "CanCon" quotient to 50 per cent during prime time, the lucrative 6–12 p.m. period. This means that the TV schedule for commercial broadcasters resembles a sandwich. In that 6 p.m. to midnight time period, Canadian programs are the bread, layered around the meat of American shows occupying the 7 to 10 p.m. time slots. But note that as a condition of their licenses, CTV must air 3.5 hours per week of Canadian drama between 8 and 11 p.m, and CanWest Global must broadcast 4 hours per week.

While the CBC is completing a Canadianization process that aims for 100 per cent Canadian content in prime time, Canada's commercial broadcasters have, for obvious reasons, shown little interest in moving in this direction. Although the CRTC is likely to impose more stringent CanCon requirements on the commercial networks in 1999, the networks always seem to be able to dodge the bullet. They put as little as possible into Canadian content and squeeze the most out of imported Hollywood productions.

The CRTC also allows simultaneous substitution. This policy allows American TV signals to be blocked when Canadian and American networks are airing the same programs during the same time periods. Indeed, Canadian broadcasters deliberately match their schedules with those of U.S. border stations so that hit shows such as *E.R.* or *Frasier* are shown simultaneously on U.S. and Canadian stations. With U.S. signals erased from the ether, Canadian advertisers have the stage to themselves. This means that there is little incentive for Canadian advertisers to try to reach Canadian audiences via U.S. border stations. The benefits of simultaneous substitution are significant. In 1995, for example, when because of scheduling difficulties with its affiliates, CTV was unable to synchronize its Friday night showing of *Due South* with that of U.S. stations, an estimated 600,000 viewers migrated to the American broadcasters. According to one estimate, simulcasting is worth $100 million annually to Canadian broadcasters.[25] Simulcasting ensures that rather than being penalized for showcasing top-rated Hollywood shows, commercial broadcasters are given every incentive to do so.

Critics of commercial broadcasters believe that they benefit from an entire ensemble of built-in rewards. Right-wing commentators often have a field day lambasting the CBC because it depends on government funding, but they conveniently ignore the fact that commercial broadcasters are also dependent on government largesse to keep them afloat. The most important break that commercial broadcasters receive from the government is that they are allowed to occupy a place on the broadcasting spectrum for what some see as very little cost. They are given an extraordinarily valuable piece of electronic real estate without having to pay the real value of the property. The main broadcasters paid just $70 million (Can.) in license fees to the CRTC in 1995–96, while cable and pay-TV franchises paid $104 million (Can.). These numbers may seem sizeable at first glance, but one has to remember that the amount paid by each broadcaster was relatively small. While journalists carp about government debt and deficits, they have never turned their sights on commercial broadcasters – asking them to pay more for "renting" the public airwaves.

Another advantage is that when networks and stations face license renewal hearings, the CRTC does not allow a rival owner to bid for the license. Unlike the oil and gas industry where leases can be acquired by other companies when contracts come up for renewal, broadcasters never have to look nervously over their shoulders thinking about what competitors might offer in their place.

Yet another benefit given to private broadcasters has been the licensing of so many cable services. CTV has become a dominant player on the cable highway with either a majority or minority stake in CTV News 1, CTV Sportsnet, Outdoor Life, History Television, The Comedy Channel, Report on Business Television, and The Women's Television Network. One is almost tempted to say that a large portion of the CBC's mandate has been redistributed to CTV through the awarding of cable licenses. So while the CBC still shoulders the responsibility of fulfilling a wide mandate, CTV not only competes against CBC in key areas that were once the public broadcaster's special preserve but it has been given (arguably) some of the most valuable real estate on the cable mountaintop. CHUM and Shaw Communications are also major players in the cable casino game. CHUM has interests in Bravo, Much Music (as well as its French-language counterpart Musique Plus), Pulse 24 (a 24-hour regional news channel serving Southern Ontario), and Space: The Imagination Station. Shaw has investments in YTV, Family Channel, Teletoon, and Movie Max among others.

Cable services such as the religious broadcaster Vision TV and CPAC claim that they have been relegated to the very back rows of the cable universe after being bumped from more prominent positions. They have charged that cable operators have given their corporate allies, broadcasters such as CTV and CHUM, the front row seats. This certainly isn't the case for all of the CTV or CHUM cable franchises, some of which are no doubt in danger of being lost in the haze of the cable universe.

Commercial broadcasters also feast on a smorgasbord of government subsidies. Commercial projects qualify for federal tax credits, support from the license fee program of the Canadian Television and Cable Production Fund (three-quarters of which comes from the federal government and the rest from the cable industry), the equity investment fund administered by Telefilm Canada, and provincial tax credits. Take, for instance, the funding package that gave life to *Flesh and Blood*, CTV's new and much-heralded dramatic series. *Flesh and Blood* cost over $1 million (Can.) per episode to make; a large sum by Canadian standards. Public money in the form of federal and provincial tax credits, investments by Telefilm Canada, and a grant from the license fee program accounted for just over 50 per cent of the costs.[26] The CBC, of course, benefits from the same mountain of subsidies. According to one estimate, a TV series bought by the CBC, produced outside of Montreal or Toronto and costing approximately $800,000 per episode, could have as much as 83 per cent of its costs covered by the public purse.[27]

Critics of commercial broadcasters claim that while Canada's broadcasting policy has created profitable television franchises, profits have yet to be used to produce memorable Canadian programming. The gamble on which the entire system rests, that sizeable profits will translate into a legacy of outstanding programs attracting a Canadian mass audience, has yet to be realized. The charge made against commercial broadcasters is that they are guilty of the broadcasting equivalent of "clear cutting." They strip the broadcasting system of its most lucrative elements and then fail to invest in the talent, infrastructure, and ideas needed to create a truly outstanding broadcasting industry. When they produce Canadian television programs, they are only going through the motions. They produce shows that follow the most conventional formulas, take few chances, appeal to the lowest common denominators, and break no new ground. John Haslett Cuff arrived at the following harsh conclusion in his 1996 *Globe and Mail* article titled "Private Sector Not Fit to Fill Shoes of Public Broadcasters":

> ... the overwhelming bulk of television produced by the private sector in Canada is mediocre, mind-numbing pap, whether comedy, drama or documentaries. And after more than three decades, neither CTV nor Canwest/Global is any more noticeably committed to producing or showing quality television. These rebroadcasting services seem to exist primarily to enrich their owners by showing either U.S. programs already available to viewers from U.S. networks or by manufacturing so-called action adventure trash (*Poltergeist, The Legacy, FX: The Series, Once a Thief*). While they kick and whine constantly about the admittedly spineless Canadian-content requirements imposed upon them by the Canadian Radio-television and Telecommunications Commission, and lobby fiercely for the demise of the CBC, Canada's private broadcasters are neither willing to provide nor capable of providing the sort of quality programming produced by the public sector.[28]

Perhaps the most devastating indictment is that even when they produce Canadian shows commercial broadcasters make few attempts to tell Canadian stories or reflect the country to itself. In fact, private broadcasters are caught in the jaws of another iron law of TV economics: the so-called "cultural discount." The brutal reality is that in order to attract international audiences, and hence be profitable, the national characteristics of a show sometimes have to be suppressed. One of the strategies in selling programs in the U.S. or overseas is to strip them of their distinctly Canadian outlook, making them look and feel as if they could take place literally anywhere. Sometimes producers go to great lengths to "deCanadianize" a show. They hide or downplay any readily identifiable Canadian features of a location or plot so that a comfort zone can be achieved with American audiences. This camouflaging or masking also works in Europe and Asia where audiences "think it's American television anyway," which is what attracts them to the show in the first place. Of course, not all successful Canadian TV exports follow this pattern. *Due South, Road to Avonlea, Flesh and Blood,* and *Traders* are examples of shows that have a unique Canadian angle or signature, and yet have sold internationally. But there is still a great deal of trepidation among producers who have come to believe that if a series is too Canadian, if it has a special Canadian flavour, then it won't be marketable globally. For producers who have to be conscious of the bottom line, avoiding "in your face" Canadian themes may be the better part of valour. *North of 60* and *Black Harbour,* both of which had strong and unmistakeable Canadian story lines and locales, never made it in the big leagues of international television.

Commercial TV's detractors paint a dismal picture of broken promises, minimal efforts to meet Canadian content obligations, and milking of the government's broadcasting policy and government subsidies for everything that they are worth without contributing anything substantial in return. To their critics, commercial broadcasters do little that is special, meaningful or uplifting, that digs deeply into Canadian life or that shows the country to itself. They claim that private broadcasters continually get the best seats at the front of the bus without having to pay the full fare. If the CBC were taken out of the equation – either broken up, melted down or sold off – the vacuum would simply be enormous. Supporters of public broadcasting make little secret of their view that the private broadcasting industry, as currently constituted, would fall far short of filling the gaping hole that would be left.

Supporters of commercial broadcasters point to programs such as *Due South, Flesh and Blood, Traders,* and *Power Play,* arguing that they have long since arrived on the scene as major contributors to Canadian drama. They have done as much to create television's land of the imagination, to make the country laugh and to attract Canadian audiences, as the CBC has, and perhaps more.

Newton Minow, a former chairman of both the Federal Communications Commission and PBS in the U.S., in speeches delivered in 1961 and 1991, made a special plea for strengthening public broadcasting as a way of offsetting the plundering commercialism of private networks. In the first of his "wasteland speeches," Minow acknowledged that television had produced many hours of wonderful entertainment and even greatness. But he was disturbed by the numbing sameness and sheer boredom produced by so much of what was on. He issued the following challenge to his audience:

> I invite you to sit down in front of your television set when your station goes on the air and stay there without a book, magazine, newspaper ... to distract you – and keep your eyes glued to that set until the station signs off. I can assure you that you will observe a vast wasteland.
>
> You will see a procession of game shows, violence, audience participation shows, formula comedies about totally unbelievable families, blood and thunder, mayhem, violence, sadism, murder, western bad men, western good men, private eyes, gangsters, more violence and cartoons. And, endlessly, commercials – many screaming, cajoling, and offending. And most of all boredom. True, you will see a few things you will enjoy. But they will be very, very few. And if you think I exaggerate, try it.
>
> Is there one person in this room who claims that broadcasting can't do better?[29]

Minow's invitation mirrors the great debate in Canadian broadcasting. The claim made by commercial broadcasters is that the CBC can and should be easily dispensed with because private broadcasters can now be the engines for quality Canadian programming. The position of those who support public broadcasting is that if the CBC were to "fade to black," to use Wayne Skene's description, commercial broadcasters would be incapable of producing anything more than a cultural wasteland.[30]

Conclusion

A central thread in this book is the notion that the Canadian public is being betrayed by those who care much more about lining their pockets than about the survival of a distinct Canadian culture or serving the needs of citizens. Government leaders, industry regulators, and private broadcasters have created a system that lavishes rewards on those who bring the most popular American programming and values to Canadians, who have, in effect, helped "Disneyize" the country. While a vigourous debate swirls around the CBC and its prospects for survival, the actions of private broadcasters are rarely placed under the spotlight.

But there may be a deeper and more pervasive phenomenon at work. It may be that Canadians have now become so oriented to Hollywood, so intoxicated by the entertainment and consumer culture created by the giant media empires, that they have lost interest in what is taking place in their own backyards. Or to put it differently, perhaps what is taking place in their own backyards now resembles what is taking place everywhere else, since to a large degree people everywhere occupy or at least share the same cultural space. John Meisel, one of Canada's leading thinkers and a former chairman of the CRTC, once proposed what many in Canada might see as an unthinkable proposition. He argued that: "Inside every Canadian whether she or he knows it or not, there is, in fact, an American. The magnitude and effect of this American presence in us varies considerably from person to person, but it is ubiquitous and inescapable."[31] One can argue that what Meisel was referring to and what Canadians have digested is not so much genuine American culture as a kind of homogenized international shopping centre culture that permeates and is being replicated all over the world.

Nonetheless, the reality may be chilling for Canadian nationalists and for supporters of the CBC. The simple fact is that Canadians do not necessarily see Hollywood TV shows as foreign or identify with Canadian programs simply because they originate in Canada. Identities are no longer clear-cut. They are multi-layered and multi-faceted. Richard Collins, an Australian scholar who has studied Canadian television, has characterized Canada as a "new society," a post-modern and post-national state where the old definitions of loyalty have been washed away.[32] *Toronto Star* columnist Richard Gwyn has arrived at similar conclusions about "the unbearable lightness of being Canadian."[33] In this context, Canadians have long seen it as their right to have as much access to U.S. television as they can possibly get, and any attempt to de-Americanize Canadian TV offerings is sure to provoke a considerable outcry. Perhaps the private networks cannot be blamed for simply giving Canadians the television that they want.

There is also the sense that the CBC has become the victim of a self-fulfilling prophecy, a kind of Catch-22. The CBC has been so battered, so beleaguered, that its very weakness has become the rationale for closing it down. Unable for budgetary reasons to compete against Hollywood drama, to be a more vital alternative at the local level, and cast adrift in a sea of cable competition, the corporation is no longer the central forum of Canada's cultural or political life. As its ratings continue to plummet, the case for supporting and maintaining a strong public broadcasting arm is no longer as compelling. The CBC's lack of firepower is used as evidence to demonstrate that public broadcasting has little appeal.

The CRTC's commitment to toughen Canadian content requirements may count for very little in the scheme of things. Although James Curran argues that effective public regulation can make private broadcasters as integral a part of a public service broadcasting system as are public broadcasters, CanCon regulations as currently structured are unlikely to do the job.[34] In a scathing indictment of the current system, W.T. Stanbury notes that CanCon requirements are geared to citizenship, not content. The CRTC awards CanCon credits based on the nationality of key production personnel, virtually regardless of the topics covered in their songs, films, or TV programs. Stanbury quotes an editorial in the *Ottawa Citizen* that complained:

> When Canadian singer Alannah Miles crooned about Mississippi and that "slow Southern style" in "Black Velvet," CanCon gave it the Maple Leaf seal of approval. Ditto for Amanda Marshall's "Birmingham" (that's in Alabama, for anyone who hasn't been south of Windsor). All sorts of country artists singing in fake Nashville drawls score, too, because they have Canuck passports tucked into their cowboy boots. In fact, very few Canadian recording artists actually make clear references to things Canadian because they know the real prize, the American market, won't know what to make of them.[35]

The task for government and for the CRTC is to devise rules of the game that will widen the media choices available to Canadians rather than just giving Canadians much more of the same thing. One obstacle will be pressures from the Americans, at forums such as the World Trade Organization, to prevent Canada from keeping protectionist policies with regard to television. Canada might have to negotiate exemptions from international law and trade practices.

Often forgotten in the debates over broadcasting policy is that threats to the country's survival are real. When federal and provincial governments devise strategies for the next Quebec referendum, they seem willing to threaten and envision fierce and costly struggles over the conditions of separation. But in their planning they seem to have neglected the most elementary fact: a national community can only exist if citizens share common experiences and assumptions. Without these connections, and without the communications policies that make these connections possible, loyalties cannot be maintained. Finding new and innovative ways to finance Canadian broadcasting is a small price to pay in the battle to maintain a distinctive Canadian identity. Preventing Canadians from becoming "strangers in television's land of the imagination" will also prevent Canadians from becoming strangers to each other.

EIGHT

The Winds of Right-Wing Change in Canadian Journalism

At first glance right-wing forces appear to be in defeat and disarray on the battlefield of Canadian politics. There have been numerous attempts by Preston Manning and by leading right-wing thinkers and activists to bring unity to conservative forces by merging the Reform and Progressive Conservative parties. The stark reality facing conservatives is that a continued fracturing of the right-wing vote is likely to ensure the Liberal Party remains in power in Ottawa indefinitely. But despite these efforts, the chasm has not been easy to bridge. Building a "big tent" party capable of providing shelter to people with a wide diversity of views seems particularly painful for parties guided by ideological purity and an unwillingness to bend on what many see as sacred principles. The egos and pride of the leaders, the different attitudes of the parties toward populist initiatives, Reform's origins in western alienation, Social Credit, and religious fundamentalism, and the fact that Reform emerged in part as an angry protest against the policies of a Progressive Conservative government make any rapprochement difficult and uneasy. Divisions between so-called fiscal conservatives – who want a smaller role for the state in the economy, governments to be run as a business, and a climate that will foster growth and investment – and social conservatives – who want greater state involvement in legislating morality whether on abortion, criminal justice or "family" values – make for quarrelsome politics.

While the Reform Party and the Progressive Conservatives continue both to pursue unity and to compete with each other – each of them growing weaker and ever more exhausted by the process – right-wingers need not despair. The right may to be unable to form a united front to contest federal elections, but a right-wing agenda dominates public debate. Whether it's the dismantling of the welfare state and the health care system, the retreat by governments from direct involvement in the economy, pressures to deliver deeper tax cuts, the widespread acceptance of free trade, or the increased salience given to law and order and "family" values, conservative perspectives have shaped the policy debate in dramatic ways.

The triumph of a right-wing agenda is not simply, one can argue, the result of failures of government programs or flavour-of-the-month ideas that have caught the momentary fancy of the public. The legitimacy of conservative viewpoints is the product, rather, of a sustained and concerted effort. A right-wing information infrastructure has been built up over the last 20 years – an infrastructure that has the capacity to shape public opinion through a variety of means. The rise of right-wing pundits, the influence of think tanks such as the Fraser and C.D. Howe Institutes, the conservative ideological tilt and corporate boosterism of Canadian newspapers are all evidence, one can argue, of the extent to which conservative institutions and ideas now dominate the public sphere.

This chapter will discuss what I see as the merging of journalism and active politics and the reasons why conservative viewpoints have achieved such a prominent position in recent policy debates in Canada. The focus will be on two simultaneous developments that are transforming the face of Canadian journalism: the rise of right-wing pundits as major actors on the Canadian political stage and the extraordinary power of media barons such as Hollinger's Conrad Black and the Sun Media's Paul Godfrey. I will also describe the emergence of think tanks as major players in policy debates.

The point is not to wage war against right-wing perspectives but to argue that it is essential for citizens to have access to a full range of views if society is to remain healthy and vibrant. To the extent that the range of opinions to which we are exposed is limited, then society as a whole becomes impoverished. While one can argue that Canadians are presently exposed to crosswinds brought by many contending views, the fear is that the developments described in this chapter can lead to distortions and abuse. The chapter is meant to be provocative, to stimulate thinking about what some see as the new shape of Canadian journalism and indeed of Canadian democracy.

Pundits and Politics

Pundits are journalists who make their living by commenting on rather than reporting the news. They are predominantly newspaper and magazine columnists, radio talk show hosts, and commentators who appear on TV news and magazine shows. Their positions and credibility are established by their colourful views, their ability to goad and entertain their audiences, and their credentials as veteran journalists who have special insights or information of some kind. Their faces and voices have become familiar to many Canadians. Although Canada has not been able to foster a class of celebrity journalists commanding huge salaries to nearly the same degree as has the United States, pundits are at the top of the journalistic food chain. Jeffrey Simpson, David Frum, Barbara Amiel, Rafe Mair, Jean Cournoyer, Jean Lapierre, Richard Gwyn, Andrew Coyne, Dave Rutherford, Norman Spector, Mordecai Richler, Peter C. Newman, Chantal Hebert, Allan Fotheringham, and Diane Francis are among the big hitters in the world of Canadian political pundits. Collectively they wield an enormous influence over public opinion, and as individuals they are far more influential than any ordinary Member of Parliament could ever hope to be.

The term "pundit" can be stretched to include academics who write for and appear frequently in the media. Michael Bliss of the University of Toronto, Alain Gagnon from McGill, David Bercuson, Roger Gibbins and Tom Flanagan of the University of Calgary, Josée Legault of the University of Montreal, Daniel Latouche at the University of Quebec at Montreal, and Guy Laforest from Laval are among those scholars who have high media profiles.

Howard Kurtz has argued that "the center of gravity" in journalism has shifted "from those who ask questions to those who seem to have the answers."[1] While columnists and other commentators have always played an influential role, that role has been magnified in recent years. The explosion of news outlets in the last 20 years has given pundits many more opportunities to be seen and heard. From Sunday morning television, to the myriad of CBC news and current affairs programs, to talk shows on private radio there is now a vast space occupied by journalists and academics who have ideas to sell, can speak in catchy phrases, and are willing to speak authoritatively and present themselves as experts on a bewildering variety of topics. On CBC alone one can see or hear the same "opinion meisters" over and over again on local TV news panels, on Newsworld programs, on morning news shows, on *The National*'s magazine segment, and on national and local radio programs.

One of the shifts that has taken place within journalism is the extent to which an increasing number of journalists have become ardent political activists. Where objectivity was once the gold standard on which the professional credibility of journalists rested, today the rules seem to have changed. Some journalists have been able to enhance their status by openly championing partisan positions and causes. We have in some senses gone back to the days of the party press, the period from 1870 to at least 1940, when fierce and zealous partisanship by journalists was the order of the day. Politics and journalism are no longer separate estates locked in a relationship of conflict and symbiosis, but are merging in new ways. In many cases the veneer of journalistic objectivity is wearing increasingly thin or becoming non-existent.

David Frum, a columnist for the *Sun* and *National Post* newspapers and a frequent guest on TV and radio panels, is part of this new breed of journalists who have made punditry and political activism into a career. As one of the driving forces behind efforts to unite the Reform and Conservative parties, Frum crosses back and forth between political action and journalistic advocacy. What makes him so valuable on the opinion circuit is that his views on virtually any topic are reliable and predictable. Frum's positions are unwaveringly and ardently right-wing. And far from hiding his political passions, he parades them and to some degree has come to symbolize them. Apparently his relentless promotion of right-wing causes reinforces rather than detracts from his success as a journalist.

Hugh Segal is another politician cum journalist. Although Segal was an assistant to Federal Conservative Party Leader Robert Stanfield, a deputy minister in the Ontario government, a Chief of Staff to Prime Minister Brian Mulroney, and a candidate for the leadership of the Progressive Conservative Party, it was as the resident Tory on *Canada AM*'s political panel and on CBC election shows that brought him to the attention of Canadians. One can argue that Segal benefits from the fact that both of these roles reinforce each other. Segal's position as a Tory insider lends credibility to his role as a pundit, while his television appearances increase his standing in the party.

Norman Spector is another example of a pundit who has hopscotched between journalism and politics. A national columnist for the *Globe and Mail* and a panelist on *Newsworld Reports,* Spector served as Chief of Staff to Brian Mulroney and then as Canadian Ambassador to Israel. Before returning to Canada he served as publisher of the *Jerusalem Post*, a paper owned by Conrad Black.

Part of the reason for the special prominence of right-wing pundits is that many public affairs programs have an adversarial structure. They use a pro-con, for and against, liberal versus conservative format. Booking someone who can represent a conservative point of view is almost mandatory. The most blatant example of the format is CNN's *Crossfire*, where conservatives and liberals are pitted against each other in what often ends up as little more than a shouting match. The same is true of the legendary *The McLaughlin Group* on PBS. Members of the group play out their adversarial roles much like actors in a sitcom.[2] Panelists almost become caricatures clashing in predictable ways. The verbal fisticuffs between liberals and conservatives are part of the entertainment. According to one observer, people tune in to watch the show in the same way that people go "to stock car races: not to see who wins but to see who crashes."[3]

This same right vs. left format, this same generic model, is also part of the Canadian media diet. CBC's *Newsworld Reports*, for instance, airs a panel consisting of Norman Spector and Michael Dector, a former advisor to Ontario NDP leader Bob Rae. A unique twist in the Canadian situation is that panelists are often chosen because they represent views in particular regions of the country. This is certainly the case on CBC Radio's *This Morning* and on CTV's *Sunday Edition*, hosted by Mike Duffy.

The important point is that people are often chosen to appear because they have an identifiable bias, because they are firmly identified with a cause. This format has become deeply entrenched within the conventions of journalism. The CBC has been particularly conscious of the need to have a variety of points of view represented in news reports and on panel discussions. As described earlier in this book, charges of biased reporting during the Meech Lake negotiations, and the controversy that erupted following the airing of *The Valour and the Horror*, made the CBC hyper-sensitive about any programming that could be construed as one-sided. The corporation responded by putting a number of internal checks in place. During elections or on particularly controversial issues such as the constitution, the CBC has instituted a kind of bean-counting exercise where every appearance is categorized and tallied to determine whether coverage has been "balanced." The CBC's handbook of journalistic standards and practices addresses the need to capture the fullest range of opinions in the following way:

> A journalistic organization, to achieve balance and
> fairness, should ensure that the widest possible range
> of views is expressed. Almost any opinion may con-
> tain a grain of truth that helps to illuminate the
> whole truth. But proper account must also be taken
> of the weight of opinion which holds these views
> and its significance or potential significance. The
> challenging of accepted orthodoxies should be re-
> ported but also should the established views be
> clearly put.[4]

Lance Bennett among other scholars has suggested that virtually all aspects of news reporting and commentary are "indexed" to reflect "the range of views expressed in mainstream government debate about a given topic."[5] As Bennett explains: "Indexing constitutes a quick and ready guide for editors and reporters to use in deciding how to cover a story. It is a rule of thumb that can be defended against questions from uneasy corporate managers and concerned citizens alike."[6]

In organizing panels, it is difficult to come up with the right combination, the combustible material that will make sparks fly. But the balancing has to have political subtlety and fit the "rule of thumb" that Bennett refers to. The CBC's most famous and successful panel was on radio's *Morningside*, a program that has faded into memory for many Canadians since it was replaced in 1997. It featured former Ontario NDP leader Stephen Lewis as the representative of the left, former Quebec and federal cabinet minister Eric Kierans as the nominal liberal, and Dalton Camp, a veteran Tory insider, as the conservative member of the panel.

Politicians have long realized that what pundits say can have a major effect on public opinion. This view is substantiated by research that has been conducted by Benjamin Page among others. According to Page: "Research has indicated that experts' views, as presented by the media, have a significant impact on public opinion: when experts speak in favor of a policy proposal, public opinion tends to move toward supporting that proposal."[7] Of course, pundits are invariably presented as experts – that's why they are invited to appear in the first place. Writer Eric Alterman has concluded, at least with regard to the American experience, that it is "the thinking of these pundits that determines the parameters of political discourse in the nation today."[8]

The trend, however, is for pundits to become surrogates or stand-ins for politicians. Political leaders realize that because of the high levels of cynicism and distrust that citizens have toward politicians, much of what they say is discounted. If the same message is delivered by a journalist it is likely be viewed as more credible, as more believable to the public.

Politicians also know that when they appear on panel discussions they will likely face tough questioning from journalists who believe that it is their job to debunk or unmask the pretensions of political leaders. Larry Sabato and others have written about the credos of "attack journalism"; the "cult of toughness," the "machismo" that pervades the journalistic culture with regard to politicians.[9] Watching political leaders run the gauntlet of cynical, "gotcha" questions has become one of the rituals of North American political life. And politicians, as much as they crave the public spotlight, are wary of the many traps that are continually being set for them. They have learned to avoid the cameras and the microphones unless they have some means of controlling the nature of the interview. Pundits, on the other hand, are likely to be treated with respect by those interviewing them. Journalists who may score points by ambushing a politician are likely to lose standing if they do the same thing to a professional colleague.

The rise of pundits, one can argue, also coincides with a continued erosion in the influence of politicians. The system of party discipline in the House of Commons makes Members of Parliament little more than spokespeople for the party line. Those who buck the party or stray off course on major issues soon pay the price. They face expulsion or demotion (as was the case with Liberal John Nunziata, who now sits as an independent, and former Reform Party stalwart Jan Brown) or are sent to languish in political obscurity at the back benches – the deadly permafrost, the Siberia, of Canadian politics. Their lack of power, and the straitjacket of party discipline, makes them unappealing to the media as prospective guests or commentators. And this lack of media exposure reinforces their powerlessness. If they are not on, not heard, not visible, then they can't reach their publics and are denied the status, the glow of importance and authority, that comes from appearing in the media.

In his book on talk radio and television in the United States, *Hot Air*, Howard Kurtz describes the new power relationships created by the prominence that pundits have achieved. Leading Washington politicians and bureaucrats carefully nurture relationships with the most influential pundits. They will often phone several times a week, lavish them with gossip and inside information, and aggressively promote themselves and their policies. The objective behind this courtship is to turn pundits into stand-ins for political parties or leaders so that their perspectives and concerns as well as their "line of the week" can be pushed on the Sunday morning TV shows and on Monday morning talk radio. Politicians use pundits to float trial balloons, attack opponents (leaving their own hands unblemished), or spread rumours.

Of course, the pundits have come to depend on these relationships. Without these contacts and tips, they would lose their value as experts with insider knowledge. The value of their own currency would diminish.

Another trend is the degree to which even routine news stories have become opportunities for punditry. Interpretive reporting has, to some extent, pushed objective journalism into the background. Reporters now feel that they are not doing their jobs unless their reports are heavily salted with their own views, their often instant off-the-cuff analysis, of the events that they are covering. As Thomas Patterson of Harvard University has described this shifting of the geological plates within journalism:

> The interpretive style elevates the journalist's voice above that of the news maker. As the narrator, the journalist is always at the center of the story, so much so that during the 1992 general election, for example, journalists spoke six minutes for every minute that the candidates were shown speaking. A viewer who watched the network news every night of the general election would have heard less from the mouths of Clinton, Bush and Ross Perot than from viewing a single presidential debate. During the 1960s, in contrast, correspondents and candidates shared equal billing on the nightly news. Today, viewers and readers are exposed mainly to the journalist's view of politics.[10]

According to Patterson, the percentage of interpretative reports on the front page of the *New York Times* exploded from 8 per cent in 1960 to 80 per cent of all stories in 1992.[11]

A report on television coverage of election campaigns by the Twentieth Century Fund condemned reporters for the editorial "kickers" or "stingers" with which they invariably end their news stories. One participant in the study argued that: "It's the sneer, the smirk, the choice of language, the often snap and harsh judgements that are made on the fly that bother people."[12]

Although punditry may have yet to penetrate into every nook and cranny of journalism, there is little dispute that in television news stories, journalists have come to occupy centre stage. They dominate the events that they are reporting on so completely that political leaders are often reduced to being props or backdrops for stories that journalists want to tell. American researcher Kiku Adatto has documented the extent to which the amount of time allotted for political leaders to be heard in TV news stories – that is, the length of sound bites – has evaporated almost to the vanishing point.[13] Sound bites have become little more than sound nibbles. During the 1968 U.S. presidential election, candidates spoke for an average of 42 seconds per quote – enough time, one can argue, for them to complete a full sentence, put forward a proposal, or enunciate an idea. During the 1996 U.S. presidential election, clip time had been reduced to less than 8 seconds.

The pattern in Canada is just as appalling. A study conducted by the Fraser Institute's National Media Archive found that the average length of a clip during the 1997 Canadian federal election was 8.2 seconds on CBC and 7.1 seconds on CTV.[14] While CBC Newsworld made a point during the election of broadcasting at least one speech by each party leader in its entirety and Canadians watched leaders nervously spar with each other in the leaders' debate, for the most part the only impressions that Canadians had of their leaders was what they gathered in the bits and pieces presented by TV journalists. Canadians are rarely exposed to their leaders for anything longer than the time it takes for them to blurt out 8 or 10 words.

Many Canadians were taken aback in December 1996 when Prime Minister Jean Chretien appeared at a CBC Town Hall meeting. The prime minister's thoughts seemed disjointed, his speech garbled, and he fumbled even the most basic questions from the audience. Prolonged exposure showed a different prime minister than the one that Canadians were used to seeing in 7-second clips on the evening news.

One wonders how events might have changed if some of the great speeches of history – Churchill's stiff-necked call to arms after the British retreat from Dunkirk in 1940, Martin Luther King, Jr.'s riveting and majestic "I have a dream" speech during the March on Washington in 1963, or John F. Kennedy's stirring "I am a Berliner" speech at the height of the Cold War – were reduced to a 7-second sound bite with journalists explaining the strategy behind the speech rather than what was said.

Politicians, of course, have long since adapted to the requirements of TV news. They come to interviews or news events prepared with colourful, biting, or humorous one-liners – the flavourful bite-size pieces that reporters need for their stories. One-liners will often be repeated a number of times so that reporters don't miss the messages that the politicians want sent. Newt Gingrich, the former Speaker of the U.S. House of Representatives, once described to reporters how he shaped his own behaviour to fit the media frame:

> Part of the reason I use strong language is because
> you all pick it up ... You convince your colleagues
> to cover me calm, and I'll be calm. You guys want
> to cover nine seconds, I'll give you nine seconds,
> because that is the competitive requirement. I've
> simply tried to learn my half of your business.[15]

Some would contend that the reduction of thoughts and proposals into tiny sound bites is the ultimate distortion, the ultimate corruption, of our democracy. What citizens see and hear of their leaders rarely extends beyond brief glimpses, pithy catch phrases, or remarks made on the fly. Leaders receive a lot less space or air time than some of the pundits who comment on them. Their pronouncements and initiatives are "framed" within a context chosen by reporters, and journalists always have the last word.

Howard Kurtz believes the new journalistic culture has created a toxic environment that rewards unwavering partisanship, entertainment rather than analysis and instant judgments.[16] The new journalism celebrates cynicism, denigrates politicians, and gives journalists control over the public agenda. In Kurtz's view, "armchair warriors" have cheapened public debate and helped to narrow rather than expand the range of views available to citizens.[17]

To some degree these arguments are overblown. We know that there are many newspaper columnists, talk show hosts, and political commentators whose insights add immeasurably to the quality of public thinking and who deserve their place at the summits of public influence. We also know that politicians have an extensive array of weapons with which to set the agenda of public debate and influence the coverage that they receive. They are not defenceless creatures unaware of and unable to meet the threats that surround them in the political jungle. Yet it is difficult to deny that punditry has come to occupy a unique place in Canadian life and that it brings its own set of dangers.

The Right-Wing Information Infrastructure

The ascent of the pundits is only one aspect of a new information environment that has emerged in the last 20 years. A number of factors, taken together, have led to the development of what I will refer to as a right-wing information infrastructure. While much of this infrastructure is amorphous, disconnected and haphazard, there is little doubt that conservative perspectives are being pushed more aggressively than in the past. This infrastructure rests on a number of foundations.

First, in the 1980s and 1990s the corporate community funneled considerable resources into so-called think tanks. The Vancouver-based Fraser Institute, the C.D. Howe Institute in Toronto, and the Canada West Foundation in Calgary are among the most influential policy-oriented research institutes. They often make headlines with timely and sometimes controversial reports on public policy issues, do contract work for governments, hold conferences and seminars, and do their own community outreach and media liaison work. Right-wingers might argue that the left in Canada has its own think tanks in the form of some university-based research centres and groups such as the Council of Canadians. But these centres clearly lack the financial muscle available to the corporate-sponsored institutes. This is especially the case for centres based in universities. Indeed, as university budgets and federal funding for basic research have been cut back, corporate money has become more important in financing university research. Corporations tend to support projects from which they can benefit directly.

According to some reports, the Donner Canadian Foundation has played a decisive role in fueling the right-wing intellectual assault of the 1990s.[18] Since 1994, it has contributed over $2 million (Can.) to support projects at the Fraser Institute, the C.D. Howe Institute, the Mackenzie Institute, and a number of universities including the University of British Columbia, the University of Calgary, and Carleton University. Projects include financing the Centre for the Study of the Public Debt at the Fraser Institute, the establishment of the Atlantic Institute for Market Studies at the University of New Brunswick, and supporting the creation of *Next City*, a quarterly magazine which takes staunchly conservative positions. Support from the foundation also helped launch another right-wing publication, *Gravitas*, which specializes in Canadian foreign and trade policy. Some see the activities of the Donner Canadian Foundation as an aggressive and inappropriate intrusion by a private American foundation which is "bred of the culture of U.S. conservatism."[19] There is concern that its mission is to spread an American vision, an American social gospel, into Canadian intellectual and political life.

A study conducted by News Watch Canada found that what the researchers characterized as right-wing think tanks received more than three times as much news coverage as left-wing centres or institutes. The study analyzed coverage in 14 daily newspapers and on CBC television and CTV news broadcasts. Right-wing research institutes included the Fraser Institute, the C.D. Howe Institute, and the Business Council on National Issues, while rivals on the left included the Council of Canadians and the Canadian Centre for Policy Alternatives.[20]

The impact that think tanks have had on governments and on the policy debate in Canada is difficult to measure. Because no major studies of Canadian think tanks have been conducted, little is known about the connections, funding, and policy influence of any of these institutions. There can be little doubt that such studies would make interesting and perhaps crucial reading. The federal government turned to think tanks during the constitutional negotiations of 1991–92 to organize five citizens' forums that proved to be critical in shaping the final Charlottetown agreement. Think tanks also produced, both before and after the 1995 Quebec referendum, a number of studies that promoted various strategies for dealing with Quebec separation. Think tanks were able to float ideas and test positions that politicians were reluctant to be associated with, but which they nevertheless wanted placed on the table of public debate. On a more mundane level, when people enter the premier's office in Alberta, for instance, they see an award from the Fraser Institute commending Premier Ralph Klein on his deficit elimination policies prominently displayed. While this is only a symbolic and admittedly inconsequential example, the existence of a connection between think tanks, conservative ideas, and government actions cannot be easily dismissed.

A second aspect of the changing information environment is the increased corporate concentration in the newspaper industry and the conservative orientation of Canada's major newspaper owners. Much of the concern surrounds Conrad Black's control, through Hollinger and Southam, of what is by one recent count 60 of Canada's 105 daily newspapers; papers reaching 2.4 million readers, 43 per cent of all circulation in Canada.[21] His holdings include the *National Post*, which was inaugurated in October 1998, as well as most of the venerable old lions of the Canadian newspaper industry – the *Victoria Times Colonist*, the *Vancouver Sun*, the *Vancouver Province*, the *Calgary Herald*, the *Edmonton Journal*, the *Regina Leader Post*, the *Saskatoon StarPhoenix*, the *Ottawa Citizen*, the *Windsor Star*, the *Gazette* (Montreal), *Le Soleil* (Quebec City), and the *Halifax Daily News*, among others. Black owns *Saturday Night* magazine and, through Southam, also has a stake in Chapters Inc., a book chain that controls roughly 35 per cent of the Canadian market.[22] Among the 400 newspapers that he owns worldwide are such lucrative prizes as the powerful *Daily Telegraph* of London, which has a daily circulation of over one million readers, the *Jerusalem Post*, and the *Chicago Sun-Times*. Hollinger also own a large swath of small-town American papers.

The concern is not only that there is too much power in the hands of a single individual but that Conrad Black is hardly an innocuous investor with only a fleeting and marginal interest in the content of newspapers. Black is by some accounts an ardent political warrior. Peter White, a Hollinger vice-president, once observed that Black was "part businessman, part media figure and part politician – though without the vagaries involved in dealing with the electorate."[23] Black holds staunch and passionately conservative views on almost all public policy issues. He strongly supported and admired Margaret Thatcher and Ronald Reagan, opposes many aspects of the welfare state, believes in a limited role for government, and has been characterized as unsympathetic to feminism and the culture of "victimization" that he feels is embedded in the politics of Quebec nationalists, natives, gays, and other groups.[24] Black actively supported Brian Mulroney's run for the Conservative Party leadership in 1983 and has donated money to the Reform Party.

Some Southam journalists are nervous about the extent to which Black's conservative views are or will be imposed on the editorial stances of their newspapers. Indeed, some feel that a cold chill has swept through newsrooms and are worried about what awaits them if their own views fail the litmus test of acceptability. While Black supposedly almost never meddles directly in the editorial process, he, like most owners, hires managers in his own image. That is, he hires people with whom he is congenial and who generally share his views about the world. David Radler, Hollinger's president and Black's chief lieutenant, once described Hollinger's operating style this way: "I am ultimately the publisher of all of these papers, and if editors disagree with us, they should disagree with us when they're no longer in our employ."[25] Radler has admitted, however, that his concerns have been voiced in at least two areas involving editorial policy. First, the *Gazette* (Montreal) is to take a much tougher line toward abuses by the sovereigntist government in Quebec against the English minority in Quebec. And second, "any Hollinger paper that wants to support a Bob Rae-type socialist government better have pretty compelling reasons. We're not going to back a political party that seeks our destruction and the destruction of the capitalist system."[26]

Black's critics believe that the newspaper baron's political passions sometimes get the better of him. At one point, he reportedly telephoned columnists at the *Daily Telegraph*, feeding them arguments and suggesting that they support the Conservative Party more vigorously. During the 1997 British general election the *Telegraph* portrayed both British Labour Party leader Tony Blair and his wife, Cherie Booth, in a particularly nasty and unfavourable light.[27] The newspaper ran pictures of Mrs. Blair that showed her in demeaning and undignified situations – looking grim or frazzled or half asleep.

Black also has strong opinions about what he sees as the failings of Canadian journalism. He has spoken and written quite frequently about what he perceives to be the intellectual lethargy and flabby-minded leftism of many of Canada's journalists. In 1989, for instance, he wrote: "For 20 years I have intermittently described large sections of the Canadian media as irresponsible, narcissistic, self-rightously biased, unqualified to exercise the power they have, over-indulged by complacent public opinion and by owners afraid to offer any ethical direction, and inadequately literate."[28] He also promised to set a new journalistic course at Southam, rooting out the diseases that he saw as having infected Southam journalists in the past:

> We're going to try and recruit the very best people we can and produce the best papers we can, and publish them to the highest standards we can. And that means separating news from comment, and not just (having) the overwhelming avalanche of soft, left, bland, envious pap which has poured like sludge through the centre pages of most of the Southam papers for some time.[29]

Part of the harsh medicine that was needed, apparently, was the hiring of a bevy of national columnists such as Diane Francis and Andrew Coyne who generally share Black's commitments and outlook.

In a review of William Kaplan's *Presumed Guilty*, a book about allegations made and legal proceedings brought against former Prime Minister Brian Mulroney during the Airbus affair, Conrad

Black blamed Southam journalists for aiding in the carrying out of what he described as a "smear" job.[30] He promised, however, that journalists under his hire would do better next time.

Media critic Rick Salutin has described Black's review:

> The "review" ends ominously. "Among the least distinguished journalistic performances [on Airbus] were some of the Southam papers," writes Black. But "they are now under new management, for which I have some authority to speak." (Talk about smug.) "When tested next on such a fundamental question of justice, we will do better." It's not every book review that can end with a guarantee of how the nation's press will report politics in the future.[31]

Critics claim that Black's drive to maximize profits shortchanges readers. There is less local coverage, newspapers are filled with cheap wire service copy, and investigative reporting is discouraged. Hollinger has become notorious for "demanning" its newspapers – eliminating as many jobs as possible in order to exact savings. But this also means that important stories or issues either may not get reported or are not reported in nearly the depth that readers require to fully understand the issues at stake.

While giant newspaper chains can achieve economies of scale by offering national advertising contracts, buying newsprint in bulk, and combining news and editorial resources, there is a danger that individual newspapers in such chains will lose their cutting edge and the charm that makes them unique. One of the most respected and influential newspaper columnists in the country, Jeffrey Simpson of the *Globe and Mail*, has lamented the drift that he sees in the newspaper industry as a result of huge monopolies tightening their grip. According to Simpson:

> We can see today that many newspapers are shrinking, in a variety of ways. They are shrinking in size, personnel, ambition, and as a consequence in their curiosity ... The actual size of newspapers has shrunk. Headlines have grown larger, as have photographs; stories have grown shorter. News holes

have declined. More commentators than ever are ideologues of the right, using their precious space less to explain than to build temples to humanity, then kick out all the humans.[32]

Michael Cobden, a former editorial page editor for the *Kingston Whig-Standard* and now a teacher of journalism at University of King's College in Halifax, believes that Black's corporate management style stifles and chokes creativity and independence. Cobden observed:

> It's not just a matter of Mr. Black's having too much influence over people's view of public affairs (though that is a danger, even if he doesn't intend it). It's a matter of the head office of his chain influencing the journalism of all its newspapers, so that they all read the same, look the same, choose the same sorts of things to write about, and write about them in much the same way, in the same tone, at the same length, in the same story form, and using the same story-telling length.[33]

Mr. Black's defenders claim that he has almost single-handedly saved and revitalized the Canadian newspaper industry. Concentration of ownership in Black's hands has saved some of the more marginal newspapers from extinction, and has led to reinvestments in newspapers like the *Ottawa Citizen* and to the redesign and revamping of others such as the *Calgary Herald.* Moreover, some believe that Conrad Black has become "the only game in town" in that he is the only major corporate player willing to make a long-term commitment to the newspaper industry. Thomson International and Power Corporation, once powerful players in the Canadian newspaper game, have divested most of their interests and are redeploying their resources elsewhere. They were scared off by declining readerships, rising costs, and the threats posed by new technologies. His supporters believe that Canadians should thank Conrad Black not only for stepping into the breach where others fear to tread but for breathing new life into what some would contend was a dying industry.

The other corporate giant, Black's principal rival, is the Sun Media Corporation. Sun Media has a hammer-lock on much of the market in Southern Ontario. It now owns the *Toronto Sun*, the *Ottawa Sun*, the *London Free Press*, and the *Hamilton Spectator* as well as newspapers in close to 20 other centres in Southern Ontario. Sun Corp. also owns the Calgary and Edmonton *Suns* and has an interest in Pulse 24, the all-news TV channel that serves Southern Ontario.

Sun President and CEO, Paul Godfrey, also has conservative views. A former elected politician, Godfrey was chairman of Metropolitan Toronto and a "Capital-C Conservative."[34] The *Suns* have their own particular brand of politics. They are known for their unabashed civic boosterism, their appeal to male working class values, and their "little guy on the street or in the subway car" suspicion of Ottawa politicians. As Christie Blatchford has described their editorial outlook, "*Sun* editorials make it clear that the paper loves, in no particular order, Tory governments and Reform ideas, breasts, more folks in jail, better controls on immigration, lower taxes, less red tape, fewer civil servants, a return to basics in education, and breasts."[35] A main concern is that before Conrad Black's takeover of Southam, the points of view found in *Sun* newspapers were offset by the existence of other perspectives, especially in cities where Southam newspapers dominated. That alternative viewpoint is not available today.

The problem of balance is compounded even further when one takes the country's self-proclaimed national newspaper, the *Globe and Mail*, into account. Long considered the voice of the Canadian establishment, the *Globe*'s positions are reliably conservative.

Some scholars would argue that the one-sided ideological tilt in the newspaper industry makes little difference at a time when citizens have access to a wide variety of sources – the CBC, specialty TV channels, magazines, books, the Internet, etc. There is also the view that citizens have the good sense to know what it is they are reading and that papers that become too narrow or too rigid in their outlook will simply drive readers away. The argument on the other side is that most people still trust newspapers and see their contents as a kind of truth. They turn to the newspaper for basic information – news about local events, sports scores, want ads, business news – and are largely unaware of the political diet being served up along with these other dishes.

Conclusion

Despite repeated failures to unite the right on the national political chess board, the entire agenda of Canadian politics has been influenced by an intellectual climate shaped more and more by right-wing journalism. This chapter described the foundation stones on which the new right-wing information infrastructure has been built. The rise of political pundits, the growing influence of think tanks, and increased corporate concentration in the newspaper industry have each played a role in propagating and legitimating conservative values.

The question, as always, is whether citizens have the information that they require to make informed judgements about the kind of country they want to live in. Studies show that information environments rich in choices and variety produce better informed and more active citizens.[36] Without the fresh air that comes from exposure to a full range of ideas, there is the potential for public life to be greatly diminished. The question is whether political debate has been slanted too far in one direction. Howard Kurtz has asked why some topics but not others are the focus for the wrath of pundits. We rarely read or hear discussions about whether corporate executives, who sometimes receive monstrous salaries, are being overpaid. Or about whether workers are being laid off "to compensate for management blunders and ill-advised mergers."[37] Or whether the medical system is really safe given the long and merciless lineups that exist for often life-saving procedures. Or whether affordable housing should be a national priority.

Those who control the levers of opinion have a tremendous responsibility to ensure that the public arena is open to a variety of perspectives. If they fail in this responsibility then it is surely an example of power and betrayal. The irony is that by continuing to wage an ideological war, the right may be undermining the very values of freedom and independence that it holds most sacred.

NINE

Confronting the Future

My intention in writing this book was to ask questions about the kind of media universe in which we are living. My aim, however, was not just to stir the pot but to warn of the tsunami that is beginning to gather force and threatens to bury us in its crashing waves. The central concern in *Power and Betrayal* is the extent to which citizens are increasingly deprived of the vital information they need to make decisions about their communities and their lives. Despite surface appearances, our media worlds are growing smaller rather than larger. They are becoming less open and less diverse even as they seem to be expanding, even exploding, in so many different directions.

I am hardly alone in sounding these warnings. There are quite a number of scholars, writers, and journalists who have written with far more eloquence and power than I have on these subjects. And I also believe that there is an aching sense of anxiety among members of the public – and this concern is reflected in public opinion surveys – that the media are failing to provide the intellectual sustenance that our society needs.

My task in this last chapter is to suggest some ways of improving the situation, some ways in which Canadian media horizons, the media avenues that we travel on each day, can be widened.

First, I must restate what I believe are some obvious truths. I believe that only the most isolated individuals would dispute the power that the media have to give us "the pictures in our heads" and to set the public agenda. People who argue that the media have little power are simply living in a dream world. At the same time, it must be recognized that the media's power is not unlimited. Audiences interpret media messages through the protective screens of their own backgrounds, needs, and values and often resist words and images that ring false or make them feel uncomfortable. Evidence garnered from the scholarly literature, however, demonstrates that the media has the capacity to be "an imposing authority" that is "virtually without peer."[1] As a leading media scholar, Todd Gitlin, has described the power of the media: "They name the world's parts, they certify reality as reality."[2]

I also believe that only someone who is totally self-interested or morally blind would deny that there are aspects of the media world that have gone wrong, that are terribly "out of order."[3] In chapter two, I describe four models of media influence. While these are not pure types, and there are truths to be found in each of the theories, they are linked by a common thread. They all deal with an imbalance, a corruption, a warping, of power relationships within the media that prevents citizens from obtaining a more meaningful picture or participating more fully in the communities in which they live.

There is no doubt that governments and regulators seem to be powerless in the face of huge global conglomerates that want to devour every morsel, every scrap on the media table, that is not yet under their control. Politicians are intimidated by the media's capacity to sway public opinion against them and by the collective muscle of media lobby groups to block or influence legislation. We are likely to look back on the late twentieth century as a unique time in history where a small coterie of corporate leaders such as Bill Gates, Ted Turner, and Rupert Murdoch were to wield almost unheard-of power. The great marauders in previous eras tended to be military and political leaders like Napoleon, Bismarck, Stalin, and MacArthur.

Corporate and technological convergence (and the two, I believe, are intertwined: each pushing and spurring the other) are transforming the cultural landscape in ways that are unprecedented. News is increasingly merging with entertainment, so that citizens are receiving a highly distorted picture of how political institutions and government policies operate. In fact, news about political life has slowly been disappearing from the screen as producers have become convinced that politics doesn't sell. Two Canadian authors, Roger Bird and Knowlton Nash, have each written a book about the sensationalism and trivia that have become the daily bread of all too many news broadcasts.[4]

Further, national and local cultures are desperately trying to find their voices amid the noisy sounds of the growing international commercial culture. While the tides of global convergence can't be pushed back, there is something to be said for keeping and savouring the special and unique flavours of national and community life. Canadians don't want their hard-won identity – an identity that, as Northrop Frye has reminded us, is still being formed, is still being articulated, is still searching for its voice – to be lost in a vast homogenous sea.[5] The processes of change described in this book are monumental developments, major openings in the ozone layer that once protected civic life and national cultures.

While many believe that new media such as cable TV and the Internet will bring greater diversity, independence, and experimentation, the reality is that the old media are imposing themselves on the new. The companies that own the old TV networks have long since occupied the most important real estate along the beachfronts of cable TV. There is also a degree to which people are attracted to web sites that amplify and connect them with the old media; web sites about TV shows, media celebrities, sports teams, newspapers, and people and events that they see or read about in the news. I do not want to take away from the genuine excitement and the hope that surrounds these new technologies and the possibilities for vital new communities and avenues of exchange that are being opened up. What I am suggesting is that we not become intoxicated by remote possibilities or indulge in pipe dreams. New power relationships may well emerge out of these new technologies, but the iron grip of current power relationships is not about to slip any time soon.

These larger developments are all reflected in changes that have taken place in the Canadian media. Canadian television is becoming more American. The CBC has been battered and bruised by over a decade of upheaval and is being chilled by the fear of further budget cuts. A single corporate entity controlled by Conrad

Black owns a huge slice of the Canadian newspaper industry. The global entertainment culture has penetrated into every neighbourhood and schoolyard, almost overshadowing local identities. Political life is less visible and less interesting to Canadians and seems as a result to be deteriorating. And a right-wing information infrastructure dominates much of our public debate.

My argument is that Canadians have been betrayed by institutions and forces at every level of the media food chain. Politicians, regulators, owners, and journalists have been guilty on too many occasions of putting ego, vanity, and profits ahead of the public interest. Politicians have both interfered with the media on some occasions and been afraid to act on others. Regulators have been weak and submissive. Owners have been willing to squeeze the system for every bit of profit that they could get out of it. And journalists have too often taken the easy road, giving consumers what they want rather than giving citizens what they need.

Much of what has been written in this book has been documented many times before in countless studies by academics and in numerous government reports. The Royal Commission on Newspapers (1981), the Task Force on Broadcasting Policy (1986), and the Report of the Mandate Review Committee on the CBC, NFB and Telefilm (1996) were among the studies that supplied a great deal of evidence and provided valuable prescriptions for change.[6] These eloquent documents with their recommendations for reform were ignored by the governments of their day.

Nothing can happen unless politicians and regulators decide to break out of the vicious circle that they now find themselves in. With regard to broadcasting, it is difficult to get tough and apply sanctions when regulators and media corporations have been dancing to the same music for decades. It is difficult to make the music stop when a whole world of expectations and behaviours revolves around making the band play on. But even small steps could go a long way toward bringing change. Some suggestions for reversing this deteriorating situation include the following:

- The CRTC must toughen Canadian content requirements. Although CanCon regulates culture to some degree, the end result of an unregulated market would be even greater control by the Hollywood entertainment conglomerates. Ted Turner and Rupert Murdoch have no interest in telling Canadian stories or reflecting Canadian realities. Guidelines have to be changed so that what qualifies as a Canadian production actually deals with Canadian issues, reflects Canadian situations, and nurtures talent in Canada. The national deficit in drama production is extraordinary. The main TV networks produce roughly 145 hours of original Canadian drama each year. This compares to over 1,000 hours produced by TV networks in France and almost 1,300 hours produced by British broadcasters.[7] It's also time for the CRTC to put teeth into the enforcement of the licenses that it bestows. Failure to live up to license requirements should mean that broadcasters must compete for their licenses in a new round of competition against all comers. Real competition, after all, is what business is all about.

- Appointments to the Canadian Broadcasting Corporation's Board of Directors should be made on a strictly non-partisan basis. Distinguished citizens from a number of different walks of life should be considered for these roles. While it's always difficult to protect public broadcasters from the heavy hand of political interference, a non-partisan board would be a symbol of integrity both within the corporation and to the public.

- The CBC should strengthen its regional presence and should be given stable funding at levels comparable to those enjoyed by European public broadcasting systems. Governments should explore new ways of funding public broadcasting. Although the public's taste for new taxes or fees of any kind is non-existent, and there are other needs in society that must be addressed when and if there are federal government budget surpluses, untapped sources of funding exist within the entertainment and communication industries.

- Journalists must step out of the stories they are covering. They should not become the stars of the show – the central focus of the events that they are reporting on. Political and community leaders who are being covered in TV news stories should be given enough "clip" time to express full sentences and communicate ideas. The reporter's voice should not be the only one heard in news stories.

- Politics and government need to be covered in some detail if a healthy democratic life is to be sustained. Health care, pensions, the problems of the education system, the politics of employment, the struggle over national unity, and the fairness and incentives of the tax system all need to be examined in a thorough way even if stories may not fit the media frame. The old "orchestra pit" theory of news reporting (one candidate says that he has a peace plan for the Middle East while the other falls off the stage into the orchestra pit: guess which one gets covered) may answer the needs of news managers to bump up their ratings. But the frame sometimes has to be expanded to fit the needs of society. Hot visuals, violence, sensationalism, and the endless pursuit of conflict give citizens a distorted view of their community and its problems. In-depth explorations of public policy issues should be part of a TV station's mandate and there should be requirements that such stories be aired regularly on local news programs.

- The newspaper industry needs a greater diversity in its ownership. Some observers are deeply worried by the prospects of an industry that can too easily become "all Conrad all the time." There needs to be a re-evaluation of the industry with a view to ensuring that a variety of perspectives continue to be expressed. Canadians cannot depend on the good will of individual owners no matter how noble their intentions might be. Since governments appear to be too weak or too intimidated to act, the commissioning of a task force report on the future of newspapers might be a useful first step. This might have the effect of forcing the issue onto the public agenda and testing various policy alternatives.

- Computers, the Internet, and media education should be promoted in the schools. Our children should be aware that citizenship depends on having and understanding the sources of knowledge that are available to them. So much of learning in the twenty-first century will depend on being able to navigate these waters.

The larger problem is how to make the media accountable in a democracy. Global corporations, media barons, and powerful journalists enjoy unrestrained power. They seem to dwell in a world beyond the reach of governments, regulators, or citizens, wielding power without apparent responsibility. While we can point fingers accusing various parties of being betrayers and accomplices, it is important to recognize that citizens also bear some responsibility. Only citizens can pressure politicians to take action, click to TV stations or channels that they believe are doing a good job while clicking others off, and make decisions about the type of TV programs that they want their children to watch. Citizens can ignore newspapers that don't present them with a diversity of views or that continually champion political crusades that have little to do with the way they live their lives or the real problems that they face.

The irony of the current situation is that many Canadians know that the media world is not what it should be. Yet they are too infected, too hamstrung, by the cynicism and passivity that the media breeds to take positive action. Perhaps we don't take the media world seriously enough, don't see the larger connections and values that it has created. The problem, as Jay Rosen once argued, is that in laughing at the media we may not realize that the media is laughing at us.[8] In the end, those who control the mass media must realize that their own prosperity depends on having open public squares, citizens who are knowledgeable and caring, and a progressive society.

UPDATE 2001

Media Conglomerates, the CBC, and Canadian Democracy

Writing about the modern mass media is a little like writing with invisible ink. Change now occurs so rapidly and at such breakneck speed that the media world of the late 1990s now seems like a distant and blurry memory. The forces of change described in the first printing of *Power & Betrayal in the Canadian Media* have if anything become even more powerful, more deeply etched into the media landscape, than at the time the book was originally published. The convergence revolution has accelerated to the point where it has become a guiding principle, almost a new religion, for the giant corporations that now control most of the Canadian media – Bell Canada Enterprises (BCE), Quebecor, Rogers Communication, and CanWest Global. At the same time, fragmentation, the other and related engine of change, has continued unabated. For example, the CRTC received 452 applications for licenses for new digital cable services in 2000. Contenders included a prospective poetry channel, a passion channel that would be devoted entirely to sex programming, and a channel that would focus exclusively on the Toronto Maple Leafs. In November of that year, 21 new digital licenses were granted. Among the 16 new English-language channels are a channel devoted to women's sports, a gay channel, a biography channel, Wisdom TV, and channels focussing on travel, books, and computers. The 500-channel universe, once the symbol of a faraway future, is now almost within our grasp.

To no one's surprise, the CBC has continued its downward spiral. In 2000, the corporation imposed further budget cuts and underwent yet another of a long series of "transformation" and "re-engineering" exercises. But all of the attempts to reconfigure and reposition the public broadcaster seem to have left it in much the same place. In a stark admission before the Standing Committee on Canadian Heritage in May 2000, the CBC's new president, Robert Rabinovitch, announced that the corporation no longer had the resources to fulfill its mandate. He contended that: "If CBC were a private sector company I would say it was structurally flawed and unless it addressed those structural problems it would be on its way to bankruptcy."[1] Meanwhile its audience numbers continue to plummet and its local and regional voices grew even fainter.

There have, however, been some unexpected turns in the road and indeed one dramatic and sudden shock since *Power & Betrayal* was first published. When the book appeared, Conrad Black held a tight grip over much of the Canadian newspaper industry. Black seemed to be at the height of his power and indeed had taken most of a lifetime to make his ascent to the highest peaks of influence and control. He had become almost the classic caricature of the newspaper baron, a man both feared and admired as part businessman, part politician, and part journalist. Indeed Black's new national newspaper, the *National Post,* had become the sharp end of the stick in a campaign to establish a new right-wing political party, the Canadian Alliance, and had altered the landscape of Canadian journalism in significant ways. It not only challenged the *Globe and Mail*'s position as Canada's national newspaper but its strong editorial positions, crusading columnists, and high-profile investigations into government impropriety helped set the journalistic and public agenda.

The shock came in August 2000 when, with little warning, Black sold his Canadian newspaper holdings to CanWest Global for $3.5 billion. Although Black will maintain a 50 per cent interest in the *Post* for a five-year period, his sudden retreat left many observers simply bewildered. Had the aging lion simply lost his taste for ideological battle, had he given up on Canada because the country had become too small for his mounting ambitions, or was it that Black saw little future in the newspaper industry and was getting out while the getting was still good?

In this update, I will review the developments that have taken place since the book was first published and analyze the impact that these changes are likely to have on the relationship between citizens and the mass media in Canada. The debate about the effects that the mass media are having on the nature of communities and indeed of citizenship has become more intense. While gazing into crystal balls is always dangerous, I will attempt to describe and make sense of the new Canadian media landscape. My conclusion is that there are both signs of hope and reasons for despair.

The Laws of Convergence

Since the first printing of *Power & Betrayal,* the pace of technological convergence has quickened. A recent report by Pricewaterhouse-Coopers found that Canada leads the world in the number of households that are online. Over 48 per cent of Canadians are now online and those who are connected spend an average of five hours per week using e-mail or navigating through cyberspace. These figures are higher than in the United States (43 per cent) or countries such as Germany and France (26 per cent).[2] And one doesn't have to look far for new technological developments that are transforming business, leisure, and education. Voice portals are now being marketed that link voice recognition, the Internet, and the telephone. Soon we will be able to send e-mails merely by speaking on the phone. The biggest challenge may be the extent to which all media will become available on the Internet. If all of radio, TV, and newspapers are piped through the Web then regulation becomes all but impossible. Programming from all over the world can spill into Canada with few barriers and little difficulty.

One other major difference since the book's first printing is that much of the euphoria and hoopla that once surrounded the Web's commercial possibilities have been toned down. The stock prices of companies such as Ebay, Amazon, and Priceline, once the darlings of e-commerce, careened into a tailspin in 2000. The outlook for commercial applications of the Internet are now much more sober and realistic.

While technological convergence has proceeded at a dizzying speed, so has corporate convergence. The trigger for much of the corporate manoeuvring that took place in Canada in 2000 was America Online's (AOL's) takeover of media giant Time Warner for a reported $159 billion (U.S.) in 1999. AOL's audacious manoeuvring, its bold leap, seemed to highlight and symbolize the convergence revolution. With more than 70 million visitors per month to its on-line properties in 2000, AOL ambition was to be able to merge and coordinate its extraordinary presence on the Web with Time Warner's dominant position in film, TV, and music production and in magazine and book publishing. Theme parks and sports franchises are also part of the mix. AOL's objective, its game plan, is to integrate and meld new technologies with old media properties in order to achieve new efficiencies, attract advertisers with multimedia deals, and promote its products on a scale that has seldom been seen before.

One media analyst described the new business model in the following way: "Content is a data engine – a brand digested through a palm pilot, TV show, on the Web, or from your car radio ... As new technology is introduced to North America, the engine is re-skinned for the environment, further establishing brand. Each distribution medium, be it the Web or your cell phone, can only enhance brand establishment, with TV being the central data bank."[3]

AOL's takeover of Time Warner was not the only deal that seemed driven by the logic of convergence. Viacom's purchase of CBS in 1999 was another instance of a giant conglomerate attempting to fit all the pieces of the media puzzle together by integrating old and new technologies. By 2000 the message from Wall Street, and indeed from Bay Street, seemed clear – media companies that had not jumped on the convergence bandwagon risked being left behind.

Convergence fever soon struck Canada with a vengeance. First, telephone and satellite conglomerate BCE took over CTV for a reported $3.2 billion. What made CTV so lucrative was not only that it owned 26 TV stations sprinkled in key markets across the country, but that it had accumulated some of the most valuable properties in cable television – CTV News 1, The Comedy Network (65%), The Sports Network (68%), Talk TV, and History Television (12%), among others. BCE then proceeded to scoop up another of the great jewels in the Canadian media crown, the *Globe and Mail.*

BCE's takeovers of CTV and the *Globe* were soon hailed as the Canadian equivalent of the AOL-Time Warner deal. BCE had emerged as a super conglomerate whose stable now included a whole panoply of old and new media properties. The company that owns Bell Canada, Telesat, ExpressVu satellite TV, the Sympatico-Lycos Internet portal, and sites such as YellowPages.ca and VMP.com. (an e-commerce retail marketplace) had added the country's largest TV network and the showpiece of the Canadian newspaper industry to its empire. BCE is also under pressure to add a major sports franchise to its arsenal.

The biggest bombshell, however, was CanWest Global's purchase of Conrad Black's Canadian newspaper empire. After more than 20 years of trying to stitch together a third national TV network out of a patchwork of independent stations, one of the great legends of Canadian TV, Izzy (Israel) Asper, finally succeeded in 2000 when he purchased TV stations in Alberta from Shaw Communications. Although his son Leonard had officially taken over the reins as President and CEO in 1999, the older Asper is still seen as the power behind the throne. Global now owns TV stations as well as newspapers in almost every major city in Canada from Halifax to Victoria. In addition, Global owns approximately 5.6 million shares in CTV and a bevy of Internet sites. Part of the shock of Hollinger's sell-off was that CanWest Global seemed to be an unlikely buyer. Global had no previous experience in the newspaper business, and as a former leader of the Manitoba Liberal Party, Izzy Asper did not share Black's ideological passions or beliefs. The fact that Global and Hollinger will co-own the *National Post* for at least a five-year period may mean that at least some clashes over editorial policy and management style will be difficult to avoid.

Perhaps the most interesting question is why did Black suddenly leave all that he had built up in Canada over the period of the last 20 years? In a requiem to Conrad Black published in the *Globe and Mail*, Doug Saunders catalogued both the lavish scale and deep fervor that characterized Black's commitment to the *National Post* in particular. The paper had reportedly lost close to $99 million in its first 21 months due in part to the large infusion of cash needed to create a new national newspaper from scratch. But the paper also had a heady, self-indulgent style. It hired a cohort of highly priced columnists and spent lavishly on headline-grabbing investigative pieces. As Saunders observed: "It had been two years of excess, unlimited spending, untamed innovation and ideological revolution, an ebullient explosion that had altered the media forever."[4]

Its effects could be felt on a number of levels. First, the launch of the new paper started a circulation war that threatened and weakened the *Globe and Mail. Globe* readership has declined from 2.34 million people who read an issue of the paper during an average week in 1997 to 2.29 million in 2000.[5] One can argue that the competition between the two national papers gave Canadians greater choice and ultimately made the *Globe* a better paper. The *Globe* was forced to recruit a new generation of writers and lost some of its stodgy conservatism.

Second, the *Post* brought a new European style to Canadian journalism: writing and headlines that were splashy, crusading, opinionated, and overtly ideological. To some degree the *Post* became both a catalyst and a cheerleader for the emergence of the Canadian Alliance Party, an intervention into national life that is almost unprecedented for a newspaper in the post-war era. The *Post* also created a news hierarchy within the Southam chain. Big city dailies such as the *Calgary Herald* or the *Montreal Gazette* would feed regional stories to the *Post* but were also relegated to a kind of farm team status where they would have to play second fiddle on big national stories "owned" by the *Post.*

There was every reason to believe that Conrad Black had relished his role as the creator of the *Post* and as the most influential newspaper owner in the country. His many speeches, columns, and pronouncements seemed to suggest a man comfortable with his immense power and with his own dedication to and prescriptions for righting the wrongs of Canadian journalism and politics. In what seemed like a final goodbye to Canada, Black wrote a "comment" that was published in Southam newspapers soon after the sale was announced. He pointed out that Hollinger was carrying a sizable debt load and that the company had been too heavily invested in Canada considering the opportunities that existed elsewhere. His retreat was a business decision, a strategic withdrawal, rather than a loss of heart or an indication of personal difficulties. Black could not resist taking a last swipe at those who were gleefully cheering his departure:

> I do not choose to reply to those who in the last week have likened me to a jackal, claimed that I have left no legacy in Canada and that I stripped little newspapers to feed large ones, declared that I have never added value to any company I was head of, or am guilty of the vast catalogue of Kafkaesque shortcomings that have been alleged against me by my self-declared enemies in the Canadian media.
>
> The authors of these lies and smears illustrate perfectly ... all the weaknesses of the country and of the journalistic craft that I have often addressed before.[6]

Speculation about the reasons for the sell-off dominated news coverage for quite some time. At least one observer noted that Black had grown more at home and more settled in London where he now lived for most of the year, was spending less time at the office, and seemed to be "withdrawing into himself."[7] Others countered this "lion in winter" hypothesis with rumors that Black had sold off his Canadian assets and was building up his war chest in order to make an even bigger strike. The theory was that Black had outgrown Canada and needed to "splash in a bigger pond."[8]

The BCE and Global takeovers were not the only big moves on the chessboard of Canadian media ownership in 2000. In another dramatic move, Quebecor Inc., owner of Canada's other large news-

paper chain, The Sun Newspapers, purchased TVA, Quebec's largest private broadcaster, and Groupe Videotron Ltee, the dominant
player in the cable market in Quebec. Quebecor is the largest commercial printing company in the world and has a strong presence
on the Internet through its Canoe and Netgraphe portals. Well aware
of the laws of convergence, CEO Pierre-Karl Peladeau has begun
talks with telephone giant Telus, which owns the wireless phone company Clearnet among other assets, in order to form a partnership
that would marry content with delivery.

The convergence bug also drove Rogers Communication, Canada's largest cable company and a key player in cell-phones, video
distribution and the magazine industry (*Maclean's*), to purchase the
Toronto Blue Jays baseball team.

While the Canadian media skyline is being dramatically altered,
it is not clear that real convergence can be easily achieved. It's one
thing to think that many different technologies and enterprises can
be linked and fitted together, it's another thing to actually do it. A
newspaper or Internet portal or sports franchise that has difficulty
making enough money on its own to survive may not be any more
successful if it is fused with other enterprises that have similar problems. While sharp and imaginative management practices may produce economies of scale and allow each venture to be promoted
by and reflected in the others, the new mega-conglomerates could
also be buried by the collective weight, the sheer size and complexity, of their new experiments. CanWest Global, for instance, a successful TV company, must now incorporate into its midst a
mammoth newspaper chain that faces enormous problems including rising printing costs, declining readership, and stiff competition
from other media. And while investors were infatuated with
dot.coms in the late 1990s, by 2000 the bubble had largely burst.
Whether Global's bevy of Web sites will pay dividends either in
the short or in the long run remains to be seen.

In short, convergence is a trend. It is not a guarantee of success.
The jigsaw puzzles may not be easy to fit together.

The convergence revolution is likely to have both positive and
negative effects. On one hand, companies such as BCE and Global

are now large enough, have enough muscle, to be able to compete effectively even against the U.S. television networks. Companies of such size certainly have the capacity to produce excellent Canadian drama and provide first-rate public affairs programming. The old industrial strategy of "Americanizing in order to Canadianize," devised when Canadian private TV companies were almost shoestring operations, may no longer be appropriate. Canadians now have every reason to expect more rather than less high quality Canadian TV. Another positive development is that Quebec-based corporations such as BCE and Quebecor, companies led by francophones, now own media properties across the country. The new wave of convergence has had the effect of re-integrating the Quebec and English Canadian media worlds. In a country that is as politically divided as Canada has been, this is an immensely important development.

But corporate convergence also has its potential downsides. The question raised by Conrad Black's foray into the Canadian newspaper business was whether too much power rested in too few hands. Convergence has, if anything, compounded and deepened the problem. Global's takeover of Black's holdings gives Global extraordinary power in most Canadian media markets. In Vancouver, for instance, a single company now owns the two major newspapers, the *Province* and the *Sun*, as well as a major TV station. While Izzy Asper's many achievements as a businessman and charitable giver are extraordinary and many observers cannot help but admire his warm and gutsy style, the question is whether one man or one company should have so much control over the information available to citizens. The capacity to intervene in and even alter public life and public consciousness is nakedly apparent. The question is an agonizing one, and it is one that is fundamental to democracy.

Canadian Public Broadcasting: The End of the Dream?

During the 1970s the Canadian media skyscape could be described as a series of low-level buildings with the CBC looming a little larger than the rest. Today four rather immense skyscrapers – BCE, Global,

Quebecor, and Rogers – hover over a smallish and rundown building, the CBC. Yet in 2000 the CBC was still able to provide services that the giants either could not or were reluctant to provide. There were, in fact, three events in Fall 2000 which highlighted the singular role that the CBC still plays in Canadian life. The first was the almost non-stop coverage provided by the CBC following the death of former Prime Minister Pierre Trudeau. The CBC appeared to go into overdrive almost immediately after Trudeau's death was announced. The crown corporation provided virtually wall-to-wall coverage chronicling not only Trudeau's life and contributions but the reactions of the public, capturing the memories and sense of bereavement that enveloped almost the entire country. The CBC had become once again the principal electronic witness to one of the great events of Canadian life.

Second, the CBC launched its big-canvas $25 million documentary series *Canada: A People's History*. The 30-hour show, produced by Mark Starowitz, chronicled Canadian history in as moving and vivid a fashion as had ever been done on television. The documentary will undoubtedly be shown in history classes across the country for years to come.

The third contribution, albeit a more controversial one, was CBC's coverage of the 2000 federal election. CBC simply provided the most in-depth reporting – covering party news conferences, airing entire speeches by party leaders, producing long-form documentaries, conducting interviews with party leaders, holding town hall meetings that brought together politicians and voters, and devoting much of its newscasts to election stories.

One particularly controversial moment came when the CBC aired a documentary on Alliance leader Stockwell Day's religious beliefs during the third week of the campaign. The documentary, which ran on *The National,* claimed that Day believed in creationism rather than evolution and that the Alliance leader had rejected the Alberta curriculum when he was the principal of a religious school in the 1980s. Day, who insisted that his private religious beliefs had little bearing on public policy, denounced the piece as "yellow journalism." It is worth noting that the Alliance Party had promised in its election platform, *A Time for Change*, to privatize the CBC's television and Internet services. Public radio would be retained.[9]

In *Power & Betrayal*, I made little secret of my view that the CBC still has a vital role to play in Canadian public life. The emergence of huge multi-platform media conglomerates and of enormous concentrations of ownership only strengthens the argument for a vibrant public broadcaster. In many communities, the CBC not only provides the kind of in-depth public affairs programming that private conglomerates tend to shun, but it is another journalistic voice in places where fewer voices are being heard. To quote an argument made in the corporation's annual report for 1999-2000:

> Canada needs a strong public broadcaster that is prepared to look beyond ratings to create platforms where artists can develop and promote their talents, and Canadians can contemplate subjects of concern to them, revel in the world's beauty, marvel at people's accomplishments or question human foibles.[10]

Power & Betrayal chronicled the extent to which the CBC had been weakened by years of budget cutting and by the cable explosion that splintered audiences and allowed private broadcasters, with the aid of the CRTC, to capture much of the prime real estate along the new cable frontier. The CBC still finds itself in a financial straitjacket with little room to manoeuvre. Now under the new president, Robert Rabinovitch, who has extensive experience in Ottawa and in the private sector, the corporation is again searching for just the right formula to guarantee its future. Although the federal government has agreed to stable funding for a five-year period (1998–2003), the parliamentary allocation dropped from $951 million in 1994–95 to approximately $760 million in 1998–99.[11] This has meant that the corporation had to depend more and more on advertising and other sources to make up the difference. Advertising and other revenue streams have now mushroomed to the point where they account for approximately one-third of total revenue. What is perhaps most alarming is that sports programming now accounts for 40 per cent of revenues. The difference was also made up through layoffs and a further tightening of the budgetary screws. Approximately 40 per cent of the CBC staff was let go during the 1990s.[12]

Rabinovitch has argued that "trying to do everything will result in the CBC bleeding to death" and that "by attempting to do the same with less, the CBC risks declining quality and declining audiences."[13] He is also worried that commercial pressures have twisted the public broadcaster out of shape, making it less distinctive, less imaginative, and less able to do the job for which it was intended. He claims that the corporation has now hit the wall and is in the midst of a profound identity crisis. His answer is to pare back everything that is not central to, that is not at the very core of, the CBC's mission. The new marching orders include reducing the corporation's dependence on commercial revenue, airing an entirely Canadian schedule in prime time, investing in children's and youth programs, strengthening its marquee news shows, and putting more money into investigative journalism and special events. The CBC will also maintain its strong presence on the Web. These initiatives could only be undertaken if other types of programming were cut. Supper-hour news shows were Rabinovitch's main target.

The plan to cut local news shows encountered heavy flak almost immediately. Opposition came principally from Liberal MPs who saw these shows as providing a much needed window for public affairs programming in their regions. Opponents argued that cutting the supper-hour shows would further centralize news production in Toronto, take the CBC out of potentially lucrative markets in places like Calgary and Halifax, and alienate audiences even more. They also pointed out that these shows had been so underfunded that they had almost been set up to fail. The shows often had only a single anchor (when studies indicate that viewers often turn to shows for friendly chit chat and a team of personalities), were poorly promoted or advertised, and often lacked the resources to cover their cities well. Critics insisted that a real commitment, a real investment, in supper-hour news shows could pay handsome dividends. The president was forced to compromise – local production would be folded into the back end of a new national supper-hour news program called *Canada Now*, which originates in Vancouver.

It remains to be seen whether Rabinovitch can refocus and re-make the CBC and find the right ingredients for success. In the meantime, the new waves of convergence and hyper-fragmentation will continue to erode its audience. The ratings for CBC TV programs dropped by 8 per cent from 1998–99 to 1999–2000.[14]

Journalism and Citizens

In *Out of Order*, a book that is now regarded as one of the classics in media studies, Harvard Professor Thomas Patterson argued that there was a disconnection between the values of modern journalism and the concerns of ordinary citizens.[15] As evidence for this claim, he compared the questions that journalists asked candidates during the 1992 U.S. presidential election with the questions that citizens asked when they had a chance to speak. Journalists were preoccupied with the horse race – who was ahead, who was behind, who was gaining, and with "insider baseball" accounts about strategies and the personal foibles of politicians. The charge was that reporters covered elections in much the same way that sports writers covered the NBA or the NFL. When ordinary voters had a chance to ask questions, the tone and the subject matter were completely different. They asked very specific questions about jobs, health care, crime, and taxes.

The quality of election reporting in the U.S. has if anything deteriorated sharply since Patterson wrote his book. Over $1 billion (U.S.) was spent on election ads during the 2000 presidential campaign, much of it flowing to the networks in the form of "soft" money. Candidates received less air time than in any previous election, and the networks were guilty of announcing winners and losers (and even getting these results wrong) while people were still voting.[16]

While we have yet to experience some of these more grotesque distortions, Canadians will not find that the picture is much different in Canada. Coverage of the 2000 Canadian federal election featured the constant reporting of polls, shrinking sound bites from the party leaders, journalists who tended to be the stars of the events that they reported on, and a wholesale neglect of the major issues that the country was facing. Voter turnout plummeted to 62.8%, the lowest voter turnout since 1896. While the political leaders must shoulder their share of the blame for a harsh campaign filled with name calling and brutal recriminations, a campaign that sharpened national divisions and raised more questions than it answered, the campaign raised important questions about the purpose and responsibility of journalism.

While the CBC came closest to the mark and there were many outstanding reports and commentaries in newspapers and by TV reporters at other networks, journalists, like some of the politicians that they were covering, often succumbed to old and tired routines.

One of the reviewers of *Power & Betrayal* contended that the book should not have been as critical of the media as it has been. I reacted to this criticism with some bewilderment. First, I had argued in the book that there is much in the media that is worthy of great praise. Almost every day Canadians can be highly entertained, deeply moved, and made to reflect on their lives because of the many delights and serious thinking on television, in newspapers, and in other mediums. Most of the journalists that I have met are first-rate professionals who are hard working, conscientious, and dedicated. But I also believe that media organizations – like other institutions such as hospitals, schools, courts, and political institutions – need to be placed under some scrutiny. If this is not done then society and democracy can easily atrophy.

In *Power & Betrayal*, I argued that those who own, control, and regulate the Canadian media system have a grave responsibility to serve their country and the needs of its citizens. I also charged that the system was out of balance – out of kilter – in some important ways and that reforms needed to be made. I still feel that way. The new Canadian media system that has been built in the last few years has the potential to deliver great benefits. It also has the capacity to do considerable harm to our public life. The new super conglomerates are amongst the most powerful institutions in our society. They have an obligation to ensure open debate, a competition of ideas, and the service of the common good.

Notes

CHAPTER ONE

1. Howard Kurtz, *Media Circus: The Trouble with America's Newspapers* (New York: Times Books, 1994), p. 13.
2. For a good discussion of the trusteeship model see William Baker and George Dessart, *Down The Tube: An Inside Account of the Failure of American Television* (New York: Basic Books, 1998), pp. 134–135.
3. Ibid.
4. Joshua Meyrowitz, "Television: The Shared Arena," in *Seeing Ourselves: Media Power and Policy in Canada*, eds. Helen Holmes and David Taras, 1st ed. (Toronto: Harcourt Brace Jovanovich Canada, 1992), p. 219.
5. Bill McKibben, *The Age of Missing Information* (New York: Random House, 1992), p. 53.
6. Jay Rosen, "Politics, Vision, and the Press: Toward a Public Agenda for Journalism," in *The New News v. The Old News: The Press and Politics in the 1990s* (New York: Twentieth Century Fund, 1992), p. 10.
7. Jürgen Habermas, *The Structural Transformation of the Public Sphere* (Cambridge, MA: Massachusetts Institute of Technology Press, 1989).
8. Quoted in James W. Carey, "The Press, Public Opinion, and Public Discourse: On the Edge of the Postmodern," in *James Carey: A Critical Reader*, eds. Eve Munson and Catherine Warren (Minneapolis: University of Minnesota Press, 1997), pp. 235–236.
9. Ibid., p. 236.
10. Quoted in Daniel Hallin, *We Keep America on Top of the World: Television Journalism and the Public Sphere* (New York: Routledge, 1994), p. 23.
11. Elihu Katz, "And Deliver Us from Segmentation," *Annals of the American Academy of Political and Social Science*, 546 (July 1996), pp. 22–33.
12. Benedict Anderson, *Imagined Communities: Reflections on the Origin and Spread of Nationalism* (London: Verso, 1983).
13. Robert Hartley, *The Politics of Pictures: The Creation of the Public in the Age of Popular Media* (London: Routledge, 1992), p. 35.
14. Barry Kiefl, "The Unique Cable TV Audience and the Future of Television," paper presented to the Advertising Research Foundation, New York, 1996, p. 4.
15. Meyrowitz, "Television," p. 218; John Mckay, "Canadians Prefer to Watch Two TV Programs at Once," *Calgary Herald*, 23 May 1997, p. D8.

16. Mandate Review Committee - CBC, NFB, Telefilm, *Making Our Voices Heard: Canadian Broadcasting and Film for the 21st Century* (Ottawa: Minister of Supply and Services Canada, 1996), p. 60.
17. Meyrowitz, "Television," p. 218.
18. Robert Hughes, *Culture of Complaint* (New York: Warner Books, 1993), p. 13.
19. Howard Kurtz, *Hot Air: All Talk All The Time* (New York: Times Books, 1996), p. 63.
20. Quoted in Canadian Broadcasting Corporation, "Talk Television" (23, 30 May 1994), transcript from the program *Ideas.*
21. Suzanne Hathaway, "Television News: Public versus Private Broadcasters" (master's degree project, University of Calgary, 1997), p. 52.
22. Jack Kapica, "All the News That's Fit to Vote On," *Globe and Mail,* 27 January 1997, p. A6.
23. Baker and Dessart, *Down the Tube,* p. 146.
24. Neil Campbell, "CTV Netcasting from Coliseum a Huge Success," *Globe and Mail,* 22 March 1996, p. A14.
25. Robert Collison, "Gzowski, " *HMHomemaker's* (Summer 1997), p. 102.
26. Canadian Media Director's Council, *Media Digest 1997–98,* pp. 29–31.
27. Robert Brehl, "Radio Firms' Earnings Soar 500%," *Globe and Mail,* 31 March 1998, p. B7; *Media Digest,* pp. 29–31.
28. Kurtz, *Hot Air,* p. 259.
29. Ibid., p. 8.
30. Benjamin Page, *Who Deliberates? Mass Media in Modern Democracy* (Chicago: University of Chicago Press, 1996), pp. 77–105.
31. David Barker, "Rush to Action: Political Talk Radio and Health Care (un)Reform," *Political Communication,* 15, no. 1 (January–March 1998), p. 85. See also *Political Communication,* 14, no. 3 (July–September 1997). The issue is devoted to "Understanding Broadcast Political Talk."
32. Casey Mahood, "Black Daily Marks Sector's Boom," *Globe and Mail,* 9 April 1998, p. B1.
33. Frank Denton, "Old Newspapers and New Realities: The Promise of the Marketing of Journalism," in *Reinventing the Newspaper* (New York: Twentieth Century Fund, 1993), pp. 10–11.
34. For a good discussion of the Canadian newspaper industry see Christopher Dornan, "Newspaper Publishing," in *The Cultural Industries in Canada,* ed. Michael Dorland (Toronto: Lorimer, 1996).
35. Ellen Hume, "The New Paradigm for News," *Annals of the American Academy of Political and Social Science,* 546 (July 1996), p. 142.
36. Ibid.
37. Mahood, "Black's Daily."
38. Anne Crawford, "Papers Should Get Under Skin of Issues," *Calgary Herald,* 13 September 1997, p. D6.

39. Quoted in Sydney Sharpe, "Newspapers Don't Face Extinction," *Calgary Herald*, 13 September 1997, p. D6.

40. John Keene, "Public Life in the Era of Communicative Abundance," Southam Lecture, Canadian Communications Association, Ottawa, May 1998.

41. Jon Katz, *Virtuous Reality* (New York: Random House, 1997), p. 159.

42. Pete Hamill, *News Is A Verb: Journalism at the End of the Twentieth Century* (New York: Library of Contemporary Thought, 1998), p. 96.

43. Tim Jones, "That Old Black Magic," *Columbia Journalism Review* (March–April 1998), pp. 40–43.

44. Gene Roberts, "Conglomerates and Newspapers," in *Conglomerates and the Media*, Erik Barnouw et al. (New York: New Press, 1997), p. 72.

45. The strongest critiques of Black's views and management style are by James Winter, *Democracy's Oxygen: How Corporations Control the News* (Montreal: Black Rose, 1997) and Maude Barlow and James Winter, *The Big Black Book: The Essential Views of Conrad and Barbara Amiel Black* (Toronto: Stoddart, 1997).

46. Quoted in Jones, "That Old Black Magic," p. 43.

47. Quoted in Casey Mahood, "Thomson's B.C. Paper Sale Raises Ire of Media Rivals," *Globe and Mail*, 21 May 1998, p. B6.

48. Frank Denton, "Old Newspapers and New Realities," p. 54.

49. Mark Abley, "Magazine Dispute with U.S. Gets Nasty," *Gazette*, 3 October 1998, p. B2.

50. Ibid.

51. See Ted Magder, *Franchising the Candy Store: Split-Run Magazines and a New International Regime for Trade in Culture* (Maine: University of Maine, 1998).

52. Abley, "Magazine Dispute."

53. For a breakdown on Internet use and non-use see Doug Saunders, "The People Who Slip Through the Net," *Globe and Mail*, 22 August 1997, p. A6; Jack Kapica, "Factoids Floating in Cyberspace," *Globe and Mail*, 25 July, 1997, p. A6; and Canadian Media Director's Council, *Media Digest 1997–1998*, pp. 13–16. I found it difficult to collect data on Internet use since the technology is gaining acceptance at a rapid rate. Some accounts, however, appear to be inflated.

54. Jack Kapica, "Factoids Floating in Cyberspace."

55. Canadian Media Director's Council, *Media Digest 1997–98*, p. 14.

56. Eileen Kahler, "Seeking Virtual Voters on the Lonely Cybertrail: A Case Study of the 1997 Alberta Election on the Internet" (master's degree project, University of Calgary, 1997).

57. Marion Just, "Candidate Strategies and the Media Campaign" in *The Election of 1996*, ed. Gerald Pomper (Chatham, NJ: Chatham House, 1997), p. 106.

58. Jon Katz, "The Digital Citizen," *Wired* (December 1997), p. 68.

59. James Carey, " 'A Republic, If You Can Keep It': Liberty and Public Life in the Age of Glasnost," in *James Carey: A Critical Reader*, p. 220.

60. James Fallows, *Breaking The News: How the Media Undermine American Democracy* (New York: Pantheon Books, 1996), p. 4.

CHAPTER TWO

1. Walter Lippmann, *Public Opinion* (New York: Free Press, 1922), foreword, p. xiv.

2. W. Lance Bennett, "Constructing Publics and Their Opinions," *Political Communication*, 10, no. 2 (April–June 1993), p. 101.

3. Lippmann, *Public Opinion*, p. xiv.

4. Ibid.

5. Ibid., p. 15.

6. Study identifying lack of knowledge about U.S. Bill of Rights, etc. cited in W. Russell Neuman, *The Future of the Mass Audience* (Cambridge: Cambridge University Press, 1991), p. 91. See also Jon Katz, "The Digital Citizen," *Wired* (December 1997), pp. 68–82, 274–275.

7. Frank Denton, "Old Newspapers and New Realities: The Promise of the Marketing of Journalism," in *Reinventing the Newspaper* (New York: Twentieth Century Fund, 1993), pp. 8–9.

8. Bennett, "Constructing Publics," pp. 103–104.

9. Denton, "Old Newspapers," p. 16.

10. Cited in Jon Katz, *Virtuous Reality* (New York: Random House, 1997), p. 178.

11. The Dominion Institute and the Angus Reid Group, National Citizenship Exam, 1997.

12. The Dominion Institute and the Angus Reid Group, The Canada Day Youth History Survey, 1997.

13. Robert Entman, *Democracy Without Citizens* (Oxford: Oxford University Press, 1989).

14. Roderick Hart, "Easy Citizenship: Television's Curious Legacy" *Annals of the American Academy of Political and Social Science*, 546 (July 1996), p. 114.

15. Quoted in Bill McKibben, *The Age of Missing Information* (New York: Random House, 1992), p. 155.

16. Ibid., p. 11.

17. Richard Cohen, "The Corporate Takeover of News," in *Conglomerates and the Media*, Erik Barnouw et al. (New York: New Press, 1997), p. 36.

18. Entman, *Democracy Without Citizens*.

19. Quoted in William Baker and George Dessart, *Down The Tube: An Inside Account of the Failure of American Television* (New York: Basic Books, 1998), p. 137.

20. Neuman, *Future of the Mass Audience*, p. 92.
21. Quoted in James Carey. "'A Republic, If You Can Keep It,': Liberty and Public Life in the Age of Glasnost," in *James Carey: A Critical Reader*, eds. Eve Munson and Catherine Warren (Minneapolis: University of Minnesota Press, 1997), p. 219.
22. Lance Bennett, "Toward a Theory of Press-State Relations in the United States," *Journal of Communication*, 40, no.2 (Spring 1990), pp. 103–125; Daniel Hallin, *The "Uncensored War": The Media and Vietnam* (Berkeley: University of California Press, 1986); Herbert Gans, *Deciding What's News* (New York: Vintage, 1979).
23. Todd Gitlin, "Introduction" in *Conglomerates and the Media*, Erik Barnouw et al. (New York: New Press, 1997), p. 11.
24. Richard Ericson, Patricia Baranek, and Janet Chan, *Visualizing Deviance: A Study of News Organization* (Toronto: University of Toronto Press, 1987), p. 16.
25. See John Fiske, "Popularity and the Politics of Information," in *Journalism and Popular Culture*, eds. Peter Dahlgren and Colin Sparks (London: Sage, 1992), p. 48. Similar thoughts are echoed in Herbert Gans, *Deciding What's News* (New York: Vintage, 1980), pp. 9–13.
26. James Fallows, *Breaking The News: How the Media Undermine American Democracy* (New York: Pantheon, 1996), p. 126.
27. Katz, *Virtuous Reality*, p. 161.
28. Timothy Cook, *Governing with the News: The News Media as a Political Institution* (Chicago: University of Chicago Press, 1998), p. 3.
29. Ibid.
30. Howard Kurtz, *Spin Cycle: Inside the Clinton Propaganda Machine* (New York: Free Press, 1998).
31. Robert Putnam, "Tuning In, Tuning Out: The Strange Disappearance of Social Capital in America," *PS: Political Science and Politics*, 28, no. 4 (December 1995), 664–683.
32. Reginald Bibby, *The Bibby Report: Social Trends Canadian Style* (Toronto: Stoddart, 1995), pp. 16, 125.
33. Harold Clarke and Allan Kornberg, "Evaluations and Evolution: Public Attitudes toward Canada's Federal Political Parties, 1965–1991," *Canadian Journal of Political Science* (1993), pp. 287–311.
34. Sheldon Alberts, "Politicians Fail Public Trust Test," *Calgary Herald*, 26 January 1997, p. A3.
35. Joseph Nye Jr., "Introduction: The Decline of Confidence in Government," in *Why People Don't Trust Government*, eds. Joseph Nye Jr., Philip Zelikow, and David King (Cambridge, MA: Harvard University Press, 1997), p. 1.
36. Joseph Cappella and Kathleen Hall Jamieson, *Spiral of Cynicism: The Press and the Public Good* (New York: Oxford University Press, 1997), p. 18.

37. Putnam, "Tuning In, Tuning Out," p. 677.

38. McKibben, *Age of Missing Information,* p. 170.

39. "David Sohn Interviews Jerzy Kosinski: A Nation of Videots, " in *Television: The Critical View,* ed. Horace Newcomb (New York: Oxford University Press, 1982).

40. See Scott Stossel, "The Man Who Counts the Killings," *Atlantic Monthly,* 279, no. 5 (May 1997), pp. 86–104.

41. Chris Dafoe, "Star-struck Newscasts Turn Criminals into Celebrities," *Globe and Mail,* 19 August 1997, p. A16; Frazier Moore, "TV News Coverage Criminal," *Calgary Herald,* 14 August 1997, p. C2.

42. Jim Calio, "National Television Violence Study," *National Association of Television Program Executives Newsletter,* 3, no. 6, pp. 1, 4.

43. Chad Skelton, "Most Canadians Believe Crime is Rising, Poll Shows," *Globe and Mail,* 28 July 1997, p. A6.

44. Ibid.

45. John Keane, "Public Life in the Era of Communicative Abundance," The Southam Lecture, Canadian Communications Association, Ottawa, May 1998.

46. John Fiske, "Politics and the Politics of Information," in *Journalism and Popular Culture,* eds. Peter Dahlgren and Colin Sparks (Newbury Park, CA: Sage, 1992), pp. 45–63.

47. Edward Herman and Noam Chomsky, *Manufacturing Consent: The Political Economy of the Mass Media* (New York: Pantheon Books, 1988).

48. Ibid., p. 2.

49. Robert Hackett, Richard Pinet, and Myles Ruggles, "News For Whom? Hegemony and Monopoly versus Democracy in Canadian Media," in *Seeing Ourselves: Media Power and Policy in Canada,* eds. Helen Holmes and David Taras, 2nd ed. (Toronto: Harcourt Brace & Co., Canada, 1996), p. 259.

50. Douglas Kellner, *Television and the Crisis of Democracy* (Boulder, CO: Westview Press, 1990), p. 18.

51. John Kirton, "National Mythology and Media Coverage: Mobilizing Consent for Canada's War in the Gulf," *Political Communication,* 10, no.4 (October–December 1993), pp. 425–441; Daniel Hallin and Todd Gitlin, "Agon and Ritual: The Gulf War as Popular Culture and as Television Drama," *Political Communication,* 10, no.4 (October–December 1993), pp. 411–424.

52. Quoted in Ell!s Cashmore, *...and there was telev!s!on* (New York: Routledge, 1994), p. 41.

53. Wilson Dizard, Jr., *Old Media New Media* (New York: Longman, 1997), p. 89.

54. Quoted in John Allemang, "Passing Judgment on TV's Best at Banff Festival," *Globe and Mail,* 16 June 1998.

55. Quoted in Baker and Dessart, *Down the Tube*, p. 27.

56. For an excellent overview of theories about public opinion formation see Samuel Popkin, *The Reasoning Voter: Communication and Persuasion in Presidential Campaigns* (Chicago: University of Chicago Press, 1994).

57. Simon's words are used in exactly this context by Bill Fox in "The Campbell Collapse: How the Failure of the Earned Media Strategy Triggered the Electoral Downfall of Canada's Oldest Political Party" (Master of Journalism thesis, Carleton University, 1994).

58. Fiske, "Popularity," p. 46.

59. Statistics garnered from Liss Jeffrey, "Private Television and Cable," *The Cultural Industries in Canada*, ed. Michael Dorland (Toronto: Lorimer, 1996), pp. 220–221, and Gun Akyuz, "Ratings: Downward Spiral," *TV World* (June/July 1998), pp. 10–11.

60. Baker and Dessart, *Down the Tube*, p. 97.

61. "Lack of 'Panic' Bad News for U.S. Networks," *Financial Post*, 6–8 June 1998, p. 18.

62. Pete Hamill, *News Is a Verb: Journalism at the End of the Twentieth Century* (New York: Library of Contemporary Thought, 1998), pp. 17, 20.

63. David Halberstam, *The Powers That Be* (New York: Alfred A. Knopf, 1979).

64. Murray Edelman, *The Symbolic Uses of Politics* (Urbana, IL: University of Illinois Press, 1964); *Constructing the Political Spectacle* (Chicago: University of Chicago Press, 1988).

65. Lawrence Martin, *The Antagonist: Lucien Bouchard and the Politics of Delusion* (Toronto: Viking Press, 1997), p. 296.

66. Joan Didion, "Insider Baseball," in *After Henry* (New York: Vintage International, 1992), pp. 49–50.

67. Quoted in Ken Auletta, "On and Off the Bus: Lessons from Campaign '92," in *1-800-President, The Report of the Twentieth Century Fund Task Force on Television and the Campaign of 1992* (New York: Twentieth Century Fund, 1993), p. 69.

68. Larry Sabato, *Feeding Frenzy: How Attack Journalism Has Transformed American Politics* (New York: Free Press, 1991).

69. Robert Reich, *Locked in the Cabinet* (New York: Alfred A. Knopf, 1997), p. 23.

70. Joe Klein, *Primary Colors: A Novel of Politics* (New York: Random House, 1996).

71. Howard Kurtz, *Spin Cycle: Inside the Clinton Propaganda Machine* (Toronto: Free Press, 1998), p. xxiv.

72. Keane, "Public Life," pp. 4–5.

73. Robert Hackett and Yuezhi Zhao, *Sustaining Democracy: Journalism and the Politics of Objectivity* (Toronto: Garamond Press, 1998).

74. Edward J. Epstein, *News From Nowhere* (New York: Vintage, 1973), p. 215.

75. Kurtz, *Spin Cycle*, p. xix.

76. Quoted in Patrick Gossage, *Close to the Charisma* (Toronto: McClelland and Stewart, 1986), p. 154.

77. Quoted in Paul Taylor, "Political Coverage in the 1990s: Teaching the Old News New Tricks," in *The New News v. The Old News* (New York: Twentieth Century Fund, 1992), p. 55.

78. See Kathleen Hall Jamieson, *Dirty Politics: Deception, Distraction and Democracy* (New York: Oxford University Press, 1992); Thomas Patterson, *Out of Order* (New York: Knopf, 1993); Larry Sabato, *Feeding Frenzy: How Attack Journalism Has Transformed American Politics* (New York: Free Press, 1991); Adam Gopnik, "Read All About It," *New Yorker* (12 December 1994); Jay Rosen, *Getting the Connections Right: Public Journalism and the Troubles in the Press* (New York: Twentieth Century Fund, 1996).

79. Gopnik, "Read All About It," p. 86.

80. Peter Goldman et al., *Quest for the Presidency 1992* (College Station: Texas A&M University Press, 1994.

81. Kurtz, *Spin Cycle*, p. 75.

82. Quoted in Goldman et al., *Quest for the Presidency 1992*, p. 119.

83. Michel Gratton, *"So, What Are The Boys Saying?": An Inside Look at Brian Mulroney in Power* (Toronto: McGraw-Hill Ryerson, 1987), p. xi.

84. Kim Campbell, *Time and Chance: The Political Memoirs of Canada's First Woman Prime Minister* (Toronto: Doubleday Canada, 1996), p. 399.

85. Joshua Meyrowitz, *No Sense of Place: The Impact of Electronic Media on Social Behavior* (New York: Oxford University Press, 1985), p. 321.

86. Murray Campbell, "Papers Vow to Respect Royal Privacy," *Globe and Mail*, 9 September 1997, p. A8.

87. Joshua Meyrowitz, "Television: The Shared Arena," in *Seeing Ourselves: Media Power and Policy in Canada*, eds. Helen Holmes and David Taras, 1st ed. (Toronto: Harcourt Brace Jovanovich Canada, 1992), p. 225.

88. Hackett and Zhao, *Sustaining Democracy*, pp. 139–140.

89. Patterson, *Out of Order*.

CHAPTER THREE

1. Mark Starowicz, "The Gutenberg Revolution of Television: Speculation on the Impact of New Technologies" in *Seeing Ourselves: Media Power and Policy in Canada*, eds. Helen Holmes and David Taras, 2nd ed. (Toronto: Harcourt Brace Canada, 1996), p. 239.

2. Quoted in Ken Auletta, *The Highwaymen: Warriors of the Information Superhighway* (New York: Random House, 1997), p. 45.

3. Ibid., p. 9.

4. Quoted in Matthew Fisher, "When Content is King," *Globe and Mail*, 15 November 1997, p. D1.

5. Auletta, *The Highwaymen*, p. 13.

6. Jeremy Rifkin, *The End of Work* (New York: G.P. Putnam, 1995).
7. Derrick De Kerckhove, *The Skin of Culture* (Toronto: Somerville, 1995).
8. Doug Saunders, "How Web and Wire Spin a News Fabric," *Globe and Mail,* 8 August 1997, p. A6.
9. Jon Katz, *Virtuous Reality* (New York: Random House, 1997), p. 154.
10. Murray Dobbin, "Unfriendly Giants," *Globe and Mail Report on Business Magazine* (July 1998), p. 74.
11. Benjamin Barber, *Jihad vs. McWorld: How Globalism and Tribalism Are Reshaping the World* (New York: Ballantine, 1996), pp. 138–139.
12. Ken Auletta, "Fourteen Truisms for the Communications Revolution," *Media Studies Journal,* 10, no. 2–3 (Spring/Summer 1996), p. 31.
13. Thomas Schatz, "The Return of the Hollywood Studio System," *Conglomerates and the Media,* Erik Barnouw et al. (New York: New Press, 1997), p. 83.
14. Ibid., pp. 74–75.
15. David Lieberman, "Conglomerates, News and Children," in Barnouw et al., *Conglomerates and the Media,* pp. 145–146.
16. Todd Gitlin, "Introduction," in Barnouw et al., *Conglomerates and the Media,* p. 7. The information on entertainment conglomerates and their holdings has been compiled from the following sources: Ken Auletta, *The Highwaymen;* William Baker and George Dessart, *Down The Tube: An Inside Account of the Failure of American Television* (New York: Basic Books, 1998); Barnouw et al., *Conglomerates and the Media;* Media Mergers, *Media Studies Journal,* 10, no. 2–3 (Spring/Summer 1996); Neil Hickey, "Will Gates Crush Newspapers?" *Columbia Journalism Review* (November/December 1997), pp. 28–36; Frank Rose, "There's No Business Like Show Business," *Fortune* (22 April 1998), pp. 86–104.
17. Quoted in Auletta, *The Highwaymen,* p. 52.
18. Quoted in Rose, "No Business Like Show Business," p. 102.
19. Quoted in J.H. Snider and Benjamin Page, "The Political Power of TV Broadcasters: Covert Bias & Anticipated Reactions," paper delivered at the 1997 Annual Meeting of the American Political Science Association, Washington, D.C., p. 31.
20. Ibid., pp. 15–16.
21. Quoted in Auletta, *The Highwaymen,* p. 26.
22. "Statements by Bosses Bolster Case Against Microsoft," *Calgary Herald,* 19 May 1998, p. E8.
23. John Merong, "The Fox News Gamble," *American Enterprise,* 8, no. 5 (September/October 1997), p. 41.
24. Ross Baker, "Murdoch's Mean Machine," *Columbia Journalism Review* (May/June 1998), p. 51.
25. Neil Hickey, "Is Fox News Fair?" *Columbia Journalism Review* (March/April 1998), p. 34.

26. Ibid.
27. Erik Barnouw, "New Look," in Barnouw et al., *Conglomerates and the Media*, p. 22.
28. Todd Gitlin, "Not So Fast," *Media Studies Journal*, 10, no. 2–3 (Spring/Summer 1996), p. 4.
29. Howard Kurtz, quoted in "The Real Dangers of Conglomerate Control," *Columbia Journalism Review* (March/April 1997), p. 50.
30. Patricia Aufderheide, "Telecommunications and the Public Interest," in Barnouw et al., *Conglomerates and the Media*, p. 162.
31. Gitlin, "Introduction," in Barnouw et al., *Conglomerates and the Media*, p. 8.
32. Auletta, *The Highwaymen*, p. 184.
33. Barber, *Jihad vs. McWorld*, p. 137.
34. Steven Rattner, "A Golden Age of Competition," *Media Studies Journal*, 10, no. 2–3 (Spring/Summer 1996), pp. 7–13.
35. Quoted in *Network - The Banff Bulletin*, Banff Television Festival (8 June 1998), p. 3.
36. Neil Postman, *Amusing Ourselves to Death* (New York: Penguin, 1985).
37. While much has been written about media framing, the best study, in my view, is still Todd Gitlin, *The Whole World Is Watching* (Berkeley: University of California Press, 1980). See also Shanto Iyengar, *Is Anyone Responsible?: How Television Frames Political Issues* (Chicago: University of Chicago Press, 1991).
38. Postman, *Amusing Ourselves*, p. 87.
39. Richard Cohen, "The Corporate Takeover of News," in Barnouw et al., *Conglomerates and the Media*, p. 46.
40. See Shanto Iyengar and Donald Kinder, *News That Matters: Television and American Opinion* (Chicago: University of Chicago Press, 1987), and Maxwell McCombs, "The Future Agenda for Agenda Setting Research," *Journal of Mass Communications Studies*, 45 (1994), pp. 171–181.
41. "News Media and Coverage," *Brill's Content* (August 1998), p. 23.
42. Neil Nevitte, *The Decline of Deference: Canadian Value Change in Cross-National Perspective* (Peterborough, ON: Broadview Press, 1996), p. 43.
43. Seymour Martin Lipset, "Revolution and Counterrevolution: The United States and Canada," in *The Revolutionary Theme in Contemporary America*, ed. Thomas Ford (Lexington: University Press of Kentucky, 1965), pp. 21–64.
44. Dempsey's point cited in Gordon Laird, "Once Upon a Time in the West," *Globe and Mail*, 14 August 1997, p. A11.
45. Seymour Martin Lipset, *Continental Divide: The Values and Institutions of the United States and Canada* (New York: Routledge, 1990).
46. Ibid., p. 212.
47. Barber, *Jihad vs. McWorld*, p. 17.

48. Marc Gunther, "They All Want to Be Like Mike," *Fortune* (21 June 1997), pp. 51–53.
49. Bill McKibben, *The Age of Missing Information* (New York: Random House, 1992), p. 42.
50. Ibid., p. 48.
51. Northrop Frye, "Sharing the Continent," in *A Passion For Identity: Introduction to Canadian Studies*, 1st ed. (Toronto: Nelson Canada, 1988), pp. 206–216.

CHAPTER FOUR

1. Bill McKibben, *The Age of Missing Information* (New York: Random House, 1992), p. 12.
2. Mark Starowicz, "The Gutenberg Revolution of Television: Speculation on the Impact of New Technologies," *Seeing Ourselves: Media Power and Policy in Canada*, eds. Helen Holmes and David Taras, 2nd ed. (Toronto: Harcourt Brace & Co., 1996), pp. 239–240.
3. See "The Future of Canadian Specialty TV Looks Even Better," *Globe and Mail*, 14 September 1998, p. C11; Doug Saunders, "Advertisers Aim to Fracture TV Audience," *Globe and Mail*, 9 August 1997, p. C3; and "Basic Facts on Canadian Media," in Holmes and Taras, *Seeing Ourselves: Media Power and Policy in Canada*, 2nd ed., p. 332.
4. Doug Saunders, "Advertisers Aim," p. C3.
5. Matthew Fraser, "Welcome to the Information Superhypeway," *Globe and Mail*, 13 September 1997, p. D1.
6. Rick Salutin, "The Unbearable Me-ness of the New Channel Universe," *Globe and Mail*, 24 October 1997, p. A14.
7. Joseph Turow, *Breaking Up America: Advertisers and the New Media World* (Chicago: University of Chicago Press, 1997), p. 3.
8. Ibid., p. 4.
9. Ibid., p. 197.
10. Ibid., p. 7.
11. Doug Saunders, "Channel Launch Called Unfair," *Globe and Mail*, 31 March 1998, p. A15.
12. Ibid.
13. Rick Salutin, "The Unbearable Me-ness."
14. The words to Springsteen's song are quoted in Porter Gibb, *It Ain't As Easy As It Looks: Ted Turner's Amazing Story* (New York: Crown, 1993), p. 339.
15. Turow, *Breaking Up America*.
16. Katz, quoted in Starowicz, "Gutenberg Revolution," p. 224. A more detailed version of Katz's position can be found in Elihu Katz, "And Deliver Us From Segmentation," *Annals of the American Academy of Political and Social Science*, 546 (July 1996), pp. 22–33.

17. Spicer, quoted in Ashley Geddes, "Spicer Predicts End of Canadian Quotas," *Calgary Herald,* 8 September 1990, p. E2.
18. Ibid.
19. Robert Brehl, "Legal Satellite Dishes Gaining Upper Hand on Grey Market," *Globe and Mail,* 15 July 1998, p. B1.
20. Michel Filion, "Radio," *The Cultural Industries in Canada: Problems, Policies and Prospects,* ed. Michael Dorland (Toronto: Lorimer, 1996), p. 126; Canadian Media Director's Council, *Media Digest 1997–1998,* p. 29.
21. Turow, *Breaking Up America,* p. 99.
22. Ibid.
23. Ibid., p. 100.
24. Ibid., p. 101.
25. "Canadians Watching Less TV," *Globe and Mail,* 6 February 1998, p. A11.
26. *CBC Annual Report 1997–98: A Summary,* p. 12.
27. Mandate Review Committee CBC, NFB, Telefilm, *Making Our Voices Heard: Canadian Broadcasting and Film for the 21st Century* (Ottawa: Minister of Supply and Services, 1996), p. 47.
28. Alan Macdonald is a colleague at the University of Calgary. His delightful and poignant descriptions and arguments seem to always bring things to life and hit the mark.
29. Quoted in Jon Katz, *Virtuous Reality* (New York: Random House, 1997), p. 60.
30. Mark Poster, "Cyberdemocracy: Internet and the Public Sphere," in *Internet Culture,* ed. David Porter (New York: Routledge, 1997), p. 205.
31. James Knapp, "Essayistic Messages: Internet Newsgroups as an Electronic Public Square," in *Internet Culture,* ed. Porter, pp. 193–194.
32. Debra Cohen and Peter Ephross, "Thousands Celebrate End of Cycle in Talmud Study," *Jewish Free Press,* 23 October 1997, p. 12.
33. Doris Graber and Brian White, "Building Cyber-Age Information Bridges Between Citizens," paper presented to the annual meeting of the American Political Science Association, Washington, D.C., August 1997.
34. John Messmer, "Early Politics on the World-Wide Web: Congressional Communication on the Internet," paper presented to the annual meeting of the American Political Science Association, Washington, D.C., August 1997; Scott Adler et al., "The Home Style Homepage: Legislator Use of the World Wide Web for Constituency Contact," paper presented to the annual meeting of the American Political Science Association, August 1997.
35. See David Taras, "The New and Old Worlds: Media Coverage and Legislative Politics," *Fleming's Canadian Legislatures 1997,* eds. Robert Fleming and J.E. Glenn (Toronto: University of Toronto Press, 1997), pp. 100–108.

36. *Darkness At Noon* (New York: Penguin, 1947) is the title of Arthur Koestler's most popular novel. For an overview of his experiences with totalitarianism see Arthur Koestler, *The Invisible Writing: An Autobiography* (New York: MacMillan, 1970).

37. Geoffry Taubman, "A Not-So World Wide Web: The Internet, China, and the Challenges to Nondemocratic Rule," *Political Communication*, 15, no. 2 (April–June 1998), p. 267.

38. Fraser, "Welcome to the Information Superhypeway," p. D2.

39. For a breakdown on Internet use and non-use see Doug Saunders, "The People Who Slip Through the Net," *Globe and Mail*, 22 August 1997, p. A6; Jack Kapica, "Factoids Floating in Cyberspace," *Globe and Mail*, 25 July, 1997, p. A6; and Canadian Media Director's Council, *Media Digest 1997–1998*, pp. 13–16.

40. John Keane, "Public Life in the Era of Communicative Abundance," paper presented to the annual meeting of the Canadian Communication Association, Ottawa, May 1998, p. 7.

41. Simon Winchester, quoted in Joseph Tabbi, "Reading, Writing, Hypertext: Democratic Politic in the Virtual Classroom," in *Internet Culture*, ed. Porter, p. 235.

42. Lucy Snowe, "Got a Date with an E-Male…," *Globe and Mail*, 23 August 1997, p. C8.

43. Quoted in William Cash, "The News That's Unfit to Print," *Globe and Mail*, 7 February 1998, p. C9.

44. Bob Blakey, "Hollywood Fears Knowles and his Web," *Calgary Herald*, 29 June 1998, p. B10.

45. Frank Rose, "Sex Sells," *Wired* (December 1997), pp. 220–221, 284.

46. Ibid., p. 221.

47. Poster, "Cyberdemocracy," p. 209.

48. Jon Stratton, "Cyberspace and the Globalization of Culture," in *Internet Culture*, ed. Porter, p. 269.

49. Roger Gibbins, whom I cherish as a wonderful colleague and friend, discussed his experiences over dinner in November 1997.

50. Patrick Brethour and Mark Evans, "Builders of the Electronic Mall," *Globe and Mail*, 11 July 1998, p. B1.

51. "Cyberspace Salesman," *Maclean's*, 22 September 1997, p. 46.

52. Brethour and Evans, "Builders of the Electronic Mall."

53. Robin Goldwyn Blumenthal, "Wooly Times On The Web," *Columbia Journalism Review* (September/October 1997), p. 34.

54. Erik Barnouw, "New Look," *Conglomerates and the Media*, Erik Barnouw et al. (New York: New Press, 1997), p. 27.

55. Anne-Marie Slaughter, "The Real New World Order," *Foreign Affairs*, 76, no. 5 (September/October 1997), p. 184.

CHAPTER FIVE

1. Quoted in Knowlton Nash, *The Microphone Wars: A History of Triumph and Betrayal at the CBC* (Toronto: McClelland & Stewart, 1994), p. 49.
2. Ibid., p. 85.
3. Quoted in William Baker and George Dessart, *Down The Tube: An Inside Account of the Failure of American Television* (New York: Basic Books, 1998), p. 73.
4. Nash, *The Microphone Wars*, pp. 158–159.
5. Quoted in Paul Rutherford, *When Television Was Young: Prime Time Canada 1952–1967* (Toronto: University of Toronto Press, 1990), p. 45.
6. For an excellent review of the "effects" literature see James Carey, "The Chicago School and the History of Mass Communication Research," *James Carey: A Critical Reader*, eds. Eve Munson and Catherine Warren (Minneapolis: University of Minnesota Press, 1997).
7. Quoted in Marc Raboy, *Missed Opportunities: The Story of Canada's Broadcasting Policy* (Montreal and Kingston: McGill-Queen's University Press, 1990), p. 247.
8. Ibid., p. 52.
9. Ibid., p. 110.
10. Rutherford, *When Television Was Young*, pp. 491–492.
11. Mandate Review Committee on the CBC, NFB and Telefilm, *Making Our Voices Heard: Canadian Broadcasting and Film in the 21st Century* (Ottawa: Minister of Supply and Services, 1996), p. 43.
12. David Whitson, "Hockey and Canadian Identities: From Frozen Rivers to Revenue Streams," *A Passion for Identity: An Introduction to Canadian Studies*, eds. David Taras and Beverly Rasporich, 3rd ed. (Toronto: ITP Nelson, 1997), pp. 302–303.
13. Quoted in Nash, *The Microphone Wars*, p. 199.
14. Ibid., p. 420.
15. Quoted in Rutherford, *When Television Was Young*, p. 77.
16. Ibid., p. 491.
17. William Thorsell, "CBC's Commitment to the Life of the Mind Helps Make Us Canadian," *Globe and Mail*, 16 March 1996, p. D6.
18. Michael Valpy, "The CBC Brings Us Bonavista," *Globe and Mail*, 26 June 1997, p. A19.
19. James Carey, "Afterword: The Culture in Question," *James Carey: A Critical Reader*, p. 336.
20. Nash, *The Microphone Wars*, p. 307; Raboy, *Missed Opportunities*, p. 131.
21. Nash, *The Microphone Wars*, p. 393.
22. Ibid., p. 292.
23. Ibid., p. 297.
24. Rutherford, *When Television Was Young*, p. 443.

25. Nash, *The Microphone Wars*, p. 363.
26. Senate of Canada, Standing Committee on Social Affairs, Science and Technology, *Proceedings of the Subcommittee on Veterans Affairs*, vol. 8 (Ottawa: Queen's Printer, 1992), pp. 91–96.
27. Senate Subcommittee, *Proceedings*, vol. 9 (1992), p. 61.
28. "Meddling by Tories at CBC Claimed," *Calgary Sun*, 16 June 1994, p. 16.
29. Quoted in Wayne Skene, *Fade to Black: A Requiem for the CBC* (Vancouver: Douglas and McIntyre, 1993), p. 218.
30. Ibid.
31. For the sequence of events within the CBC see David Taras, "The Struggle Over *The Valour and the Horror*: Media Power and the Portrayal of War," *Canadian Journal of Political Science*, 28, no. 4 (December 1995), pp. 725–748.
32. Confidential interview.
33. Skene, *Fade to Black*, p. 200.
34. "The Valour and the Horror and the Shame," *Globe and Mail*, 12 November 1992, A20.
35. Quoted in Nash, *The Microphone Wars*, p. 534.
36. Timothy Findley, "Point-Counterpoint: Ethics in the Media, " *Journal of Canadian Studies*, 27 (1992–93), p. 198.
37. Senate Subcommittee, *Proceedings*, vol. 9, pp. 96–97.

CHAPTER SIX

1. Quoted in Knowlton Nash, *The Microphone Wars: A History of Triumph and Betrayal at the CBC* (Toronto: McClelland and Stewart, 1994), p. 391.
2. Ibid.
3. The notion of indexing is best explained in Lance Bennett, "Toward a Theory of Press-State Relations in the United States," *Journal of Communication*, 40, no. 2 (1990), pp. 103–125.
4. Interview, 18 January 1996, Ottawa.
5. Interview, 18 January 1996, Ottawa.
6. Interview by author, June 1992, Ottawa.
7. Elly Alboim, "Inside the News Story: Meech Lake as Viewed by an Ottawa Bureau Chief," *Meech Lake and Canada: Perspectives From The West*, eds. Roger Gibbins et al. (Edmonton: Academic Printing and Publishing, 1988), pp. 235–245.
8. John Meisel, "Mirror? Searchlight? Interloper?: The Media and Meech," *After Meech Lake: Lessons for the Future*, eds. David Smith, Peter MacKinnon, and John Courtney (Saskatoon: Fifth House, 1991), pp. 147–168. See also Elly Alboim, "Response to Mirror? Searchlight? Interloper?: The Media and Meech," *Electronic Journal of Communication*, 2, no. 1, pp. 63–68.

9. Interview by author, June 1992, Ottawa.

10. Gadi Wolfsfeld, "Promoting Peace Through the News Media: Some Initial Lessons From the Oslo Peace Process," *Media, Ritual and Identity*, eds. Tamar Liebes and James Curran (London: Routledge, 1998), pp. 219–233.

11. Ibid., p. 232.

12. Rheal Seguin, "Spicer Assails Media 'Ayatollahs'," *Globe and Mail*, 21 January 1992, p. A1.

13. Laurier Lapierre, "Meet the Notables Who Dictate What Quebeckers Think," *Globe and Mail*, 21 March 1992, p. D1.

14. Quoted in Alain Saunier, "Don't Blame the Media," *Globe and Mail*, 23 April 1992, p. A19.

15. Interview by author, June 1992, Ottawa.

16. See David Taras, "The Mass Media and Political Crisis: Reporting Canada's Constitutional Struggles," *Canadian Journal of Communication*, 18, no. 2 (Spring 1993), pp. 131–148.

17. James Curran, "Crisis of Public Communication: A Reappraisal," *Media, Ritual and Identity*, eds. Liebes and Curran, p. 195.

18. Interview with David Bazay, 16 January 1996, Toronto.

19. Ibid.

20. Quoted in Mordecai Richler, "From the Ottawa Monkey House ... to Referendum," *Belling the Cat: Essays, Reports and Opinions* (Toronto: Alfred A. Knopf Canada, 1998), p. 336.

21. Guy Laforest, *Trudeau and the End of a Canadian Dream* (Montreal and Kingston: McGill-Queen's University Press, 1995).

22. Interview, 15 January 1996, Toronto.

23. Interview, 16 January 1996, Toronto.

24. Michel Cormier, "Referendum '95," *Scan* (November/December 1995), p. 4.

25. Quoted in Erin Research, *Report on CBC/SRC Quebec Referendum Coverage, 1995*, p. 20.

26. Fraser Institute, "From Over-Confidence to Crisis: How English-Language TV Favoured the Federalist Position in the 1995 Quebec Referendum," *On Balance*, 8, no. 10.

27. Cormier, "Referendum '95."

28. Quoted in Erin Research, *Report on CBC/SRC Quebec Referendum Coverage, 1995*, p. 26.

29. Nevill Nakivell, "Media helped the Yes Side's Cause," *Financial Post*, 7 November 1995, p. 17.

30. Interview, 18 January 1996, Ottawa.

31. Kenneth McRoberts, *Misconceiving Canada: The Struggle for National Unity* (Toronto: Oxford University Press, 1997), p. 230.

32. Quoted in Erin Research, *Report on CBC/SRC Quebec Referendum Coverage, 1995*, p. 26.
33. Ibid., pp. 36–44.
34. Ibid.
35. Quoted in Roger Landry, "Media and the Unity Issue," *The Media Series: A Collection of Addresses* (Toronto: Canadian Journalism Foundation, 1997), p. 6.
36. Cormier, "Referendum '95," p. 5.
37. Interview, 22 January 1996, Montreal.
38. McRoberts, *Misconceiving Canada*, p. 229.
39. Interview, 24 January 1996, Quebec City.
40. Interview, 24 January 1996, Quebec City.
41. Fraser Institute, "From Over-Confidence to Crisis."
42. Stephen Entwisle, "Clear As Mud: The CBC's Treatment of the 1995 Referendum Question" (Graduate Program in Communications Studies, University of Calgary, 1998).
43. Interview, 16 January 1996, Toronto.
44. Interview, 26 January 1996, Toronto.
45. Interview, 19 January 1996, Toronto.
46. Pierre Elliot Trudeau, " 'Lucien Bouchard, Illusionist'," *Montreal Gazette,* 3 February 1996, p. B3.
47. Richler, "The Ottawa Monkey House," pp. 333–334.
48. Interview, 15 January 1996, Toronto.
49. Interview, 19 January 1996, Toronto.

CHAPTER SEVEN

1. Quoted in Danny Schechter, "Media Summits," *Media Studies Journal* (Spring/Summer 1996), p. 84.
2. Michael Medved, *Hollywood vs. America* (New York: Harper Collins, 1992), p. 3.
3. Anthony Keller, "Have Can-con, Will Travel," *Globe and Mail,* 13 September 1997, p. C3.
4. Canadian Film and Television Production Association, *The Canadian Film and Television Production Industry: A 1998 Profile* (Ottawa, 1998), p. 2.
5. Gayle MacDonald and Doug Saunders, "Can West-Shaw Swap Rejigs Broadcast Market," *Globe and Mail,* 19 August 1998, pp. B1, B4.
6. Mandate Review Committee CBC, NFB and Telefilm, *Making Our Voices Heard: Canadian Broadcasting and Film for the 21st Century* (Ottawa: Minister of Supply and Services Canada, 1996), p. 67.
7. Ibid., p. 35.
8. Ibid., p. 61.

9. Hugh Segal, *Beyond Greed* (Toronto: Stoddart, 1997), p. 95.

10. Daryl Duke, "The Final Cut?" *Canadian Forum*, 14, no. 7 (November 1996), p. 17.

11. W.T. Stanbury, "Canadian Content Regulations: The Intrusive State at Work," *Fraser Forum* (August 1998), p. 73.

12. MacDonald and Saunders, "Can West-Shaw Swap," p. B4; Canadian Broadcasting Corporation, *Annual Report 1997–98: A Summary*, p. 12.

13. Suzanne Hathaway, "Television News: Public versus Private Broadcaster" (master's degree project, The University of Calgary, 1997).

14. Mandate Review Committee CBC, NFB, Telefilm, *Making Our Voices Heard*, p. 73.

15. Canadian Broadcasting Corporation, *Annual Report 1996–97*, p. 33.

16. "The Future of Canadian Specialty TV Looks Even Better," *Globe and Mail*, 14 September 1998, p. C11.

17. Quoted in Peter Waal, "Your Move Ivan," *Canadian Business* (11 September 1998), p. 57.

18. Mark Starowicz, "The Gutenberg Revolution of Television: Speculations on the Impact of New Technologies," *Seeing Ourselves: Media Power and Policy in Canada*, eds. Helen Holmes and David Taras, 2nd ed. (Toronto: Harcourt Brace Canada, 1996), p. 246.

19. James Curran, "Crisis of Public Communication: A Reappraisal," *Media, Ritual and Identity*, eds. Tamar Liebes and James Curran (New York: Routledge, 1998), pp. 175–202.

20. Liss Jeffrey, "Private Television and Cable," The Cultural Industries in Canada: Problems, Policies and Prospects (Toronto: Lorimer, 1996), p. 245.

21. Jeffrey, "Private Television," p. 245.

22. Jacquie McNish and Janet McFarland, "Izzy Asper Ascends to TV's Throne," *Globe and Mail*, 22 August 1998, p. B5.

23. Ibid.

24. Stanbury, "Canadian Content Regulations," p. 12.

25. Ellen Vanstone, "Simulcast Sins Drive Up Blood Pressure and Ad Revenue," *Globe and Mail*, 13 May 1997, p. A17.

26. Stanbury, "Canadian Content Regulations," p. 61.

27. Ibid.

28. John Haslett Cuff, "Private Sector Not Fit to Fill Shoes of Public Broadcasters," *Globe and Mail*, 7 October 1996, p. C1.

29. Newton Minow, "The Wasteland Speech," in Newton Minow and Craig Lamay, *Abandoned in the Wasteland: Children, Television and the First Amendment* (New York: Hill and Wang, 1995), p. 188.

30. Wayne Skene, *Fade to Black: A Requiem for the CBC* (Vancouver: Douglas and McIntyre, 1993).

31. John Meisel, "Escaping Extinction: Cultural Defence of an Undefended Border," *Southern Exposure: Canadian Perspectives on the United States*, eds. David Flaherty and William McKercher (Toronto: McGraw-Hill Ryerson, 1986), p. 152.

32. Richard Collins, *Culture, Communication & National Identity: The Case of Canadian Television* (Toronto: University of Toronto Press, 1990), p. xxii.

33. Richard Gwyn, *Nationalism Without Walls* (Toronto: McClelland & Stewart, 1996).

34. Curran, "Crisis of Public Communication," p. 178.

35. Stanbury, "Canadian Content Regulations," p. 55.

CHAPTER EIGHT

An earlier version of this chapter was published in the *Canadian Journal of Communication*, 21, no. 4 (Autumn 1996), pp. 485–495

1. Howard Kurtz, *Hot Air: All Talk All The Time* (New York: Random House, 1996), p. 19.

2. Ibid., p. 22.

3. Ibid., p. 24.

4. Canadian Broadcasting Corporation, *Journalistic Standards and Practices* (1995), pp. 30–31.

5. Lance Bennett, "Toward a Theory of Press-State Relations in the United States," *Journal of Communication*, 40, no. 2 (Spring 1990), p. 106.

6. Ibid., pp. 107–108.

7. Benjamin Page, *Who Deliberates? Mass Media and Modern Democracy* (Chicago: University of Chicago Press, 1996), p. 109.

8. Eric Alterman, *Sound and Fury: The Washington Punditocracy and the Collapse of American Politics* (New York: Harper Collins, 1992), p. 5.

9. See Larry Sabato, *Feeding Frenzy: How Attack Journalism Has Transformed American Politics* (New York: Free Press, 1991); Thomas Patterson, *Out of Order* (New York: Knopf, 1993); Kathleen Hall Jamieson, *Dirty Politics: Deception, Distraction and Democracy* (New York: Oxford University Press, 1992); and Jay Rosen, "Politics, Vision, and the Press," *The New News v. the Old News: The Press and Politics in the 1990s* (New York: Twentieth Century Fund, 1992).

10. Thomas Patterson, "Bad News, Bad Governance," *Annals of the American Academy of Political and Social Sciences*, 546 (July 1996), p. 102.

11. Ibid.

12. *Report of the Twentieth Century Fund Task Force on Television and the Campaign of 1992* (New York: Twentieth Century Fund, 1993), p. 8.

13. Kiku Adatto, *Picture Perfect: The Art and Artifice of Public Image Making* (New York: Basic Books, 1993), p. 25.

14. "Election '97: CBC and CTV National Television News Coverage," *On Balance*, 10, no. 7, p. 8.
15. Quoted in Timothy Cook, *Governing with the News: The News Media as a Political Institution* (Chicago: University of Chicago Press, 1998), p. 114.
16. Kurtz, *Hot Air*, p. 4.
17. Ibid.
18. Krishna Rau, "A Million for Your Thoughts," *Canadian Forum* (July/August 1996), pp. 11–17.
19. Ibid., p. 12.
20. Brent Stafford, "Right-wing Research Agencies Quoted Much More Often," *NewsWatch Monitor*, 1, no. 1 (Summer 1997), pp. 1, 3.
21. Maude Barlow and James Winter, *The Big Black Book: The Essential Views of Conrad and Barbara Amiel Black* (Toronto: Stoddart, 1997), p. 10.
22. Ibid., p. 7.
23. Quoted in John Partridge, "Citizen Black," *Globe and Mail*, 25 July 1987, p. D6.
24. See Conrad Black, *A Life in Progress* (Toronto: Key Porter, 1993); Richard Siklos, *Shades of Black: Conrad Black and the World's Fastest Growing Press Empire* (Toronto: William Heinemann Canada, 1995).
25. Quoted in Michael Valpy, "Hollinger's Swallowing of Southam is Bad News," *Globe and Mail*, 28 May 1996, p. A19.
26. Quoted in Barlow and Winter, *The Big Black Book*, p. 15.
27. Madelaine Drohan, "Blair's Wife Feels Heat of Tory Press," *Globe and Mail*, 5 March 1997, pp. A1, A3.
28. Quoted in Barlow and Winter, *The Big Black Book*, p. 126.
29. Ibid., p. 127.
30. Conrad Black, "Mulroney Rises Above Airbus Smear," *Calgary Herald*, 10 October 1998, p. I11.
31. Rick Salutin, "It Seems Some Reviewers Are More Equal Than Others," *Globe and Mail*, 22 October 1998, p. A18.
32. Jeffrey Simpson, "Our Industry is Chasing Its Tail," *Globe and Mail*, 18 April 1996, p. A10.
33. Michael Cobden, "Worried about the Heavy Hand of Hollinger," *Globe and Mail*, 6 May 1997, p. A21.
34. Richard Mackie and James Rusk, "Opposition Strategists Fear Godfrey's Political Power," *Globe and Mail*, 25 July 1998, p. A3.
35. Christie Blatchford, "Star, Sun Are Worlds Apart," *National Post*, 29 October 1998, p. A4.
36. Marion Just, Ann Crigler, Dean Alger, Timothy Cook, Montague Kern and Darrell West, *Crosstalk: Citizens, Candidates and the Media in a Presidential Campaign* (Chicago: University of Chicago Press, 1996).
37. Kurtz, *Hot Air*, p. 366.

CHAPTER NINE

1. Shanto Iyengar and Donald Kinder, *News That Matters* (Chicago: University of Chicago Press, 1987), pp. 116, 133.
2. Todd Gitlin, *The Whole World Is Watching* (Berkeley: University of California Press, 1980), p. 2.
3. The phrase is taken from Thomas Patterson, *Out of Order* (New York: Basic Books, 1993).
4. See Roger Bird, *The End of News* (Toronto: Irwin Publishing, 1997), and Knowlton Nash, *Trivia Pursuit: How Showbiz Values are Corrupting the News* (Toronto: McClelland and Stewart, 1998).
5. Northrop Frye, "Sharing the Continent," *Divisions on a Ground: Essays on Canadian Culture* (Toronto: House of Anansi Press, 1982).
6. *Royal Commission on Newspapers* (Ottawa: Supply and Services Canada, 1981); *Report of the Task Force on Broadcasting Policy* (Ottawa: Supply and Services Canada, 1986); Mandate Review Committee CBC, NFB and Telefilm, *Making Our Voices Heard: Canadian Broadcasting and Film for the 21st Century* (Ottawa: Minister of Supply and Services Canada, 1996).
7. Mandate Review Committee CBC, NFB and Telefilm, p. 76.
8. Address by Jay Rosen, Queen's University Public Forum on Television, Kingston, Ontario, May 1992.

UPDATE 2001

1. Robert Rabinovitch, Opening Remarks to the Standing Committee on Canadian Heritage, 16 May 2000 (transcript), p. 2.
2. Tamara Gignac, "Canada a nation of surfers," *Calgary Herald,* 17 November 2000, p. A10.
3. Beverley Milligan, "Surfing the interactive tidal wave," *Playback,* 13 November 2000, p. 26.
4. Doug Saunders, "Post Mortem," *Globe and Mail,* 5 August 2000, p. A7.
5. "Globe readership down over 3 years," *National Post,* 17 November 2000 (accessed through www.nationalpost.com).
6. Conrad Black, "Comment," *Calgary Herald,* 9 August 2000, p. A15.
7. Eric Reguly, "Black needs a splash in bigger pond," *Globe and Mail,* 2 August 2000, p. A5.
8. Ibid.
9. Canadian Alliance, *A Time for Change: An Agenda of Respect for All Canadians,* p. 7.
10. Canadian Broadcasting Corporation, *Annual Report, 1999–2000,* p. 2.
11. Rabinovitch, *Opening Remarks,* p. 3.
12. Ibid., pp. 13, 9.
13. Guylaine Saucier, "Message from the Chair," *CBC Annual Report,* p. 2.

14. *CBC Annual Report*, English Television, p. 5.

15. Thomas Patterson, *Out of Order* (New York: Alfred A. Knopf, 1993).

16. Ruth Marcus, "Costliest Race in U.S. History Nears End," *Washington Post*, 5 November 2000 (accessed through www.washingtonpost.com).